THE BIG-ASS BOOK OF CRAFTS

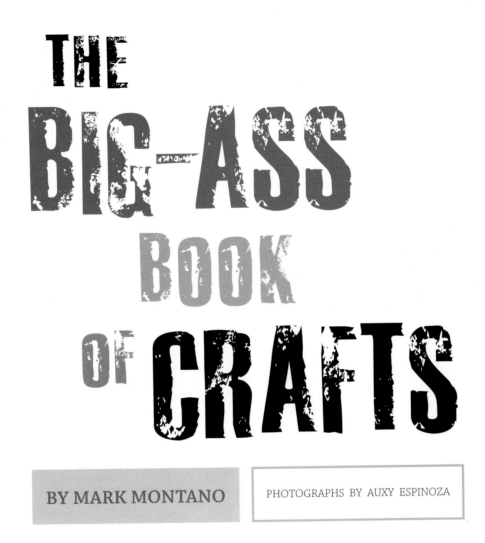

BY MARK MONTANO

PHOTOGRAPHS BY AUXY ESPINOZA

SIMON SPOTLIGHT ENTERTAINMENT

New York London Toronto Sydney

NOTE TO READERS

All activities in this book should be performed with adult supervision. Common sense and care are essential to the conduct of any and all activities described in this book. Neither the author nor the publisher assumes responsibility for any loss, damages, or injuries that may occur, and the author and publisher hereby expressly disclaim responsibility for any loss, damages, or injuries, however caused. Neither the author nor the publisher endorses any of the products, tools, or services referred to in this book or assumes any responsibility for use of any such products, tools, or services. All trademarks of products are property of their respective owners. Be sure to read and follow all instructions and warnings that accompany any products, tools, or services referred to in this book. Due to differing conditions, materials, and skill levels, the author and publisher disclaim any liability for unsatisfactory results. Nothing in this book is intended as an express or implied warranty of suitability or fitness of any product, tool, service, or design.

S|S|E

SIMON SPOTLIGHT ENTERTAINMENT
An imprint of Simon & Schuster
1230 Avenue of the Americas, New York, New York 10020
Text copyright © 2008 by Mark Montano
Photographs copyright © 2008 by Auxy Espinoza
All rights reserved, including the right of reproduction in whole or
in part in any form.
SIMON SPOTLIGHT ENTERTAINMENT and related logo are trademarks
of Simon & Schuster, Inc.
Designed by Jane Archer
Manufactured in the United States of America
First Edition 10
Library of Congress Cataloging-in-Publication Data
Montano, Mark.
The big-ass book of crafts / by Mark Montano ;
photographs by Auxy Espinoza.—1st ed.
p. cm.
ISBN-13: 978-1-4169-3785-2
ISBN-10: 1-4169-3785-4
1. Handicraft. 2. House furnishings.
3. Interior decoration. I. Title.
TT157.M6347 2008
745.5—dc22
2007039253

CONTENTS

This book is dedicated to all the people who
think they aren't talented or crafty. . . . I promise
you that if you just look, you'll find that you are.

INTRODUCTION

My good friend Nadia (one of the craftiest people I know and a total inspiration to me) told me something one day while I was in the process of writing this book. She said, "Make sure your crafts are *home worthy*." At first the statement seemed simple, but then I began to think about how important it is and what it means. Anyone can paint a chicken on a ceramic pitcher, but does that mean it's worthy of your home? Does that mean it's something you created that is worthy enough to show off? Does it reflect who you are and express your personality? I hope that what you find in this book inspires you to make crafts that are beautiful, functional, fun, and—most important—home worthy. I happened to be moving into a new home as I was writing this book, and I had endless space to fill, walls to decorate, windows to dress up, and lighting fixtures to play with. It was a blank canvas, and my goal was to fill it with home-worthy creations. While you probably won't devote an entire year to making enough craft projects to fill your house, that's just what I did. Here is the result.

Take your time, have a blast, enjoy the process, and feel free to let me know how it turns out. I'm always available at markmontanonyc@aol.com, and I love hearing about successful crafting adventures!

TWO IMPORTANT THINGS TO REMEMBER AS YOU EMBARK ON YOUR YOUR CRAFTING JOURNEY: Newspaper is crucial! Always have a stack on hand to cover your workspace. It will make cleanup a breeze and ensure that you don't get paint and glue on your tables and floors. And remember to always use safety glasses or goggles to protect your eyes when using power tools.

ARTSY FARTSY

B e warned, my friends. If you make *any* of the projects in this book, you will be labeled by your friends and family as "artsy fartsy." If you can deal with it, then you are good to go. If you cannot deal with it, well, then close the book and take up tap dancing. (But then you will just be known as that nutty tap dancer from down the street.) I don't think there is anything wrong with being called "artsy," but the fartsy part I can do without.

If, like me, you're able to embrace your artsy side, you'll probably agree that there is nothing sadder than a bare wall or an empty table. The following projects can be used as a remedy for those sad surfaces. Go crazy and go BIG! Use your imagination and have a blast. Embrace your artsy fartsy self. Who cares what people say, anyway?

ANTIQUE COLOR-COPIED PRINTS

Make new, inexpensive art look ancient and amazing! When I go to museums, I am always fascinated with how beautifully worn the sketches are. The yellowed edges, the watermarks, the stained paper—they each seem to have such a history. Somehow the passing of time has made them look even better. So I began to wonder how I could duplicate this effect to make some of the images that I like to color-copy and frame look aged. This is what I came up with.

YOU'LL NEED:

- Pot of very strong coffee or tea (best if left out for a day or two)

- Tray large enough for your artwork to lie flat on and not overlap itself (Try a cookie sheet if it's in good shape—not rusty or warped.)

- 4 or more paperweights; smooth rocks or unopened cans will do (I like rocks. They're free!)

- Color copies of anything you want to antique (I like old fashion plates, which I find in Dover Books— you can go to any local bookstore, though—and even some of my own pencil sketches from my life drawing class in college.)

- Spray bottle

OPTIONAL: *A place outside in the sun in the middle of a hot day*

1. Pour your coffee or tea into the tray.

2. Dip your color copies into the coffee/tea quickly, making sure it gets wet but not so soggy that it could tear. (Paper can get weak and fall apart, so you have to work fast and set it aside.)

3. Lay the wet artwork flat on the newspaper.

4. Place some small weights on the corners of your project. This will keep the edges from curling up as the paper dries.

DON'T WORRY: *If puddles of coffee or tea form in places on the artwork. That only helps enhance the overall effect of the process.*

5. When the artwork is dry, if it's not as antique-looking as you'd like, you may want to spray some more coffee/tea on it by using your spray bottle and letting it dry again. You can repeat this process, depending on how worn you'd like the piece to look.

6. Once you get the effect you want and the artwork is completely dry, flatten it further by putting it between some books or magazines before you frame it. (If the paper is wrinkled or wavy, it won't look authentic!)

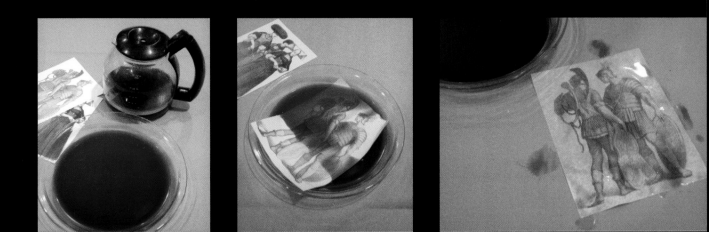

SUBSCRIPTION-CARD ARTWORK

You know how annoying it is to open a magazine and have to rip out all of the subscription postcards? I just hate it. I also hate when they fall out as I'm reading. So I figured out a way to use them as art, and now when I open a magazine, I'm always happy to see them. A positive side effect of crafting is that if you can take just a few things that annoy you and make them into something beautiful, you'll be a lot happier. Trust me on this!

YOU'LL NEED:

- Subscription postcards from a magazine
- Tempera paints in dark colors, like blue, gray, green, red, and deep orange
- Blue painter's tape
- 1"-wide, flat art brush
- Rubber stamps of things, like birds, leaves, trees, and faces (or anything else you want)
- Embossing powder in gold or silver
- Embossing heat gun (or hair dryer if you don't have one)
- Embossing stamp pad

HERE'S HOW:

1. Place tape on the edges of your subscription card, covering ¼" all the way around.

2. With your art brush, fill in the area inside the tape with the tempera paint. (You should use one color.)

> **DON'T WORRY:** *If you can see printing underneath. It's part of the art!*

3. When the paint dries, ink your rubber stamp with the embossing ink pad and press firmly onto the painted area, making sure to center the image.

4. Sprinkle the gold or silver embossing powder while the ink is still wet. (You will see the particles stick to the stamp's design.)

5. Set the embossing powder with your heat gun or hair dryer.

> **DON'T WORRY:** *If your paper warps. Just press it overnight in between some books.*

6. Remove the tape and place your card in a simple frame, and you've got some great art!

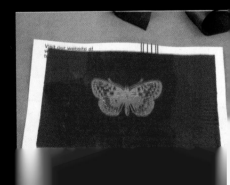

DRAG ART

This project could not be simpler, and it always turns out beautifully. There is no right or wrong way to do this craft, so have fun, and if you don't like what you've created, simply keep draggin' paint onto your canvas until you do.

YOU'LL NEED:

- Canvas in the size of your choice

- A couple of 2" × 12" strips of sturdy cardboard

- Acrylic paints in any colors

> **HINT:** *Try colors that match, like different blues with greens, or reds with oranges that have hints of yellow.*

- Rubber gloves

HERE'S HOW:

1. Squirt blobs of each paint color along the entire top of your canvas. Dribble some farther down on your canvas as well.

2. With your cardboard strip pressed firmly against the top of the canvas, drag the paint down the entire canvas, making sure to cover all the areas of the canvas with the paint. It's a smearing action, and you will see your modern art piece emerge before your eyes.

> **SUGGESTION:** *Be generous with the paint, and even overlap some of the colors, so that when you drag it down, they'll blend together. The thicker the paint, the cooler it looks.*

> **DON'T WORRY:** *If you miss a spot; you can always fill it in when it's dry.*

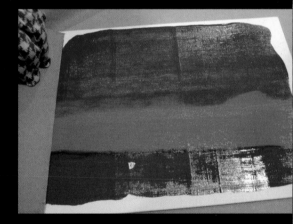

3. Now it's time to frame your art and hang it up. That was easy, wasn't it?

KID ART

Nothing makes me happier than a wall of original art done by my nieces and nephews. For this project, just toss some cookies in the oven and break out the art supplies for an afternoon. This particular masterpiece was drawn by Anais Hernandez, age ten. It is of my friend (her uncle) Cristian. I think the likeness is amazing, and everyone who has seen this drawing knows exactly who it is of!

YOU'LL NEED:

- Kids, preferably nieces and nephews. If you don't have your own, borrow some!

- Art supplies like crayons, markers, and pastels

- Large sketchpads (Strathmore makes wonderful quality pads in sizes as large as 18" × 24"!)

- Premade cookie dough

- Frames or framing place

HERE'S HOW:

1. Put the cookies in the oven, and clear off the living room floor so everyone has plenty of room to spread out.

2. Challenge each child to draw you or one another, making sure they center their art and have lots of white space around each figure.

3. Be sure you let them know how talented they are.

4. Frame your masterpieces and display them proudly.

Silhouette-like images can be found among cave paintings and on ancient Greek vases. The term and what most people think of as silhouettes originated in early eighteenth-century Europe. The first silhouettes were painted images, taken from a subject's shadow and reduced in size. Now you can create them with a camera and some black spray paint! What took hours and hours a hundred years ago can literally take twenty minutes today . . . if you're quick.

YOU'LL NEED:

- Black spray paint (high gloss or matte; it's up to you)

- Camera (regular or digital; both will work)

- Scissors good for making very small cuts

HERE'S HOW:

1. Take profile photos of your friends and family. (I like to use digital because you can print out the image at any size you like.) These are my friends Melanie and Russ.

2. Once you have taken your photos and printed/developed them, carefully cut around the image.

3. Once your image is cut out, coat it with black spray paint and let dry.

4. Set in any sort of frame that you like. I mounted mine on plain white paper with book-page matting. (I like the way the black letters pick up the black of the silhouettes.)

> **HINT:** *Make sure to cut out every detail, like eyelashes, messy hair, an Adam's apple, and eyeglasses. The details are what make the silhouette realistic.*

ART SWITCH PLATES

Sometimes it's hard to find the light switch in a room when it's painted the same color as the wall. I gotta tell you, this drives me nuts! I didn't want this to happen in my house, so I decided to make each light-switch plate a mini piece of art. When I get tired of a design, I just switch it out. Light-switch plates are inexpensive and incredibly easy to replace.

YOU'LL NEED:

- Images to apply to your light switch (Try using a color copy of a cool greeting or postcard. Even some great wrapping paper would work for this project. There are tons of decorative papers available at Michaels, an arts and crafts store.)

- Krylon Spray Adhesive

- Elmer's glue

- 1"-wide paintbrush

- Scissors

- Very sharp craft knife, so that you can make intricate cuts

- Krylon Acrylic Crystal Clear

- Sharpened pencil

OPTIONAL: *Metallic gold paint*

1. Cut your images to the size of the light-switch plate.

> **NOTE:** *You can use any image you like, as long as you remember that there will be a square cut out for the light switch (right in the center). So, if you are using an image of a face, take care to lay out the image so that it's not disturbed by the screws or the switch.*

2. From each corner of your image, cut in about ⅜", at a diagonal toward the center, so that the corners lie flat over the curved edges of the light-switch plate.

3. Spray the back of the image with your spray adhesive.

4. Apply the image to the face of the light-switch plate, making sure the sides are sticking to the plate.

5. Working from the back side of the plate, use your craft knife to cut an X in the rectangle where the actual switch will go. (This will make four tiny triangles.)

6. Spread a light coating of Elmer's glue on the triangles and fold them in, front to back, to adhere them to the back of the plate.

7. Now, working from the front of the project, hold your plate up to the light, so you can see through the image, and carefully cut a small X over each of the screw holes (again creating tiny triangles).

8. Push your sharpened pencil through the holes, so that the triangles remain inside the screw holes.

9. Spray the surface of the plate with Krylon Acrylic Crystal Clear at least three times, waiting for the coat to dry at least ten minutes between each application. (Remember, light-switch plates get used a lot, so you want to protect your masterpiece!)

10. Mount on your wall and light up your life.

FOR THE GOLD LIGHT-SWITCH PLATE:

1. Cover the plate with metallic gold paint, and let it dry.

2. Cut out your image and apply it by using spray mount or by applying Elmer's glue to the back of the image.

3. Spray the surface of the plate with Krylon Acrylic Crystal Clear at least three times, waiting for the coat to dry at least ten minutes between each application.

3-D PHOTO

This is a 3-D photo of my friend Rich and Gus the Wonder Dog. The 3-D effect makes it seem like Gus is about to jump out of the frame for a game of fetch!

YOU'LL NEED:

- Shadow box (mine was 5" × 7")

- 4 duplicates of a 5" × 7" photo (If you only have one photo, you can take it to a copy shop and have it color-copied four times on card stock.)

- Scissors

- 1 sheet of ½"-thick Styrofoam

- Craft knife or the Styro Wonder Cutter Plus (I prefer the Styro Cutter as it's the easiest tool I've ever used for cutting, and it's precise.)

- Krylon Spray Adhesive

- Elmer's glue

1. Take a good look at your photo and decide which parts are going to be raised in your 3-D project.

> **HINT:** *When you look at a photo of a group of people, the ones in the front should be raised the most, the people in the back would be raised less, the trees and bushes even less, and the sky and clouds not at all.*

2. From a copy of your photo, cut out the items that will be raised the most. This will be your top layer.

3. Using a second copy of your photo, cut out the images that will be your next layer. (Trust me, it sounds confusing, but it will make sense once you start doing it.)

4. Now cut out what will be your final raised layer from your third photo. You have one untouched photo left. That will be your background image on which you will apply the three layers.

5. Lay out all of your images on the Styrofoam and trace around each image. Set aside your cutouts.

6. With your craft knife or Styro Wonder Cutter Plus, cut out your shapes from the Styrofoam.

> **SUGGESTION:** *Cut out your shapes just a bit smaller than the traced area, so that you don't see the Styrofoam peeking out when you put your project together.*

7. Adhere your images to the Styrofoam shapes with your spray adhesive.

8. Start putting your shapes on top of one another. With Elmer's glue, glue the top layer to the second layer, the second to the third (make sure the glue is dry between each piece before gluing to the next piece), then the whole piece to the bottom layer (the untouched photo).

9. Frame your 3-D photo in a shadow box and hang for your enjoyment!

BRONZE BABY SCULPTURE

Creepy? Maybe a little. But it's more than just a scary bronze baby. It's a way to make something simple look like a work of art. Take this technique and use it on any interesting object you find just lying around the house. I think you will find it's an amazing way to make something look like a million bucks.

YOU'LL NEED:

- Cheap plastic baby doll (I got mine at a 99¢ store)
- Round lid from a jar (It should be big enough to fit your doll's feet.)
- Elmer's glue
- Household Goop glue
- Spray paint, in each color: dark brown, silver metallic, and gold metallic
- Spray bottle filled with water

HERE'S HOW:

1. Glue the doll to the top of the lid with the Household Goop glue so that it stands on its own.

2. When the Household Goop is dry, drip Elmer's glue onto the doll and smear it around so the doll looks like it's sculpted.

3. After the Elmer's glue is dry, spray the entire sculpture with the dark brown spray paint.

4. Wait about five minutes for the paint to dry, then spray the sculpture with water. While it's still wet, spray it with the silver metallic spray paint.

5. After the paint has dried, spray it with water again, and then coat it with gold metallic paint until you get the bronze effect.

6. Let the paint dry and place it artfully in your home.

RANDOM-CUT PAPER MASKS

There truly are no rules for this project. It's about enjoying yourself and coming up with something that you like. Keep this one between us, though, since my friends think these are masks from an extinct Siamese wandering tribe. Sadly, people who are less crafty than we are will believe anything!

YOU'LL NEED:

- Large piece of paper to use as your background
- Paper in contrasting colors, at least 8½" × 11"
- Scissors
- Glue stick
- Frames

OPTIONAL: *I surrounded a basic wooden frame with wooden clothespins glued around the edges. For my larger masks, I just used poster frames but still got a great effect. You decide what works best for you.*

HERE'S HOW:

1. Fold one sheet of colored paper to one quarter its original size by folding it in half from top to bottom, then folding it in half again from left to right.

2. Draw swirls and squiggles on one side of your folded paper.

3. Carefully cut out around the shapes, using them as a guide but not following them perfectly. (It's just a way to guide your scissors in different directions, to get an interesting shape when you unfold the paper.)

4. Cut out a face pattern from another sheet of colored paper. (I dig the pointy ears on mine.)

5. Glue the face to your background paper.

6. Apply your unfolded crazy-cut paper above the face, so it looks like a hat.

7. Frame your mask and enjoy.

15

DAVID HOCKNEY PHOTO COLLAGE

Many art historians believe that Pablo Picasso invented what we refer to as "collage." He was one of the first artists to use collage in his work by pasting pieces of painted canvas to other canvases. However, I believe that collage was inevitable ever since the Chinese invented paper around A.D. 105–107. It appears in twelfth-century Japanese art, as a background for calligraphy, and it spread like wildfire all over the world from there.

David Hockney used photographs for his collages in a way that has inspired artists all over the world. Today, with the use of digital photography and computers, and the ability to print photos at home, a photo collage is a wonderful way to spend the day creating personalized art.

YOU'LL NEED:

- Photo that you can manipulate in a photo program on your computer
- 3" × 4" photo paper
- Large sheet of paper to mount your work on
- Glue stick
- Scissors
- Computer printer

OR (IF YOU DO NOT HAVE A COMPUTER):

- Disposable 35-mm camera with at least 36 exposures
- Large sheet of paper to mount your work on
- Glue stick
- Scissors

HERE'S HOW TO MAKE THE COLLAGE USING A COMPUTER:

1. On your computer, duplicate the photo you want to use about fifteen times.

2. Crop a small portion of your image from each photo until you have captured each section of the picture in a different photo.

> **FOR EXAMPLE:** *If you are making a collage of a face, section off the hair, the left eye, the right eye, the nose, the chin, and so on until all of the image is represented collectively in your cropped photos.*

3. Print out your photos.

4. Artfully arrange your photos on a large piece of paper so you can see what it might look like when it's framed.

> **SUGGESTION:** *Overlap some of the photos, extend an arm, make someone have three eyes to make it interesting. You'll be surprised at how your art will evolve.*

5. Carefully glue the images to one another with the glue stick, being careful not to mess up your layout.

6. Mount on the piece of paper and frame.

HERE'S HOW TO MAKE THE COLLAGE USING A DISPOSABLE CAMERA:

1. Pick your subject. I like to photograph friends with a natural background during a beautiful, sunny day.

2. Stand far enough away that you can photograph a good amount of the background of your subject.

3. Starting at the upper left-hand side of your subject, photograph each part of him/her, subtly moving the camera from left to right, taking photos as you move along, until the entire subject has been photographed in sections.

4. Take your disposable camera to get developed.

5. See steps 4–6 in "Here's How to Make the Collage Using a Computer" above on how to assemble your collage.

3-D BLOSSOM BOX/ORIGAMI FLOWERS

If you've ever been in a room with small windows or no windows at all, then you can see how 3-D floral projects can come in handy. They're perfect for a cubicle or a drab office because they are flower arrangements that never have to be watered, and they give the feel of being outdoors.

YOU'LL NEED:

FOR THE 3-D BLOSSOM BOX:

- Shadow box frame
- Twigs
- Hot-glue gun
- Paper on which to mount your flowers
- Elmer's glue
- Scissors
- Glitter glue in gold and pink
- Green, yellow, and pink construction paper or cardstock
- Krylon Spray Adhesive

FOR THE 3-D ORIGAMI FLOWERS:

- Box frame with ½" depth
- Pages from an old book
- Box of long ball-point straight pins
- Scissors
- Paper on which to mount your flowers
- Small black buttons (one for each flower)
- Elmer's glue

FOR THE 3-D BLOSSOM BOX:

1. Cut out your flowers and leaves.

2. Fold each petal and leaf lengthwise to add a 3-D effect.

3. Cover the back of your shadow box with blue paper, using the spray adhesive for an even application.

4. With the hot-glue gun, attach your twigs to the paper.

DON'T WORRY: *If your twigs aren't perfect; just glue them together to make them the shape you want.*

5. Carefully apply the flowers and leaves to the twigs using small dabs of Elmer's glue.

6. When the flowers are dry, dot the gold glitter glue in the center of each flower.

7. Dot the pink glitter glue along the twigs.

8. Frame your masterpiece.

FOR THE 3-D ORIGAMI FLOWERS:

1. Cut out your flowers.

2. Fold each petal lengthwise to add a 3-D effect.

3. Arrange the flowers on the paper that you will be framing.

4. Stick your flowers in place using the pins.

5. Glue the flowers in place one at a time using Elmer's glue.

6. Remove the pins after ten minutes so they don't get too set into the glue.

7. After the glue has dried for about an hour, attach your buttons to the center of your flowers. (You can keep the buttons in place with the pins.)

8. Frame your masterpiece.

POSTCARD QUILT ART PIECE

Every time I see a stack of postcards at a coffee shop, I grab a handful. I'm drawn to the color, the variation, the way people advertise their events—you name it. I take them home and pin them to my inspiration board, and at the end of the year, I sew them together to make a postcard quilt. So the next time you're out getting coffee, take a look at those stacks, because they're a great way to find out what's going on in your neighborhood, and they can be used in some pretty cool artwork.

YOU'LL NEED:

- Sewing machine with a zigzag stitch
- Tons of postcards with images that you like
- Scissors

HERE'S HOW:

1. Trim your postcards so they are all the same size. (I like mine to be 4" wide, so that when I sew them together, they make nice rows.)

2. Start sewing the postcards together, side by side, with the zigzag stitch on your sewing machine, making rows that are about 24" long.

> **DON'T WORRY:** *If your quilt isn't "perfect." This project is organic and can turn out many different ways. Just start sewing your cards together and see what happens.*

3. Once you have about six or seven rows, it's time to start sewing them together. Lay out your rows in the order you are going to sew them.

> **HINT:** *Since this is paper and not fabric, you will have to add to your quilt by sewing one row at a time. You cannot do it in pieces because, unlike fabric, you will only be able to get one row at a time inside your sewing machine without crumpling your quilt.*

4. Sew two rows together, and then add on your third row, then your fourth, and so on, until you've sewn all of them together.

5. Once you have completed your quilt, you may find that it's a little lumpy. Place it under a large stack of books overnight to flatten it out.

6. Pin your new art to the wall and be inspired!

LIVING DOLL

My niece loves all kinds of dolls, so I decided a really fun way to make art with her would be to dress up paper dolls with real fabric and flowers. This has been done forever—from ancient Chinese dolls to puppets—so I thought I would give it a modern twist.

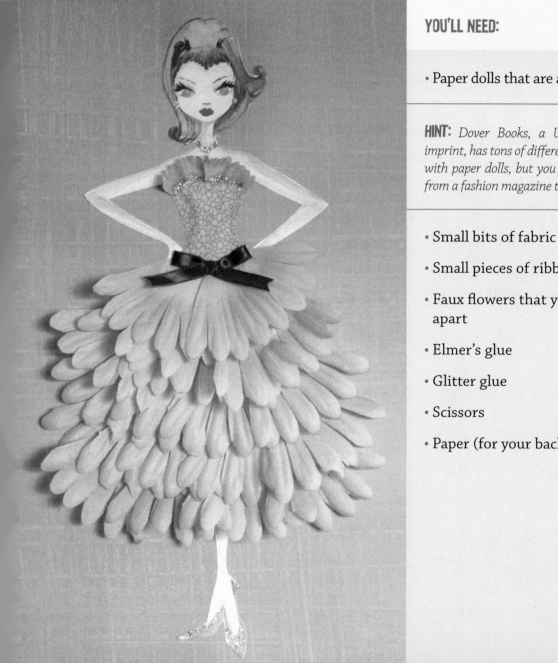

YOU'LL NEED:

- Paper dolls that are about 8" tall

> **HINT:** *Dover Books, a UK publishing imprint, has tons of different books filled with paper dolls, but you can use pages from a fashion magazine too.*

- Small bits of fabric
- Small pieces of ribbon
- Faux flowers that you can cut apart
- Elmer's glue
- Glitter glue
- Scissors
- Paper (for your background)

1. Cut out your paper doll and attach it onto your background paper with Elmer's glue.

2. Cut out a top for your doll from a piece of your fabric. (I used blue fabric and cut out a basic tube top.)

SUGGESTION: *If you are using a paper-doll book, you can use the clothing clip-on shapes as templates.*

---

3. Glue the top onto your doll (and if you have one, you can glue the fabric onto a clip-on top shape, then attach the whole thing onto your doll).

4. Cut out a skirt for your doll from a piece of fabric different from the top (and if you have one, you can glue the fabric onto a clip-on skirt shape).

5. Carefully take apart the faux flowers so that you can use them on your skirt.

6. Before you start gluing them down, place the flowers on the skirt to see how you would like to arrange them.

7. Starting from the bottom of the skirt, glue on faux petals, all the way up to the waistline of the skirt.

8. Once the glue is dry, tie a small bow with a small bit of ribbon and glue it over the waistline of the skirt.

9. Glue the skirt to your doll, or attach the clip-on skirt if you glued your fabric onto one.

10. Glue other bits of the flower to the top, as a corsage or trim.

11. When the glue is dry, add some glitter glue for earrings and to sparkle up the shoes.

12. Carefully place your doll in a box frame and enjoy!

PAINTED WOOD RUG

There are terrific alternatives to traditional rugs these days. I particularly like the bamboo and wooden rugs, which are highly durable and easy to keep clean. Since I am such a huge fan of painted rugs, I thought I'd marry the bamboo rug and the painted rug to see what would happen. It was pretty easy to do. The key is covering it with polyurethane once you're happy with the painting so it lasts forever.

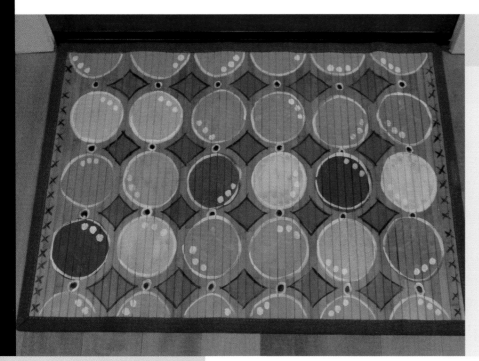

YOU'LL NEED:

- Bamboo rug or wood slat rug

- Acrylic paints

- Artist's brushes

- Pencil

- Oil-based polyurethane

- 3"-wide brush (for applying polyurethane)

HERE'S HOW:

1. For the design shown, I simply used the top of a jar to trace my circles and painted them in various colors. You can use any design you want.

2. Once the paint is completely dry, cover the rug with several coats of polyurethane, and let it dry for several days.

MAKE SURE: *When you are brushing on the polyurethane, you do not get it on the fabric sides of the rug.*

3. Thanks to the polyurethane, if the rug gets dirty, you can easily mop or wipe off the mess!

This is a great way to dress up a wall, soundproof a room, and add some warmth to your home. Use a fabric that matches your upholstery, and watch the room come alive. I like this project because I get bored with my walls and I can change out the panels as often as I want.

YOU'LL NEED:

- JT21 staple gun (This is a staple gun that is easy to handle and great for small upholstery projects like this.)

- 1½' × 5' wooden-framed painter's canvas

- 2 yards of fabric

SUGGESTION: *In case you choose a fabric with a repeat in the pattern (as in the fabric pictured), make sure you take a tape measure to the store with you so that you buy enough fabric to properly center your pattern.*

- Iron and ironing board

- Pushpins or thumbtacks

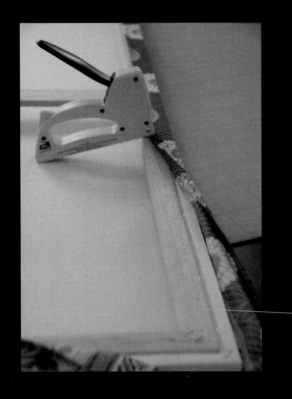

1. Iron the fabric.

2. With the fabric facedown on your workspace, center the canvas above the fabric and lay it facedown as well.

3. Cut away excess fabric so you aren't working with oodles of extra fabric, making sure you don't cut off too much. You should have enough fabric left that you should be able to fold the fabric edge over the canvas's.

> **SUGGESTION:** *If you are working with a wooden-framed artist's canvas, use where the canvas was trimmed as a guide for where your fabric should be cut.*

4. Tack the fabric in place with pushpins or thumbtacks so it doesn't shift.

5. Once you have your fabric centered and secured to the canvas, place one staple in the center of each side to keep it in place. (Make sure you staple the inside part of the frame, so you can't see the staple.)

6. Turn the canvas over to see that your pattern is still centered properly, because the fabric can shift during stapling.

7. Flip the canvas back so you can add more staples to each side. Each time you staple, also staple directly across on the opposite side of the canvas, pulling the fabric lightly, so that it's tight across the front of the canvas.

8. After every few staples, turn the canvas over to check that the fabric is still centered.

9. Continue to add staples directly across from one another until you have staples on all sides of the canvas, ½" apart.

10. Remove the pushpins and hang the canvas on your wall.

SPRAY PAINT AND WATER TECHNIQUE

I like to experiment with paint techniques, and this is one of my favorites, because you never know how it's going to turn out. Now, this is more of a technique than a craft, and you can use it in many different ways for various projects.

YOU'LL NEED:

- Glass plates, picture frames, small glass containers— whatever you want to spray

- Gold metallic, silver metallic, brown, and light blue spray paint

- Spray bottle filled with water

HERE'S HOW:

FOR THE BLUE-AND-GOLD GLASS PLATE:

1. Spray water on the back of a glass plate, and then immediately apply gold metallic spray paint.

2. When the gold paint is dry, spray the entire back of the plate with blue spray paint.

FOR THE BROWN-AND-SILVER PICTURE FRAME:

1. Cover the entire frame with brown spray paint.

2. When the brown paint is dry, spray the frame with water, and then immediately apply the silver metallic spray paint.

FOR THE SMALL CONTAINER:

1. Spray the outside of the container with water, and then immediately spray it with silver metallic spray paint.

2. When the silver paint is dry, cover the inside of the container with brown spray paint.

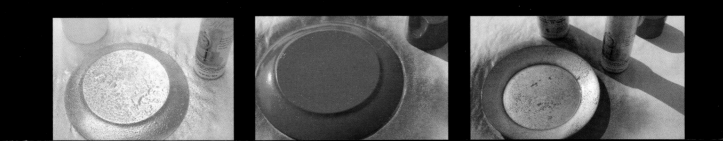

SIMPLE VINTAGE POSTERS

I have to be honest here; I'm not a huge poster fan. I love real art. But I truly *do* enjoy enlarged vintage images. Images from vintage books, like Dover Books, is the way to go for something amazing and impactful in your home.

YOU'LL NEED:

- Vintage images (available at Doverpublications.com, Barnesandnoble.com, Amazon.com) or any superdetailed black-and-white image you would want to see enlarged

- Office supply store, such as Staples

HERE'S HOW:

1. Ask a Staples employee to supersize your image. They can make any image 2' × 3', which is standard poster size.

SUGGESTION: *If you would like to have your poster laminated, Staples can do that, too.*

2. Take your new poster to a frame shop, or pop it in a poster frame yourself.

If an artist inspires you, it's important to have his or her work all around you! I love the Italian Renaissance, and Botticelli is one of my favorite artists of that era. I like to have postcards and reproductions of his art displayed throughout my home. It's sometimes hard to find small pieces of art without ripping them out of a book, so I decided to search the Internet for a few images. I found printable pieces of Botticelli's (and many other artists') art that I could put up around my house. Simply conduct a Google image search for an artist, and see what you find.

YOU'LL NEED:

• 8½" × 11" piece of wood

> **SUGGESTION:** *Use an old cutting board or even a cheap old plaque from a discount store that you can cover. I found the one in the picture for two bucks!*

• Color printout of a work of art by a favorite artist

• Set of acrylic paints with gold, reds, and colors that are in the painting you print out

• Small paintbrushes

• Krylon Spray Adhesive

• Elmer's glue

HERE'S HOW:

1. Attach your printout to the wood with the spray adhesive.

2. Paint around the edges of the wood with gold paint, making sure to go over the edge of the image as well.

3. Try to match one color in the painting, and add some of it to the piece of art without changing the image too much—don't add a mustache if she doesn't have one! (I like to add some color in the background and on places where there is white and black. This will give the painting some dimension.)

4. Rub some red paint around the edges of the wood with your finger, making sure to blend the gold and red paints nicely.

5. When the paint is dry, cover the entire painting with Elmer's glue or decoupage paste to seal it and give it some more texture.

I was tired of putting everyone I knew into art, so I decided to make myself into a litho. A lithograph (or litho) is a graphic image or impression of a subject that still represents the subject, but leaves out the finer details and small lines. It was really easy, and all it required was some colored paper, a little time, and money toward framing.

There are two ways to do this project. Both are pretty easy but take a little bit of experimenting, so make sure you have some time before you start. Once you master them, you will be well on your way to becoming a wonderful artist!

MAKING A SINGLE LITHO USING A BLACK–AND–WHITE COPY MACHINE:

YOU'LL NEED:

- Photo that is crisp, clear, and in which the subject's head takes up the majority of the photo

> **SUGGESTION:** *School photos are great for this project, as are professional portraits, because the face is prominent in the photo.*

- Copy machine that lets you adjust the darkness and lightness of the copies

HERE'S HOW:

1. Set the copy machine to enlarge your image by 25 percent and lighten your image by just a bit. (Most copy machines have bars that are highlighted to indicate lightness. You'll want to go one bar at a time.)

2. Replace your original photo with the copy you've just made. Before you make a copy of *that* copy, set the copy machine to enlarge your image by another 25 percent and lighten by another little bit.

3. Once your photo is large enough that you no longer see its minor details, continue lightening the image, but do not enlarge it.

4. When your image looks like a litho, resize the image to any size you'd like. (Don't lighten!)

5. You can have your litho framed and hung for your viewing enjoyment!

> **HINT:** *You want the image to be only white and black. There should be no gray tones at all. The only reason you're enlarging and then lightening the photo is to try to remove all the fine details of your image.*

> **SUGGESTION:** *To get four of these images on a page, make four copies at 25 percent of the original size and paste them to one page for your master copy. Then you can copy this master copy onto colored paper, and this will create a repeated-image Warhol litho.*

MAKING A REPEATING LITHO USING YOUR COMPUTER:

HINT: *It helps to be a little computer savvy to do this project. I'm not, but managed to figure it out on my Mac.*

YOU'LL NEED:

- Electronic file of the photo you want to work with

- Photo-editing program, such as Hewlett-Packard Image Editor

- 16 sheets of colored paper, 8 each of two different colors of paper in the same color family

- Double-sided tape

DON'T WORRY: *About buying a photo-editing program. These programs are pretty standard with most inkjet printers.*

HERE'S HOW:

1. Creating a litho on your computer is so easy! Just poke around your photo-editing program until you find something that says "litho"! Select this option and pop your photo into the print mode, then start playing with the image. It should automatically change the lightness/darkness of the image for you.

2. If by chance you don't have a litho setting, you should change your photo to a black-and-white one, and then play with the contrast setting until you reach the desired image.

SUGGESTION: *I know this might sound difficult, but if you have ever printed a photo from your computer, it's pretty easy to figure out. I'm not very techy, but I managed to do it easily. You just have to experiment.*

3. Print out four images per page on each of the sixteen sheets of transfers.

4. Overlap each page evenly by ¼" and attach them to one another using the double-sided tape to form four rows and four columns, alternating colors.

SUGGESTION: *Do this on a large surface or on the floor, attaching row upon row, until you form a square.*

BEAN WALL PANEL

I've always like gluing things. Pasta, beans, rocks, beads—you name it. I wanted to make a wonderful bean canvas for this book, to show that even the most silly crafts can be fun to make, and look very sophisticated. I hope you like this piece as much as I do. I think it's beautiful, and I had a blast making it, too!

YOU'LL NEED:

- 1 bag each of long-grain rice, red beans, pink beans, white beans, split-yellow peas, and green lentils

- Large canvas, at least 12" × 18"

- Pencil

- Ruler

- Elmer's glue

- Krylon Acrylic Crystal Clear

- Latex paintbrush with 2"-long, soft bristles

HERE'S HOW:

1. Draw a border around your canvas, about 2" from the edge.

2. Using your ruler, draw a line down the exact center of the canvas.

3. Draw a vase and vines (like I did) on the canvas, inside the border, or make up your own pattern.

> **MAKE SURE:** *That your drawing is symmetrical. Mine is a bit off, but I don't really mind that much.*

4. Start by setting the main/outside lines with darker beans by drawing over your pencil lines with a thick line of Elmer's glue and placing the beans onto the glue, end to end. (I went around the edges and outlined the vase with the dark red beans.)

> **SUGGESTION:** *If you decide to create your own image, you'll want to draw a layer of glue over the outside lines of your objects. You should, however, still use a dark-colored bean for these outside lines.*

5. Next, fill in each leaf with glue and sprinkle on some lentils until you have filled in the shape.

6. Working in small areas, make sure to fill in the vase and flowers with your beans and peas.

> **SUGGESTION:** *Before you start to glue the beans and peas down, experiment with colors to see how they are going to look next to one another. If you came up with your own image, choose whatever color beans you'd like. You don't have to stick to the list provided. Use your imagination!*

7. When you have finished your leaves, vines, flowers, and vase, apply glue to the areas not covered with beans, peas, and lentils, and sprinkle with rice.

8. When the glue dries, coat the entire piece with the Krylon Acrylic Crystal Clear and let it dry. Be generous with the coating, as it will keep in place anything that could be loose.

9. Let the entire panel dry overnight before hanging it up.

LEMON
TEA
SUGAR SCRUB
FOR FACE
AND
BODY

OLIVE OIL
BODY
SOFTENER

CRUSTY
FOOT
BALM

Lip Shine!
Yummy

Lip Shine!
Yummy

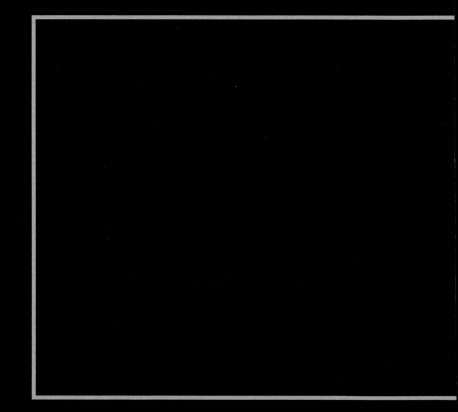

MARK'S SPECIAL TOOTHPASTE!

VITAMIN E FACE SCRUB

BODY WORSHIP

I was in a fancy-schmancy store one time, looking at some organic body products. I started to read the ingredients, and they seemed to contain almost everything I had in my cabinets at home! I jotted down some of the ingredients, did some Internet research, and started to experiment, like a mad scientist on a mission. What I found was that olive oil is amazing for moisturizing, salt is fantastic for exfoliating your face and body, and peppermint oil has one thousand uses and works wonderfully in homemade products. Before mass production, this is what people used to stay healthy and beautiful. Mix and match ingredients, and have a blast getting gorgeous! (And, by the way, making your own products is a lot more cost-effective than buying the fancy-schmancy stuff.)

SUGGESTION: *I store all of my homemade products in jars and bottles from The Container Store. They have containers in all shapes and sizes, and they look great lined up in my bathroom!*

NOTE: *Be aware of potential allergic reactions and test all homemade products on a small patch of skin on your arm before fully applying.*

VITAMIN E FACE SCRUB

This scrub will take off the dead skin cells and moisturize your face all at once. I love it and use it every few days. You'll love it too. Put some in the palm of your hands, gently scrub your face in a circular motion, then rinse well. Follow with some more moisturizer if you need it; if not, you're done. You can also use this scrub on your elbows and knees, by just scooping some onto a washcloth and scrubbing it on your joints.

YOU'LL NEED:

- 1 cup finely granulated salt
- 15 drops vitamin E oil
- 2 teaspoons olive oil
- ¼ bar unused glycerin facial soap (or your regular facial soap)
- Large mixing bowl
- Cheese grater
- Moisture-proof container

HERE'S HOW:

1. Grate the bar of soap with the cheese grater.

DON'T WORRY: *If the glycerine soap sticks together as you grate. It will separate when you start to mix it up.*

2. Pour your salt, vitamin E oil, and olive oil into the large bowl, and mix well.

3. Add your grated soap, and mix thoroughly.

4. Pour the mixture into your container.

LEMON LIP SHINE

Making your own lip shine is easy, fun, and inexpensive. Also, you can put anything you want in it to suit your tastes. It's just like cooking! If you don't like lemons, think about using things like melted chocolate chips or cinnamon oil, or even almond oil would be nice. Make a great label, and package it for your friends!

YOU'LL NEED:

- 2 tablespoons Crisco or vegetable shortening
- 1 tablespoon grated paraffin wax (You can get this at the grocery store.)
- 10 drops vitamin E oil
- 10 drops lemon oil
- Bowl
- Small, handsome containers

HERE'S HOW:

1. Combine all the ingredients together in your bowl.

2. Microwave the mixture for thirty seconds. If that doesn't melt everything, then nuke it for another ten seconds, until it's completely melted.

3. Pour the mixture into your small containers, and let it cool to room temperature.

SUGGESTION: *Double and triple your recipe to make more lip shine for you and your friends!*

LEMON TEA SUGAR SCRUB

I've used this for more than a year, and now my skin glows. Just put some onto your palms and gently scrub your face with it, or scoop some onto a washcloth and give your body a scrub. It's best to do it in the shower or tub, however, because it can get a little messy!

YOU'LL NEED:

- 1 cup sugar
- 3 tablespoons Epsom salt
- 10 teaspoons olive oil
- 2 teaspoons honey
- 3 green tea bags
- 1 lemon to zest (I prefer organic.)
- Grater or zester
- Large mixing bowl
- Beautiful container

HERE'S HOW:

1. Grate your lemon rind and set aside the zest.

2. In the large mixing bowl, combine and mix the sugar, Epsom salt, and loose tea (just rip open the bags and sprinkle the leaves in).

3. Add in the olive oil, and mix.

4. Add the honey, and combine well.

5. Add the lemon zest.

6. Mix everything in the bowl, then fill up your container.

7. Make a label, and start using it for yourself, or give it to a friend to enjoy!

WHY IN THIS ORDER? *Because the other ingredients break down the honey so it mixes in evenly.*

OLIVE OIL BODY LOTION

This is a way to nourish your skin in more ways than one. Feed your skin with olive oil and watch how soft it becomes. Just so you know, I've tried this myself and it works.

YOU'LL NEED:

- 1 cup unscented body lotion

SUGGESTION: *You can use any brand of lotion for this project because the body lotion is a base. The real moisturizing and softening comes from the olive oil.*

- ¼ cup virgin or extra virgin olive oil
- Plastic or glass container or lotion bottle

OPTIONAL: *15 drops peppermint or lemon oil*

HERE'S HOW:

1. Put the lotion, peppermint or lemon oil drops (if desired), and olive oil together into your container/bottle, and shake vigorously.

2. Use all over your body, and enjoy!

NOTE: *These are just a few of the properties of peppermint oil and lemon oil: Peppermint is believed to help smooth and relax muscles when inhaled or applied to the skin, and it's great for its cooling properties, which is why I'm a big fan of using it in the summer. Lemon oil is believed to help fight against infections, plus soothe headaches, migraines, and muscular problems. You can see why it would be nice to add either oil to a lotion.*

RELAXING BATH CRYSTAL BODY SCRUB

This stuff is the absolute best. Who doesn't enjoy kicking back and exfoliating after a long day of making crafts?

- 2 pounds Epsom salt (usually packaged in a 1-quart milk carton. You'll need one carton.)

- 20 drops lavender oil (very relaxing)

- 5 teaspoons olive oil

- ½ bar unused body soap of your choice (preferably unscented)

- Cheese grater

- Large mixing bowl

- Beautiful glass container and scooper for your product

OPTIONAL: *3 drops food coloring to give the scrub color*

HERE'S HOW:

1. Finely grate your soap, then set aside the shavings.

2. In the big bowl, mix the Epsom salt, lavender oil, and olive oil.

HINT: *At this point, you'd drop in your food coloring, and combine thoroughly into the mixture, until you have the tint you like.*

3. Mix in your grated soap.

4. Pour the entire mixture into a glass container, pop the scoop on top, and seal.

SUGGESTION: *I like to keep my body scrubs in containers on the side of the tub. If you do too, look for containers that are made completely of glass or plastic, or glass with plastic lids, so that they stay looking nice. Metal lids get rusty when exposed to moisture.*

5. Now go and scrub that stressful day away!

CRUSTY-FOOT BALM

After having hosted *10 Years Younger* on TLC, I've spoken to many dermatologists throughout the years, and all of them have told me that the best way to soften hard, crusty feet is to use petroleum jelly. It's that simple! Now, being crafty and not really a person to use just plain old petroleum jelly, I decided to add a little mint oil to the jelly, to give it a nice cooling effect while it softened my feet. This recipe is so simple, you will love it—and so will your significant other. No more sandpaper feet!

YOU'LL NEED:

- ½ cup petroleum jelly
- 25 drops peppermint oil
- Small glass container with a screw-on lid
- Small spoon
- Old pair of socks

HERE'S HOW:

1. Fill the glass container with the petroleum jelly.

2. Heat the jelly in the microwave for thirty seconds. If the jelly hasn't melted, continue to microwave in thirty-second intervals, until the jelly is liquefied.

3. Add in the peppermint oil, and stir well.

4. Let the mixture harden for a few hours. (You can put the container in the fridge if you are impatient!)

5. Before you go to bed, smooth the balm on your feet and wear an old pair of socks, or put the balm on before you leave the house in the morning. (Trust me, this stuff really works!)

We all want beautiful, white teeth, but sometimes the harsh bleaches in whitening toothpastes can make your teeth sensitive. After a little bit of research, I came up with something that actually worked and didn't hurt my teeth. Plus, I feel wonderful after I use it. I switched out my regular toothpaste for this concoction, and have been smiling bright ever since. One more little secret: It's really economical. I mean *really*!

YOU'LL NEED:

- 1 lime to zest (I prefer organic.)
- 1 cup baking soda
- 20 drops mint oil or peppermint oil
- Zester, or the tiny little part of a cheese grater
- Fantastic-looking lidded jar

HERE'S HOW:

1. Zest the lime rind, being careful to stop grating when you reach the pith (the white part of the fruit).

2. Let the zest dry for about two hours.

3. Put the zest, baking soda, and mint/peppermint oil into your jar and, with the lid tightly screwed on, shake well.

4. Dip your toothbrush into the shaken mixture and brush away those stains!

SUGGESTION: *If you want the zest to be really fine, let it dry overnight, and then grind it with a mortar and pestle.)*

NOTE: *While brushing, you will get little pieces of lime in between your teeth. Just rinse well, or floss your teeth. After a week, try your normal toothpaste, and you will notice how much it tastes like chemicals.*

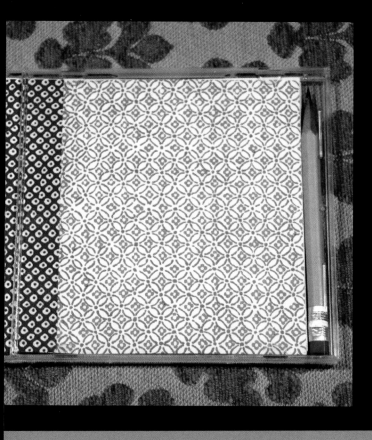

BORED AT MY DESK

When I worked at a desk job (let's not talk about it too much; I try to forget that time in my life), I was always in the copy room, doing things I should not have been doing. No, not copying my butt, but rather making photo albums, stationery, and cool pieces of art. My cubicle looked like a mini museum, and it's amazing I got any work got done at all in between craft projects. I was actually told once that perhaps I had too many distractions in my little world, and to clean it up.

At that point I knew that things in the corporate world had to change. There is no reason your office or work space has to be boring. Everything you use on a daily basis, even your tape dispenser, should be fun and scream your name. That way, when someone borrows your stapler, you'll know it's yours when you reclaim it, because you have glued a plastic banana onto it! Make your containers special by adding flowers to your pens. Do anything to brighten your day and environment! Oh, and when you get a second, make copies of your butt; it's really fun!

CD JEWEL CASE NOTEBOOK

Nothing is more annoying than trying to find a note you wrote to yourself on the back of a gum wrapper. This craft is a great way to always have pencil and paper on hand, and because of the hard plastic shell, it's always in good shape. I keep a CD case notebook in my car, and my notes and business cards are always in one place. Make one for yourself, or give it to one of your disorganized friends!

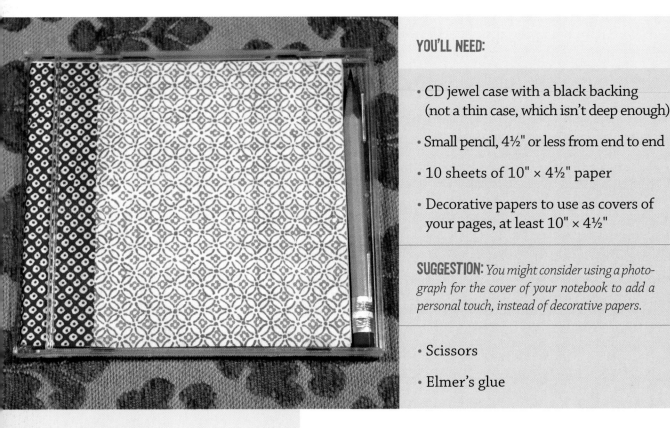

YOU'LL NEED:

- CD jewel case with a black backing (not a thin case, which isn't deep enough)
- Small pencil, 4½" or less from end to end
- 10 sheets of 10" × 4½" paper
- Decorative papers to use as covers of your pages, at least 10" × 4½"

SUGGESTION: *You might consider using a photograph for the cover of your notebook to add a personal touch, instead of decorative papers.*

- Scissors
- Elmer's glue

HERE'S HOW:

1. Remove the black plastic inside your CD case (this is the part that holds the CD in place), as well as the paper with the album cover and liner notes.

2. Fold your 10" × 4½" paper in half lengthwise so that it's 5" × 4½" (just smaller than the dimensions of the case).

3. Fold your decorative paper the same way.

4. Put your blank pages inside the decorative cover.

5. If you want, glue on another piece of paper (like I did with the blue dots) for a nice detail on the spine.

6. Place the notebook and the pencil into the case, and you are good to go!

This is a project that would look wonderful on any desk. The graphic beauty of dominoes, I find, can enhance any room or surface.

YOU'LL NEED:

- Household Goop glue

- ¼ yard of Ultrasuede or sticky-back craft felt

- Transparent tape

- Grease pencil

FOR THE SQUARE BOX:
- 49 dominoes

FOR THE LONG RECTANGULAR BOX:
- 61 dominoes

FOR THE PENCIL CUP:
- 18 dominoes

FOR THE SQUAT BOX:
- 29 dominoes

FOR THE SQUARE BOX:

1. To create the sides and bottom of the box, apply Goop glue to the edges of eight dominoes, then join them together, side by side, in the shape of a square, creating two rows of four dominoes each.

2. Make five of these eight-domino squares.

3. When the five squares are dry, lay one square flat on your work area (this will be the bottom of the box) and glue the four remaining squares to the edges of the bottom piece to create the walls of the box.

4. You will need to add a small line of glue on the outside vertical edges of the corners where the sides of the box meet.

SUGGESTION: *It might help to lean two of the opposite sides in about ⅛" at the top when gluing the sides of the box together. Use a bit of clear tape on the corners to keep the sides of the box in place while the glue dries. This might cause the sides to dry leaning in at a slight angle, but that's okay; it will just enhance the homemade effect!*

5. For the lid, glue eight dominoes together, as you see in the second photo below, with a ninth domino on its side. (This will be a handle.)

6. On the underside of the lid, mark off with your grease pencil where the center of each stabilizer domino will go. The stabilizer dominoes should be placed approximately ¼" from the edge of each side of the lid to fit inside. (These four dominoes go under the lid and sit inside the walls of the box so the lid doesn't slip off.)

7. Glue the four dominoes to the underside of the lid, one per wall, and let them dry.

8. Once the box is dry, glue your sticky felt or Ultrasuede square to the bottom by putting a small amount of Goop glue around the edges of the material, pressing down firmly.

FOR THE LONG RECTANGULAR BOX:

1. Create the long sides of the box by gluing together eight dominoes in a row side by side. (Make two of these long sides.)

2. For the short sides, glue together two columns of two dominoes (four total) to form a rectangle. (Make two of these sides.)

3. Make the base by gluing together two columns of eight dominoes (sixteen total) in a long, flat rectangle.

4. When the sides and base are dry, glue the walls to the base to make the box.

5. You will need to add a small line of glue on the outside vertical edges of the corners where the sides of the box meet.

6. Creating the lid is similar to the way you make the lid for the square box. Glue sixteen dominoes together, with the seventeenth set on its side in the middle, for the handle. Use the photograph on page 49 as a guide. (Don't forget to add your four stabilizer dominoes.)

FOR THE PENCIL CUP:

1. The sides are created by gluing together four dominoes to form a rectangle. (Make four.)

2. The bottom is created by gluing together two dominoes to form a square.

3. With the bottom of the holder flat on your work space, glue on the sides of the pencil cup.

4. Put a line of glue along the outside vertical edges of the dominoes forming the corners, leaning two opposite sides in so they touch the neighboring sides ever so slightly.

FOR THE SQUAT BOX:

1. To create the base, follow the instructions in step 1 for the square box.

2. Make each of the four sides of the box by gluing together two dominoes, short end to short end.

3. When the sides are dry, glue them to the base.

4. To make the lid, use the same instructions for the lid from the square box project, remembering to add your stabilizer dominoes.

5. After the glue dries, glue on some Ultrasuede or sticky felt for the bottom, and you're done!

3-D PHOTO BRIGADE

My friend Steve has a habit of cutting out photos of people and standing them up on his desk when he is bored. It's strange, but I love it, so I asked to borrow the idea. I think it's a great way to show off your photos, and I enjoy being surrounded by my family's and friends' smiling faces.

YOU'LL NEED:

- Glue stick

- Lightweight cardboard (an express-mail envelope would be perfect)

- Scissors

- Craft or X-Acto knife

- 3" × 5" photos of friends and family

HERE'S HOW:

1. Cut your photos in any way that you like. I like to cut out the backgrounds, keeping the faces and upper bodies.

2. Trim the cardboard into a rectangle that measures about 3" × 1½".

3. Using the craft or X-Acto knife, score a line on the cardboard ½" in from the edge, the entire length of one of the approximately 3" edges, and bend it 90 degrees.

4. Glue the ½" bent part to the back of the photo with the glue stick, leaving about ⅛" between the bottom of the photo and the base so that it can lean back at a very slight angle.

5. Make a bundle of these and see how your day improves.

SUGGESTION: *Whenever possible, print the photos from your computer so you don't have to cut up the actual prints.*

At least ten times a day I need to jot down an idea for a craft project. I was always looking for the perfect journal, notebook, or writing pad to keep my notes in, and I finally decided to make my own. Now you can too.

YOU'LL NEED:

- Sturdy corrugated cardboard (I like the shipping boxes from the post office or from shipping services such as FedEx!)

- Any paper or fabric you'd like (to cover your book)

- Paper for the inside of the book (This can be any kind of paper, from construction paper to copy paper, as long as it can be cut to the size of the book you are binding.)

- Krylon Spray Adhesive

- X-Acto knife or box cutter

- Rubber cement or Elmer's glue

- Ruler

- Pencil

OPTIONAL: *Krylon Acrylic Crystal Clear for a shiny finish, and any colored ribbon for a beautiful bookmark*

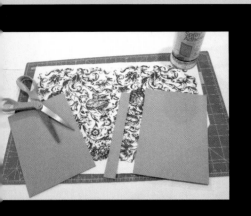

1. Create the front and back covers of your book by cutting the cardboard into two equally sized pieces.

2. To create the spine for your book, cut a piece of corrugated cardboard that is ½" wide and matches the length of your front and back covers.

3. To begin putting the cover together, lay out your fabric/paper facedown.

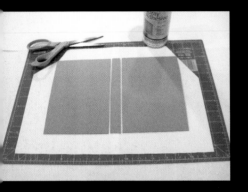

HINT: *Try using specialty wrapping paper from a craft store, or make your own by taking an image and color copying it. If the paper isn't big enough for your book, simply glue sheets of your image together to create the size you need.*

---

4. Lay all your cardboard pieces on top of the fabric/paper, side by side. The spine should be in the middle, the front cover on the left of the spine and the back cover on the right. There should be a ⅛" space between the spine and the front and back covers.

5. Using a ruler and a pencil, trace around your pieces of cardboard. (This will help you remember exactly where to place the pieces later on.)

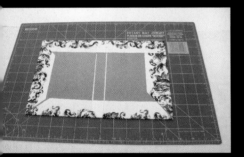

6. Measure and mark off 1" from all sides of the fabric (meaning, you should have a 1" space between the marked-off lines and the outside edges of the cardboard).

7. Remove and set aside your cardboard pieces. Using the lines you've marked off, trim off the excess fabric/paper. Make sure not to cut out the drawings of your cardboard pieces! (You should wind up with a piece of fabric with the tracings of the front and back covers and the spine. There should be the 1" space between the edge of the fabric/paper and the edges of the tracings.)

8. Remove the cardboard, and spray the entire underside of your fabric/paper with the spray adhesive.

9. Using the tracings you made earlier as a guide, carefully place your cardboard pieces onto the fabric/paper cover. (They will be hard to move once they are laid down.)

10. Cut off each corner of the book cover. The cut should be made at the corners of your front and back covers, and at an angle, so that the pieces that fall off are little triangles of fabric/paper.

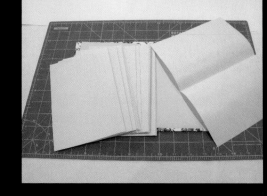

11. Before the spray adhesive dries, fold the edges of the book cover over, so that they stick to your cardboard.

> **HINT:** *Now is a good time to spray the front cover with some Krylon Acrylic Crystal Clear. It makes your book look professional—and last much longer! Plus, I think it adds a nice finish.*

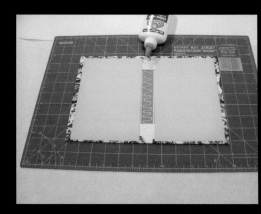

12. Next, you will need to prepare your endpapers, which are the pages that will be glued to the inside front and back covers of your book. Use something bright and colorful and that contrasts with your cover. Your endpapers (you'll need only two sheets) should be trimmed to match the size of your cardboard pieces minus ¼" from the top, bottom, and one side.

13. Cover your endpapers with spray adhesive and carefully place them onto your inside front and back covers, leaving ¼" between the endpaper and the top, bottom, and outside edge (the one farthest from the spine) of each cover.

14. Cut the paper you're going to fill the book with to the same size as your endpapers.

> **SUGGESTION:** *I have a paper cutter that I use to make my own block of paper. It's uneven, but I don't mind—I like the homemade feel of it. However, if you want something cut perfectly, head over to Staples and have them cut your paper for you to the size that you want. They do a good job, it'll turn out perfect, and it's not terribly expensive.*

15. Add rubber cement or glue to the spine on the cover, and carefully set your block of paper onto the spine, lengthwise, adhering the paper to the book cover.

16. Stand your creation spine side down, with bookends pressed against both sides. Let the book dry overnight. In the morning, you will have a bound book. Congratulations!

BABY HEAD PAPERWEIGHT

Yes, people will think you are weird for making this, but that's okay!

YOU'LL NEED:

- Hollow doll's head
- Plaster of Paris (Plaster of Paris comes in powder form, and all you do is add water. Just follow the instructions on the box.)
- Small, flexible plastic cup (to mix the plaster of Paris)
- Black and gold spray paint
- Spray bottle filled with water

HERE'S HOW:

1. Mix the plaster of Paris in your flexible plastic cup.

2. Fill your doll head with the plaster and let it dry, per the directions on the box.

> **HINT:** *Make about ¼ cup of plaster at a time so you don't make too much.*

3. Spray the head with black spray paint.

4. When the paint is dry, spray the head with water, and then immediately spray it with the gold spray paint.

5. Let the paint dry completely.

6. Place the head on a pile of papers or just set it on your desk to spark some interesting conversation.

SPIRAL–BOUND NOTEBOOKS

I love having personalized stationery and notebooks around the house. They're better than just plain old pads, and you can match them to your decor. Make notebooks with photos of your friends or with your favorite piece of art for covers. Anything that can be laminated can become a notebook cover. This project will make two notepads measuring 8½" × 5½". These are such fun and creative things to make!

YOU'LL NEED:

- 2 4¼" × 5½" images (for the front and back covers)

> **HINT:** The dimensions of your images depend on what kind of notebooks you make. For small notepads, your images should be 4¼" × 5½". For a full-size notebook, the images should be 8½" × 11".

- Stack of 8½" × 11" copy paper

- Access to a laminating machine

HERE'S HOW:

1. Go to a copy center, such as Staples, and have your images laminated side by side onto an 8½" × 11" lamination sheet.

2. Cut the lamination sheet in half so that you get two laminated images, which you'll use for your notepad's covers.

3. Have the copy paper cut in half, widthwise. (I would say one hundred sheets is about the maximum you should bind.)

> **NOTE:** To make an 8½" × 11" notebook, just have the copy center laminate two 8½" × 11" images onto two lamination sheets, and you won't have to have either the sheet or the paper cut.

4. Have the copy center bind your books, either with plastic or wire spiral binding.

5. It's really that easy, and the results are amazing and make great presents!

ULTRASUEDE DESK BLOTTER, PLACE MAT, OR TABLE RUNNER

Ultrasuede is my favorite fabric, and this project uses one of my favorite techniques: using fabric glue to put Ultrasuede designs onto Ultrasuede! It's easy and you can get some fantastic results. Just let your imagination run wild. . . .

YOU'LL NEED:

- ½ yard of Ultrasuede (for the base of your blotter or mat. You'll need more for a table runner, so measure your table before going to the store.)

- ¼ yard each of two different colors of Ultrasuede (for the patterns)

- Scissors

- Fabric glue

HERE'S HOW:

1. Cut your base fabric to the size of a desk blotter or place mat (I like a base that is about 12" × 18"), or longer for a table runner.

2. Starting at one end of the fabric, cut ⅓"-deep decorative notches along the border of your base fabric. Your notches should be 2" apart.

3. Cut out any pattern you'd like from one of the two colors of Ultrasuede, and glue to the center of your base fabric.

HINT: *Make different center patterns by just folding the Ultrasuede in half and experimenting with shapes!*

4. Cut out the patterns you'll glue around your central pattern from your remaining color of Ultrasuede. Adhere those pieces any way you'd like.

5. Once the fabric glue is dry, you're ready to use your blotter/mat/runner!

¼" Scale: ¼" = 1"

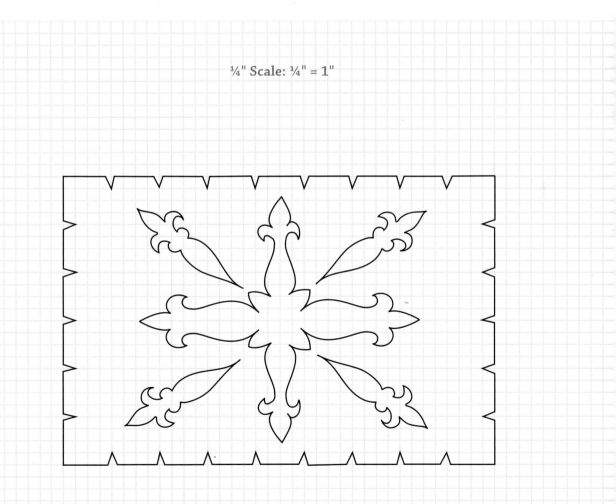

ULTRASUEDE-COVERED CONTAINERS

This is a terrific way to recycle cans and small boxes, and at the same time make your desk at work the envy of all others. It will also make your workspace feel more organized, simply by having matching containers for your paper clips and pushpins.

YOU'LL NEED:

- Several containers, such as old tea tins, empty cans, and boxes
- Piece of paper (to draw your template on)
- Ultrasuede, in any color
- Gold spray paint
- Ribbon, in a matching pattern or color to the suede (to use as trim)
- Brass charms (I like ordering from FancifulsInc.com. They have an amazing selection to choose from!)

- Hot-glue gun and glue sticks
- Elmer's glue
- Scissors
- Ruler
- Pencil

SUGGESTION: *If you use empty cans, make sure they're cleaned and dried, and that the label has been removed.*

HERE'S HOW:

1. You will need to make a template for your Ultrasuede. Wrap the paper around your container, marking off its height and length.

2. Trim the excess paper so that you're left with a rectangle that should wrap perfectly around your container. Set the template aside.

SUGGESTION: *If you're using a recycled aluminum can, you can use the label as your template and save yourself a step! Just be careful that when you remove the label from the can, you don't rip it.*

3. Spray the top, bottom, and inside of the container with gold spray paint.

4. While the spray paint dries, place your paper template onto the Ultrasuede. Using the template as a guide, trim off the excess suede so that the paper and the suede are the same size.

5. After the paint dries, tack the suede onto the container, using the hot-glue gun.

HINT: *Alternate between using the hot-glue gun and the Elmer's glue so you have a nice bond. (Hot glue is great for adhering something short-term, and the Elmer's is great for making sure it's permanent.)*

6. If you are working with a cylindrical container, when the glue is dry, bend your brass charm so it curves like the curve of your can and adheres flat to the can over the area you want to apply it. (They bend easily, so be careful!)

7. Place a dab of hot glue and of Elmer's glue onto the charm, then apply it to the side of your container.

8. Lay the container flat, with the side with the charm facing up. This is so the glue can dry without the charm slipping off.

9. After the glue has dried, you're ready to accessorize *any* desk!

PEN FLOWER ARRANGEMENT

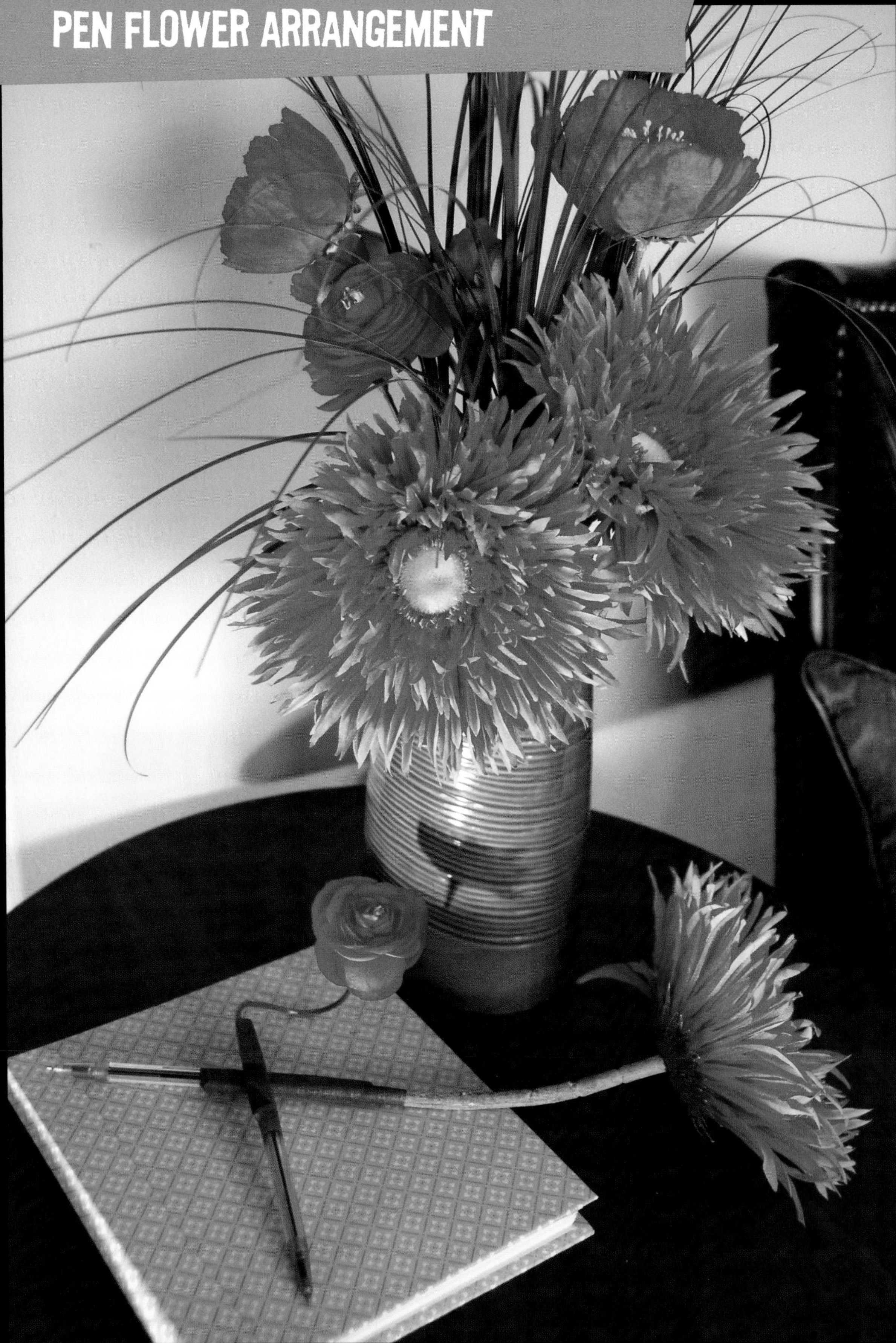

Okay, so, I always need a pen and can rarely find one around. This project is a terrific idea—to spruce up a desk area and ensure that you'll always have a pen handy.

- Ballpoint pens (as many as you want)

- Faux flowers (one for each pen)

- Vase with a big mouth (so that it's easy to retrieve a pen. I got mine at Michaels, an arts and crafts store.)

- Floral tape

MAKE SURE: *To get faux flowers with wire stems, not plastic, strawlike stems.*

- Ruler

- Wire cutters

- Scissors

HERE'S HOW:

1. Measure the length of your pen and subtract 2" (if your pen is 6" long, then your measurement would be 4").

2. Determine how long you want the stems of your flowers to be. (This depends on the height of your vase.)

3. Subtract the pen length you came up with in step 1 from the stem length you came up with in step 2 (trust me!).

4. Trim the flower's wire stem to the length of your measurement from step 3, using the wire cutters.

5. Wrap the bottom 2" of the stem around the end of the pen (the part that doesn't write) and tape them together using the floral tape, as tightly as possible.

6. Fill your vase with as many "flowers" as you need to create a bautiful arrangement, and you are all set to write!

SUGGESTION: *Use greenery around the edges and among your "flowers" so that your arrangement looks as real as possible.*

CAN I HAVE A LIGHT?

magine this: It's midnight, and you have to get out of bed to pee. Instead of turning on a light (the shock of the glare will keep you up for the next two hours), you try to maneuver your way through the room in the dark, only to stub your toe. It's all over. You're now watching the late, late, late show and reruns of *Oprah* because you can't get back to sleep.

All of this could have been avoided if you had taken some time earlier that week to create a fantastic light fixture for yourself. Each of the following lamps is perfect for that wonderful glow that makes even the most tired people look lovely and the most mundane TV dinner a romantic experience. And it won't traumatize you with its brightness in the middle of the night.

GLOWING CRAFT–PAPER HANGING LANTERN

I couldn't decide where to put this lantern after I made it. It looked fantastic in my small bathroom, giving a dramatic effect and a nice glow that didn't wake me up in the middle of the night. Then in the summer, when I needed some outdoor light that wasn't too bright, I strung it up, and it had such a beautiful impact. It almost looked like the moon. A very oddly shaped moon.

YOU'LL NEED:

- Snap-in socket-and-cord set, with a switch on the cord and a candelabra base (for use with chandelier or night-light bulbs)

HINT: *The best place by far to get lamp parts, I've found, is Lampshop.com.*

- 2 16"-diameter wire planting baskets from a nursery (These come in all shapes and sizes and are wonderful bases to work with when making hanging lanterns.)

- Thin craft paper, any color

- 2' of thin wire (or twist ties)

- 25-watt (or lower) lightbulb

- 1"-wide paintbrush

- Krylon Acrylic Crystal Clear

- Elmer's glue

- Scissors

- Wire cutters

1. Wire the mouths of your baskets together using the small-gauge wire and wire cutters. This will create the shape that you are going to cover with the craft paper.

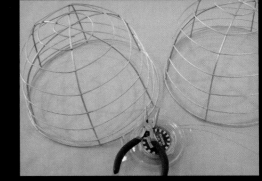

2. Cut your craft paper into strips that are about 1½–2" wide and about 10" long.

3. Water down your glue just a bit, so that it's easy to spread. Use a ratio of one part water to two parts glue.

4. Paint glue along your strips and attach them to the basket. Overlap the strips by about ¼" so they adhere to one another, making sure to leave a hole at the top and the bottom.

> **HINT:** *Be generous with the glue, and don't worry if you miss a spot with the craft paper. You can always add some smaller pieces later.*

5. Once you've covered the entire structure, let it dry. You will notice that after the glue dries, the paper tightens around the wire baskets, and you will be able to see the structure underneath.

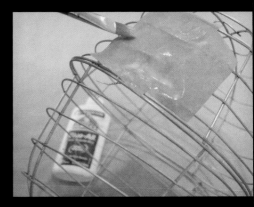

6. Carefully cover the lantern in three layers of Krylon Acrylic Crystal Clear coating, which will make it sturdy, letting the coating dry in between layers.

7. Tie a loose knot in the light cord, about 6" from the bulb socket.

8. Screw in your lightbulb and let it slip through the top hole and into the lantern.

9. Thread some wire through the hole in the knot of the cord (you might want to loop the wire once or twice, to secure it to the cord), then twist the wire around the wire hook that should have come with your basket (attaching it to the base of the hook should be fine).

10. Hang from a hook and see how wonderful it looks!

DRINKING-STRAW STARBURST HANGING LIGHT

One of my favorite things to do is use everyday items in an unexpected way. I've always loved straws, because they come in a thousand variations, from fluorescent colors to bendy and striped. This lamp is a terrific way to brighten up a kids room and spark the imagination.

YOU'LL NEED:

- Roll of 20-gauge wire

- 6" snap-in socket-and-cord set, with a switch on the cord and a candelabra base

- Very small, low-wattage lightbulb, such as one used for a night light

- 300 drinking straws, any color

- Wire cutters

- Needle-nose pliers

1. Cut off about 20" of your 20-gauge wire.

2. Take fifteen straws and wrap the wire tightly around the center of the bundle. This will fold the straws in half, with both ends of the straws on one side and the centers on the other side.

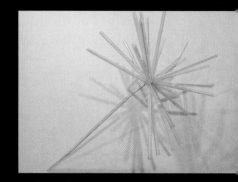

3. Secure the straws together by tightly twisting the wire around the center of the bundle. Keep twisting the wire to the ends to create the twisted wire stem below the bundle of straws.

4. Thread the wire through another straw, and insert the stem inside of it so that the wire is hidden. You should have a small tube of straw covering your bouquet's stem and a long piece of wire coming out of the other end.

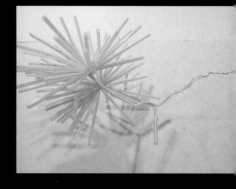

5. Cut the wire from your cluster, but leave a piece about 1" long. Bend the excess wire up to secure the straw, which is hiding the wire, to the bouquet.

6. Make about fifteen straw clusters.

7. Tie a loose knot in the light cord, about 4" above the bulb's socket.

8. Insert the ends of about eight of the straw clusters into the cord knot and twist them around the cord so they are secured.

9. Keep inserting the stems into the cord knot, and for some variation, wrap some of the stems around the other stems until you have used all of your stems and have a cluster shape you like.

> **MAKE SURE:** *Your straws are not touching the lightbulb, so that you avoid an accidental fire. It's a very low wattage anyway, so I assure you it's unlikely anything could happen. But it's better to be safe than sorry.*

10. Hang your lantern and let there be light!

TWIG CHANDELIER

When I moved into my new house, I was faced with a light fixture in my dining room that needed to be covered up. Until I find the perfect chandelier, I'm going to keep making my own and enjoying them as my moods change. Often, we find ourselves in apartments where we cannot change the light fixtures, so this is a great way to add some interest to your ceilings and bring some nature into your home. Even though my crafty moods change with the direction of the wind, this twig chandelier may be up for the long haul.

YOU'LL NEED:

- Twigs in various sizes, ranging from 1'–4' in length

- Elmer's wood glue

- Large pinecone

- 20-gauge wire

- Wire cutters

- Faux leaves and small silk flowers (I used wood roses because they were falling off a tree in my front yard.)

- 3 12"-long pieces of heavy twine

- 3 2"-long eye screws

- Scissors

- Copper and gold acrylic paint

- Brown spray paint

- 1"-wide artist brushes

- Hot-glue gun and glue sticks

- Ladder

1. Start by experimenting with the twigs and arranging them into shapes that you like. (I prefer crisscrossing them into a triangle, for a base, and building from there.)

2. For this project, we'll use the triangle base. First, take three twigs and create a triangle. Tie the twigs together with your wire. This base will be the part of your chandelier that will be closest to the ceiling.

3. Start adding twigs on top of the base. Once you have a structure that you like, add lots of wood glue wherever you see twigs touching and let the glue dry overnight.

4. After the glue has dried, wrap wire around the areas where the twigs crisscross, to secure the twigs to one another and to make your structure sturdy.

5. Paint the entire structure with brown spray paint and let it dry.

6. Hang the chandelier over your existing light fixture by screwing in your eye screws into the ceiling, so you form a triangle around your light fixture.

7. Tie the twine to your twig chandelier. The distance between each twine should be the same as the distance between each eye screw on the ceiling.

8. Tie the twine to the eye screws.

9. Paint your flowers and leaves with brown spray paint so they match the twigs.

10. After the paint has dried, add your flowers and leaves to the structure, using the hot-glue gun, while the chandelier is up and you can see how you want to place your flowers/leaves. (There is a lot of going up and down on a ladder, so be careful!)

11. Add some copper and gold acrylic paint in various places to highlight the chandelier.

12. Carefully use wood glue to secure your pinecone to the center of your chandelier.

13. If you have any holes in the chandelier that need filling, add some small branches and secure them into place with wood glue, after covering them with brown spray paint.

14. You're now ready to enjoy your fabulous creation!

LAMINATED CHANDELIER

Many of the light fixtures original to my house have a metal ring around the edge and protrude down from the ceiling. Others have a disk suspended over the lightbulb. Any of these can be covered up and beautified with this simple method.

YOU'LL NEED:

- Lots of pages from a book
- Scissors or paper cutter
- Large needle and a thimble, or tiny hole puncher
- About 300 ornament hooks
- Double-sided tape, or regular transparent tape
- Access to a laminating machine

HERE'S HOW:

1. Laminate your pages and cut them into squares and rectangles of different sizes.

> **DON'T WORRY:** *If your shapes aren't "perfect." It doesn't matter if they are, so you can't go wrong with this!*

2. Using your needle or hole puncher, poke a hole in two opposing ends of each laminated square and rectangle.

3. Insert the ends of one hook through the holes of two squares or rectangles. Hold up one of the shapes and thread another hook through its other hole. (You're creating a chain of squares and rectangles.) Continue creating chains of shapes until you think you've made enough to cover your fixture (you can always add more if it's not enough).

> **HINT:** *Have fun with the pattern of your chain by alternating squares and rectangles!*

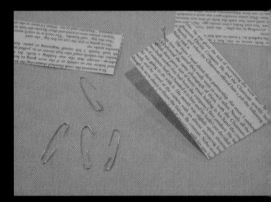

4. Tape the strips to the metal part of your light fixture.

5. Shorten and lengthen the strips until you get the size you like, then enjoy how you've beautified your light fixture!

TISSUE-PAPER-COVERED INDUSTRIAL HANGING LAMP

These lamps are absolutely gorgeous, and they look like they cost a fortune. Make one or two for your home, and prepare to see how jealous your friends get!

YOU'LL NEED:

- Lamp wiring kit, with socket, switch, and cord (You can lengthen the cord with an extension cord if you want.)

- 25-watt (or lower) lightbulb

- 2' × 5' roll of galvanized steel 23-gauge hardware cloth (This looks like a mesh wire.)

- Straight-cutting tin snips

- Work gloves (The hardware cloth can easily scratch you.)

- Galvanized steel duct roof cap, in the size of your choice (I'd chose the 8" or 6" sizes because it's easier to get your hand in to change the bulb.)

- 2' of small-gauge wire

- Package of tissue paper, any color, or 2 yards of a thin cloth (try muslin, burlap, or gauze), in a neutral shade

- Krylon Acrylic Crystal Clear or Elmer's glue

- 1½"-wide paintbrush

- Household Goop glue

- Drill and ½" diameter drill bit

HERE'S HOW:

1. Drill a ½" hole into the center of your steel roof cap.

2. Measure the circumference of the roof cap, then and add 2" to the measurement.

3. Cut the hardware cloth to that measurement, with your tin snips. (Don't forget to wear the gloves!)

4. Roll the cloth into a tube, so that it fits inside the steel cap, then remove it but keep the tube shape.

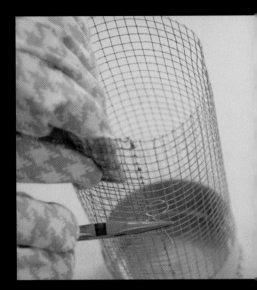

5. With your gauge wire, fasten little ties along the edges of the tube to secure its shape.

6. Slip the tube of hardware cloth into the roof cap.

7. Squirt some Household Goop glue along the inside rim of the cap so that the top of the tube is glued to the steel cap.

8. Cut the tissue paper/fabric into small squares, about 2" × 4".

9. Using the Krylon Acrylic Crystal Clear or Elmer's glue, wet the pieces with a brush and apply them to the hardware cloth, in a nice even pattern. (Make sure to cover the entire hardware cloth.)

10. After the Krylon is dry, give the hardware cloth another coat so the lamp is nice and sturdy.

11. Wire your lamp kit through the hole in the roof cap by inserting the cord through the top of the lamp. (Make sure to follow the directions that came with the kit!)

12. Screw in your lightbulb, hang the lamp from a hook, and there you have it: a beautiful suspending lamp!

> **SUGGESTION:** *Leave the bottom of the lamp open so you can reach in and change the lightbulb when it burns out.*

This lamp looks great on side tables, and you can select marbles in colors that complement your decor!

YOU'LL NEED:

- Push-thru side out socket (This has the cord coming out of the socket.)
- 25-watt (or lower) lightbulb
- 1" of threaded rod
- Check ring with a ⅜" diameter
- 1" diameter rubber washer
- Mason jar
- Enough marbles to fill the jar, any color
- Clip-on lamp shade
- Drill and ⅜" diameter drill bit

HERE'S HOW:

1. Drill a hole into the center of your jar's lid.

2. Put your threaded rod through the hole. However high you want the bulb to be from the lamp's base is how much threaded rod you should leave above the lid.

3. From the top side of the lid, screw your push-thru side out socket onto the threaded rod.

4. Place your rubber washer on the threaded rod on the underside of the lid, then screw on your check ring. Make sure to tighten the ring to keep everything in place.

5. Fill the jar with marbles.

6. Screw on the lid. You should be left with the socket pointing upward.

7. Place in your lightbulb and clip on your lampshade. Voilà!

TWO-LITER SEA-CREATURE LAMP

Kids love this lighting fixture. It's like having a lamp and a pet in one!

YOU'LL NEED:

- Snap-in socket-and-cord set, with switch and a candelabra base
- 15-watt chandelier lightbulb
- 2 emptied and cleaned 2-liter soda bottles
- Craft knife
- Scissors
- Goof Off glue remover

HERE'S HOW:

1. Remove the labels from the bottles and rub off the glue using Goof Off. (It's the only thing I've found that works.)

DON'T WORRY: *If the Goof Off leaves an oily residue. Just wash the bottles with soap and water in the sink, and it'll come off.*

2. Cut the base off one of the bottles, using your craft knife to create a hole, and then using the scissors to finish the cut.

3. Cut ¼" strips in the bottle, from the bottom up to the neck. Do this all the way around the bottle, until the whole thing is cut up.

4. Repeat steps 2–3 with the second bottle.

5. Stack the bottles on top of each other, so that one bottle is nested inside the other and the necks are fitted together.

6. Thread the light cord through the bottom of the cut bottles, so that the socket is surrounded by the cut strips.

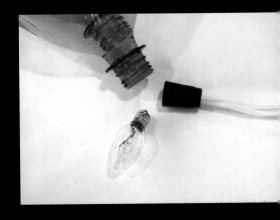

7. Screw in the lightbulb and hang the lamp from a hook. It's that easy!

> **SUGGESTION:** *Several of these lamps in a cluster look wonderful. Using different-colored lightbulbs also looks great. However, when experimenting with different-colored bulbs, always make sure to use a 15-watt bulb or less.*

KITCHEN UTENSIL LAMP

This is the ultimate in kitchen kitsch. I love two things about this lamp: the conversations it starts and how beautiful the shadows are when it's the only light on in the house.

YOU'LL NEED:

- Silver or brushed steel lamp base, with lamp harp

- 25-watt (or lower) lightbulb

- 10" diameter lampshade with washer top (These are the kinds that work with a harp. I took apart an old lampshade for mine.)

- 20 forks and 20 spoons (made of cheap stainless steel, and make sure you can bend them easily!)

- Drill and ⅛" diameter drill bit

- 20 S hooks

- Household Goop glue

- Chandelier lightbulb

HERE'S HOW:

1. Attach your washer-top lamp's wire to the harp and secure to the lamp base.

2. Bend the handles of the forks in half backward, making sure they are bent consistently at the same point.

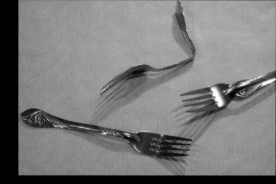

3. Drill holes into the handles of all of the spoons, at their ends.

4. Hang the forks over the lamp's wire, leaving equal spaces in between each fork and making sure the tines of the fork are facing outward.

5. Attach each spoon to one end of an S hook, then hang the whole thing on the wire from the other end, in between the bent forks. Make sure the concave sides of the spoons are facing outward.

6. Once you have everything in place, add a dab of Household Goop to the underside of the forks and S hooks, where each touches the lamp's wire.

7. Let the glue dry, then screw in your chandelier bulb and let the light shine.

DRINKING-STRAW WALL SCONCE

Straws are a great material for crafts because they are abundant and easy to work with. This is a nutty wall sconce, and I am making no excuses for it. I like it, and that's all that counts! Two of these joined together at the mouths would also make a great pendant lamp. Hang it on the wall, and you'll have an amazing art piece that also functions as a light.

YOU'LL NEED:

- 250 straws, any color
- Night-light
- Extension cord
- Unused deep-fryer basket, with handle and ¼" holes

HERE'S HOW:

1. Working from the inside of the deep-fryer basket, fold your straw in half and push each end of the straw through two adjoining holes.

2. Repeat this process until you have pushed straws through all the holes in your deep fryer.

3. Plug your night-light into one end of the extension cord.

4. Wrap the extension cord around the handle of the fryer basket, so that the nightlight hangs inside of your lamp.

5. Bend in the handle if you'd like (as seen in the photos to the right) or hang the basket from its handle from a nail on the wall. The inside part of the basket should be facing toward the wall.

6. Plug in the other end of the cord and enjoy your nutty sconce!

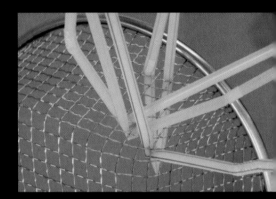

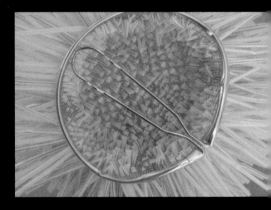

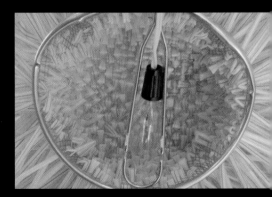

BASKET LAMP

Ninety-nine cents stores are filled with wicker baskets that might not look great by themselves, but put two of these together, mouth to mouth, and you have a terrific lamp that, in clusters of three, will make your back porch into a classy outdoor living room.

YOU'LL NEED:

- 2 baskets that are the same size

> **SUGGESTION:** *Find baskets that have a bottom rim and a separate woven bottom.*

- Lamp kit, with about 15' of cord
- 25-watt lightbulb
- Heavy-duty craft knife, or small craft saw
- Drill and ¼" diameter drill bit
- Elmer's wood glue

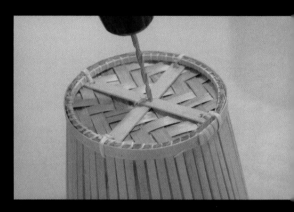

HERE'S HOW:

1. Drill a ¼" hole in the bottom of one of your baskets. This will be the lamp's top.

2. With the heavy-duty craft knife, or craft saw, cut, as cleanly and evenly as possible, a large hole in the bottom of your second basket. If you can, try to remove the entire bottom. This will be the lamp's bottom, and allow you to change the bulb when it burns out.

3. Lay one basket over the other, so that the mouths are aligned. Glue the mouths together with Elmer's wood glue.

4. When the glue is dry, wire your light socket set through the ¼" hole at the top.

5. Hang from a hook and enjoy!

NIGHT-LIGHT BOXES

Call me immature, but I love a night-light. The soft glow seeping through the quiet night as I make my way to the fridge for a midnight snack of a two-foot-long submarine sandwich and an entire bag of cookies . . . Heaven.

YOU'LL NEED:

- About 50 wooden clothespins (for a 6" × 8" frame), or about 90 wooden clothespins (for an 8" × 10" frame)

- 2 identical, flat wooden frames with square edges (I got mine for a song at Ikea!)

- Elmer's wood glue

- Extension cord

- Night-light from a dollar store (They have tons!)

- Masking tape

- Color-copied image to fit your frame

- Craft knife

1. Frame your image in one of the frames. This will be the face of your light box.

2. Remove the metal springs from the clothespins. You'll need the wooden pieces to create the "sides" of your light box.

3. Take the glass out of the frame that will be the back of your light box. (You won't need it anymore, and you can use it for the tin frame project on pages 328–30.)

4. Stand your frames up on their sides one in front of the other, with the fronts of the frames facing the same direction.

> **SUGGESTION:** *Prop the frames up with books or whatever it takes to keep them parallel to each other.*

5. To create the sides of the light box, put a layer of glue along the top edges of the frames. Place your clothespins facedown, across the frames and next to each other to make the first side of your box.

6. Let the glue dry, and repeat this process on each side of your frames until you have a box.

7. Remove the cardboard from the back frame of your box once the glue is dry.

8. With the craft knife, cut out a ½" × ½" hole at the bottom of the cardboard piece you've removed. This hole is for the extension cord to go through.

9. Fit the night-light into the hole you've made, with the plugs coming out of the back of the cardboard. Secure the light with tape, then plug it into the extension cord. (You should have the night-light on one side of the cardboard and the plug on the other.)

10. Replace the cardboard onto the back frame, with the extension cord coming out of the ½" × ½" hole.

> **WARNING:** *Even though the night-light is a low wattage, make sure that the bulb is not touching the cardboard and that the bulb is separated from the cardboard by the plastic shade.*

11. You're done; now go enjoy a midnight snack!

DECOUPAGE READING LAMP

My friend Duran (cool name, right?) says that lamps are the jewelry of the home. I couldn't agree more. You can show anyone who enters your home how special you are by your accessory choices, and lamps are a great place to start. This one was made with a very boring base that desperately needed some attention!

YOU'LL NEED:

- Lamp with a base that has large surfaces
- Black-and-white copies of antique images
- Pages from a book
- Elmer's glue
- 1"-wide, flat art brush
- Scissors
- Krylon Acrylic Crystal Clear
- Cup of water

HERE'S HOW:

1. Cut your book pages into 2" × 2" squares.

2. Cut out your antique images and make sure they're not too large for your lamp base.

3. Water down your Elmer's glue with 1 teaspoon of water for every tablespoon of glue.

4. Apply the book pages to the lamp base using the glue mixture. Completely cover the lamp.

5. When the pages are dry, apply your black-and-white antique images.

6. When the entire lamp base is dry, spray with several coats of Krylon Acrylic Crystal Clear. (This will protect your work and make it easy to dust.) Enjoy!

PUNK PAPER LANTERN

My favorite thing about this lantern is that it looks just as cool without a light in it as it does with one. I think it works well with graphic projects, such as my Andy Warhol–inspired litho project, and it also looks great next to the drag paintings.

YOU'LL NEED:

- Round paper lantern (Try PearlRiver.com.)
- Package of Crayola finger paints (These work really well, and they come in a wide range of vivid colors.)
- Paper cups
- Hook
- String

OPTIONAL: *25-watt lightbulb*

HERE'S HOW:

1. Assemble your lantern and hang it with a hook and string so you can work with it more easily.

2. Water down your paints so they will drip more easily. Mix a 1:1 ratio of paint and water in a paper cup.

3. Crease the lips of the cups into spouts so you can better control the paint as you pour.

HINT: *Lay some newspaper down on the floor to catch the paint when it drips.*

4. Pour one color of the paint along the top rim of the lantern so that it drips down its outside. It doesn't matter what color you choose to start with.

5. Pour the next color over the lamp. Repeat with as many colors as you like.

6. When the paint is dry, unhook the lantern, rehang it upside down, and repeat steps 4–5.

7. Add a lightbulb to this lamp or use it as a piece of art. I like it because it looks wonderful, day and night.

POPSICLE–STICK TRAMP ART LAMPSHADE

Tramp art refers to an art form that uses any kind of found materials, such as matchsticks, Popsicle sticks, bottle caps, or even cigar rings. I've always loved it, because it is eco-friendly, and you can make just about anything with these recycled items if you put your mind to it.

YOU'LL NEED:

- 500 Popsicle sticks

- Elmer's Wood glue

- 3" diameter washer-top ring

- Large newspaper spread, at least 22" × 30"

- Scissors

- Amazing Goop craft glue

- Ruler

HERE'S HOW:

FOR THE DODECAGON HALF OF THE LAMPSHADE:

1. You will need to cut a dodecagon, with sides that are 3" long, out of newspaper. I know it sounds daunting, but no worries; just follow my lead! (A dodecagon has twelve equal sides.)

2. Fold your large sheet of newspaper in half lengthwise, and then fold it in half again, widthwise.

3. Lay the newspaper down in front of you, like a diamond. The open edges should be facing away from you and the folded tip pointing toward you.

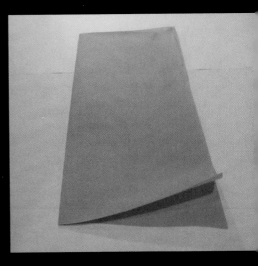
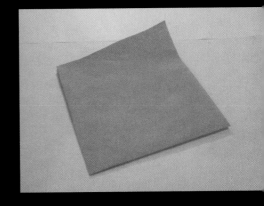
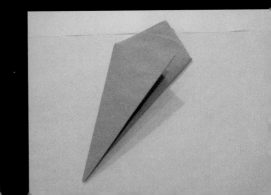

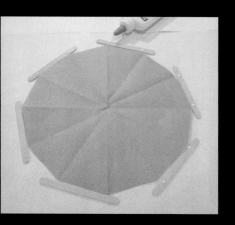

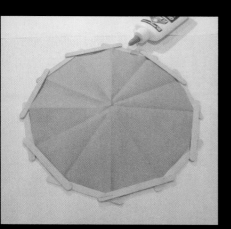

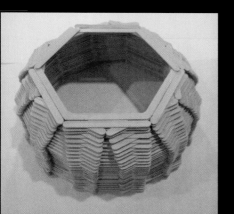

4. Fold the left point of the diamond over to the right, a little more than halfway to the right point. Now fold the right point over to the left side, going over by a little more than halfway. You will have created a shape that looks like a long, thin kite.

5. Starting from the folded tip of the newspaper, measure 5½" on the two long sides of the triangle and mark the measurements. Connect the dots, then cut along the line and unfold. You now have a dodecagon.

6. Flatten your dodecagon and lay on top of another piece of newspaper.

7. Place six Popsicle sticks, one along every other side of the dodecagon.

8. Place six more Popsicle sticks in between the first six, overlapping them. You'll connect the layers by placing a dab of glue wherever they intersect. This is the bottom ring of your lampshade.

9. Repeat steps 7–8 until you have twenty layers of sticks.

10. For your twenty-first through thirtieth layers, start pushing your Popsicle sticks toward the center, about ⅛" per row, so it starts to narrow as you continue upward. At about the thirtieth layer, you won't be able to add height to your lampshade anymore because the Popsicle sticks will be touching end to end. Also, since the structure is becoming more narrow, you will only need six sticks per layer at the top, and your hexagon half will fit on top nicely. This is the bottom half of your lampshade.

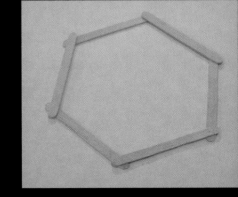

FOR THE HEXAGON HALF OF THE LAMPSHADE:

1. To create the top half of your shade, you'll make a hexagon, which has six equal sides. (This one you will have to fudge a bit, so pay attention.) Glue six Popsicle sticks end to end so they form a hexagon.)

2. Like the dodecagon, you'll build the hexagon half with layers that each narrow ⅛" as you continue upward, until the top row forms a Star of David .

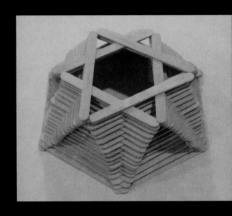

FOR THE LAMP:

1. When the glue on the top half of the shade is dry, adhere it to the bottom half of the lampshade.

2. When the glue on the top and bottom halves is dry, glue your washer-top ring into the lampshade with Amazing Goop glue and let it dry. (It should fit snugly toward the top.)

3. Attach the washer-top ring to your lamp's harp and start to brag.

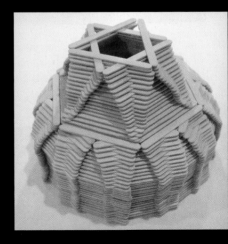

COPPER-TUBE LANTERN

This lantern provides so much warmth to a room. I love mine!

YOU'LL NEED:

- Lantern that opens at the top (Most of them do.)
- Copper-tube cutter for ½" diameter tube
- 2 90-degree ½" copper elbows
- 3 copper ½" Ts
- 4½' of copper tubing
- Household Goop glue (I love this stuff and would eat it if I could!)
- Tea light or votive candle

HERE'S HOW:

Mini coupe-tubes

1. Use your copper-tube cutter to cut your copper tubing into pieces of the following lengths: four 4" pieces, two 5" pieces, and two 14" pieces.

2. Join two of the 4" pieces together with a copper T.

3. Attach a 14" piece to one end of your now 8" piece of joined tubing.

4. Attach an elbow to the other end of the 14" piece.

5. Join the 5" piece to the copper elbow. (Can you see it taking shape?)

6. Repeat steps 2–5, and you'll have both sides of your lamp.

7. Hang the handle at the top of the lantern on one of the pieces of copper tubing at the top, and attach the 5" pieces together at the top with the third copper T. Adjust the handle so that the lantern hangs from the center.

8. Bend and twist the sides of your lamp until it's shaped properly and symetrically.

9. Carefully separate the joints and add a bit of Household Goop glue so that they stay in place once reattached.

10. Time to put in your candle and enjoy your new lantern!

COPPER-TUBE CANDELABRA

Copper and candles offer the perfect mood lighting for any occasion.

YOU'LL NEED:

- 6 ½" copper elbows
- 4 ½" copper Ts
- 6 5" pieces of copper tubing
- 1 8" pieces of copper tubing
- 2 4" pieces of copper tubing
- 6 glass hurricane candleholders with ½" base, and 6 tea lights

HERE'S HOW:

1. Join two 5" pieces of copper tubing together by inserting one piece into the left hole of the copper T and the other piece into the right hole, creating a 10"-long joined piece.

2. Make two more of these joined pieces (three total).

3. Repeat step 1, except use the 4" pieces of tubing, so you make an 8" piece.

4. Attach the 8" piece of copper tubing into the center hole of the T of the 8"-long piece you've just made. You will now have a large copper T shape.

5. Join the 10"-long pieces to the three ends of the T shape.

6. Attach copper elbows at the end of each 10"-long piece, adding a bit of glue so they stay in place.

7. Bend and twist the tubing into the shape that you see in the photo above, with all of the elbows facing upward.

8. Insert the glass nubs that are located at the bottom of the glass hurricane candle holders inside the copper elbows and add the tea lights.

STANDING WOODEN CANDELABRA

If you want a romantic candlelight dinner, this is the ideal way to do it without cluttering the dining table. Now you'll have more room for desserts!

- 2 decorative 8½"-long, 2"-wide wooden scroll brackets

- 4 plain 2"-wide wooden shelf brackets

- 1 piece of 2×2 pine, cut to a length of 5'

- Elmer's wood glue

- Beige spray paint, or any color you'd like (I'm sure mine will be many different colors throughout its life in my home.)

- Masking tape

- Household Goop glue

- 5 glass votive holders and 5 votives

HERE'S HOW:

1. Working on a large, flat surface (not the floor), use the wood glue to attach the shorter sides of the wooden scroll brackets to one end of the 2×2, on opposite sides and flush against the wood, as seen in the picture.

2. Glue two of the plain, wooden shelf brackets flush against the wood (basically, repeat step 1 but put the brackets on the other end of the pine). This will begin the base of the candelabra.

3. After the glue is dry, attach a third bracket on one of the remaining sides of the base of the 2×2.

4. Give the glue a couple of hours to dry, then rotate your candelabra so that the third bracket hangs over the edge of your work surface. Glue the fourth bracket to the base end of the 2×2.

5. After the glue is dry, cover the entire piece with spray paint.

6. Finally, glue on the five glass votive holders with the Household Goop glue, insert a votive in each holder, and light away!

CAN WE TABLE THAT?

T he table is a pretty useful piece of furniture. I'm not sure we ever really think about how much that flat surface with legs—where we put our stuff, eat our dinners, pay our bills, and get frisky if we're really lucky—is a part of our everyday lives. My theory about anything that plays such a big part in your life is that it should be special, beautiful, and reflect who you are. I have always considered a table to be a blank canvas that I can cover in any way possible. Glue, paint, mosaic—you name it, it's on a table in my house. Even duct tape has found its way onto one of my little creations.

One of my favorite tables to work with is the Parsons style of table from Ikea, which is a small square table that retails for less than fifteen dollars. It's perfect for covering in fabric, spray painting, stenciling, and decoupage. My second favorite kind of table is the one abandoned on the sidewalk in front of someone's home. There it is: chipped and water stained, with one wobbly leg; just waiting for someone like me to put it back together and turn it into a beautiful masterpiece. Before you get rid of a table, make sure you have exhausted every option for it. Otherwise, you will want it back after you see it reincarnated in my house. Finders keepers, I say!

HARLEQUIN AND DECOUPAGE TABLE

Whenever I'm driving down the street and see a wonderful piece of furniture left out for the dump, I have to rescue it and see if there is anything I can do to give it another life. It's a great way to exercise my creativity and to present a friend with something wonderful. I found the table I used for this project on a street in L.A.

YOU'LL NEED:

- Old table that deserves another life

- Several paper images (I chose antique fashion images.)

- Spray paint, any type, in beige

- Light blue brush-on latex paint, any brand

- ½"-wide art brush

- Several small-bristled art brushes

- Krylon Spray Adhesive

- Oil-based polyurethane, any brand

- 2"-wide brush (for the polyurethane)

- Medium-grit and fine-grit sandpaper

- Ruler

- Pencil

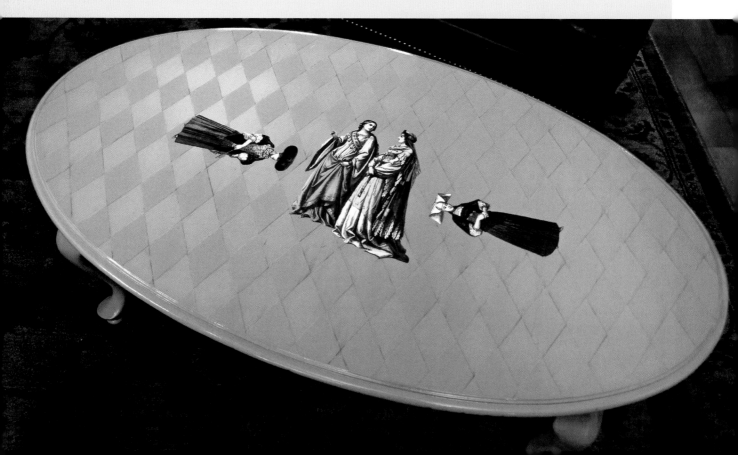

1. Sand your piece of furniture with the medium-grit sandpaper to remove dirt and create a smooth surface for your work, and wipe off the dust.

2. Cover the furniture with the beige spray paint; this will be your canvas.

3. With your ruler and pencil, draw diagonal parallel lines, about 2½" apart, across the top of the table.

4. Draw diagonal parallel lines (also 2½" apart) across the table in the other direction, intersecting the first set of lines to make a diamond pattern, called "harlequin."

5. Fill in every other diamond with light blue latex paint, using your art brush. (Sorry! This is going to take awhile. Even for the most seasoned painter, it's a long process, but it's well worth it.)

> **SUGGESTION:** *Paint around the edges of your table, like I did, to give your work some dimension. The painted edge also works as a frame.*

6. When your harlequin pattern is dry, spray the backs of your paper images with the Krylon Spray Adhesive, and apply them anywhere you'd like on the tabletop.

7. Coat your table with a small amount of the oil-based polyurethane, and let it dry.

8. After the polyurethane is dry, very, very, *very* lightly sand the tabletop with the fine-grit sandpaper, wipe the dust off, and apply another coat of the poly-urethane.

9. After that layer of polyurethane is dry, your table is done!

FABRIC-COVERED TABLE

This is not just a craft project; it's a technique that you can use on just about anything. I want you to really think about something that needs a face-lift and try to use this technique. It's easy, it looks amazing, and you can get wonderful results. It's a great way to toss another print into your decor or create a table (or another piece of furniture) that is completely unique.

YOU'LL NEED:

- Table that needs a face-lift

- Minwax Polycrylic Protective Finish (or a water-based acrylic coating)

- 1"–3"-wide latex paintbrushes

- 1 yard of cotton fabric (or more, if you are covering a larger table)

- Scissors

- Chalk

HERE'S HOW:

1. You will be working with the tabletop first, since it's the largest part you'll have to cover. Center the design of your fabric on the tabletop.

2. Mark off the edges of the tabletop with chalk, which is where you're going to make cuts.

3. Carefully trim your fabric so it's the exact size of the tabletop.

4. Paint a thin coat of the Minwax Polycrylic Protective Finish on the tabletop. This will serve as the glue, to keep your fabric in place.

5. Lay your fabric on top of the thin layer of "glue," positioning it so it's once again centered.

6. Paint over the fabric with a generous amount of Minwax.

7. While the Minwax dries, measure the amount of fabric needed to cover the sides and legs. Repeat steps 3–6, except, of course, you'll be attaching the fabric to the sides and legs of the table.

8. After the Minwax dries, you're ready to show off your creation!

DON'T WORRY: *If you don't have big pieces left. You can patch pieces of cloth together, and your table will still look amazing.*

CHECKERBOARD PARSONS TABLE

This table is a great-looking piece, and it's the perfect size for any room. The table pictured has fewer, larger squares, but for a real checkerboard, follow the instructions here for placing eight squares on a side.

- 24" × 24" Parsons table (I got mine at Ikea for less than fifteen dollars.)
- 4 12" × 12" (standard size for floor tiles) self-stick floor tiles in contrasting colors
- Ruler
- Pencil
- Goof Off glue remover
- Olfa craft knife (for scoring tile; they work the best)

HERE'S HOW:

1. Using the pencil and ruler, mark off each tile into 2½" × 2½" squares.

2. With the knife, score along the lines you drew, and break the tiles into sixteen squares each, yielding sixty-four squares total.

3. Place the tile squares on the table in a checkerboard pattern, so you know where to adhere the pieces before you start sticking them down.

4. Carefully peel the backings and place the tiles onto the tabletop, one at a time.

5. Once you've finished sticking your squares down, wipe off the excess glue and pencil markings with Goof Off.

6. Use anything—from a real set of checkers to hard candies—for your checkerboard pieces, and enjoy the game.

> **WARNING:** *It's hard, but not impossible, to remove the tiles once they are stuck to the table. Make sure you know where the squares are to be placed, just to avoid the hassle.*

OUTDOOR COFFEE TABLE

This project is not as difficult as you might think, but it does take some time. If you are really having trouble finishing it, ask a savvy friend for some help.

YOU'LL NEED:

- 1 4' × 4' sheet of ¾"-thick birch plywood
- 2 4' × 4' sheets of ½"-thick birch plywood
- 4 16"-long pieces of 2×4 wood, any type
- 4 48" (this is standard size) poplar slats
- Jigsaw
- Hammer
- 20 1"-long wood nails (sometimes called "round wire nails")
- 24 2"-long wood screws
- Drill and ⅛" diameter drill bit (for starter holes) and Phillips head 2" screw bits for wood screws
- Paint or wood stain, any color

HERE'S HOW:

1. Drill holes through the top of your table into the 2×4 pieces of wood (the legs).

2. Place the 2" side of your 2×4 leg at the corner of the tabletop, facing the center, then screw the legs into the ¾"-thick plywood, using two wood screws per leg. Each leg should be at a 45-degree angle from each corner, pointing toward the inside of the table.

3. Using the half fleur-de-lis image below as a pattern, place the enlarged image on the ½"-thick plywood and trace it onto the wood four times. Repeat on the second piece of ½"-thick plywood.

4. Use the jigsaw to cut out the shapes. Your results will be eight fleurs-de-lis halves.

These pieces will be used as a decoration on the corners of the table.

5. Nail these shapes to the underside of the edge of the table. Use three wood nails for each piece, and make sure each piece is evenly spaced and that the 2" side of the table legs are visible. Screw the shapes to the leg as well, using two screws per side.

6. Nail the shapes to the legs as well, to secure.

7. Attach your poplar trim along the edges of the table with wood nails.

8. Stain or paint your table, then watch as your neighbors go green with envy!

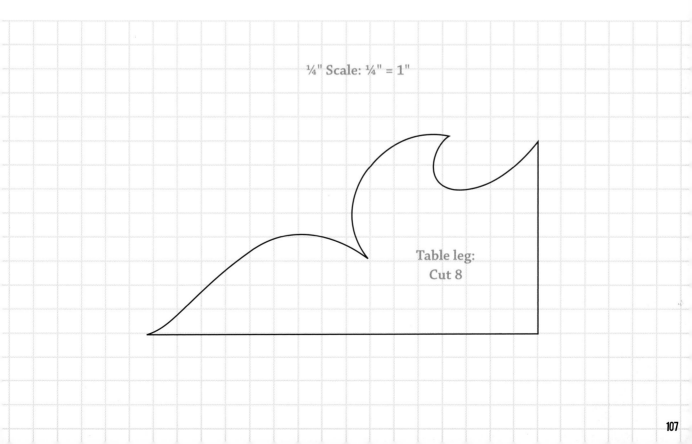

¼" Scale: ¼" = 1"

Table leg:
Cut 8

GAME TABLETOP

Poker is now a national pastime, and more and more people are forming poker clubs and playing at home. My weekly poker game with the gang is one of my favorite social activities, and I decided it was finally time to make a real game tabletop. This one was pretty easy to construct, and I can take it off my dining room table and store it when I'm not using it.

YOU'LL NEED:

- 4' × 4' piece of ½"-thick plywood
- Jigsaw
- Medium-grit sandpaper
- Playing cards
- 1 yard of green felt
- Brown spray paint, any brand
- Krylon Spray Adhesive
- Elmer's glue
- Minwax Polycrylic Protective Finish
- 3"-wide latex paintbrush
- Scissors
- Pencil

HERE'S HOW:

1. Measure 14" in from each corner on all four sides of the square, drawing a dot with your pencil to mark each measurement. Connect the dots across the corners. The resulting shape, inside your lines, should be an octagon.

2. Cut off the corners with a jigsaw, using your pencil lines as a guide.

3. Sand the edges to make them smooth.

4. Cover the tabletop with brown spray paint. Don't worry about painting the center, though. You only need to paint about 12" in from each side. (The felt will cover the unpainted part.)

5. Cut your felt into a 36" square.

6. Measure in 10" from each corner of the felt and draw a dot with your pencil to mark each measurement. Connect the dots across the corners. The resulting shape, inside your lines, should be an octagon.

7. Cut off the corners of the felt, using your pencil lines as a guide, and cover your felt octagon with Krylon Spray Adhesive.

8. Center the felt on the tabletop, hiding the unpainted center.

9. Glue playing cards into any pattern you'd like around the edges of the table.

10. When the glue is dry, brush Minwax Polycrylic Protective Finish over the cards and the wood, but do not get any on the felt.

11. Once the tabletop is dry, you can place your new tabletop over an existing table, or a foldout card table, for a professional poker game at home.

ROPE SIDE TABLE

Okay, my friends can usually tell which pieces of furniture in my house I made and which pieces I bought. But they mistook this piece for an expensive purchase. Something about things wrapped in rope just makes a fantastic statement. I wonder what my cat would look like covered in rope? Hee, hee! I went through a ton of hot glue and rope for this project, but it was well worth it.

YOU'LL NEED:

- 300'–350' of ¼" Manila rope (This usually comes in 50' spools and costs less than five dollars for 50'. Just look around and I know you'll find it for a bargain.)

- 2 18"-high plastic trash cans with mouths that are about 12"–14" in diameter (I got mine at the dollar store.)

- Round particle board tabletop, with a 24" diameter and ¾" thick (standard at stores such as Home Depot and Lowe's)

- Hot-glue gun and glue sticks (about fifty)

- Household Goop glue

- Krylon Color Creation Crystal Clear Top Coat

- Heavy-duty scissors

1. Glue the bottoms of your trash cans together with the Household Goop glue. This will create your table's base.

2. Glue the tabletop onto the base. Be generous with the Household Goop glue; the excess will be covered by the rope.

3. Once the glue is dry, attach the rope around your table base with the hot-glue gun, wrapping the rope from the bottom of the base all the way up to the underside of the tabletop. (This will take some time, so be patient!)

> **HINT:** *Apply glue to both the rope and the trash can to make your rope really stick.*

4. For the tabletop's surface, start at the center and glue the rope outward in a spiral, all the way to the outside edge.

5. Once your table is covered in rope and after the glue has dried, protect it with several coats of Krylon Color Creation Crystal Clear Top Coat, then enjoy being the envy of all your friends.

ROUND—MIRROR TILED MOSAIC TABLE

You've seen tons of broken-mirror mosaics, made with randomly shaped shards. How about using something different? These round mirror tiles spruce up a tabletop instantly. And just face it: Almost anything looks better with disco mirrors and some gold paint!

YOU'LL NEED:

- Round table, any size (My table has a 30" diameter tabletop, and it took about eight hundred round mirror tiles that ranged in size from ⅜" to 1".)

- Enough round mirrors to cover your tabletop (Try Michaels, an arts and craft store)

- Amazing Goop craft glue

- Krylon Premium Metallic spray paint, in 18KT Gold (I have tried many gold paints, and Krylon makes the best metallic paints, hands down. I used gold on my table. You can choose any color that you like.)

- Bathroom-tile grout, any brand

- Medium-grit sandpaper

- Spackle knife

- Sponge

- Bucket of cold water

- Masking tape

- Newspaper

HINT: *Check out secondhand stores and furniture outlets for simple, inexpensive tables to use for this project. Remember, just a bit of paint and some creativity can go a very long way! The table I used for this project was fifteen dollars from Goodwill.*

HERE'S HOW:

1. Sand your tabletop surface. This will create a nice, rough surface, which will make your glue stick on much better.

HINT: *Sanding a surface before you paint or use glue will help the paint and glue stick better and, ultimately, last longer.*

2. Glue on your tile mirrors with the Amazing Goop craft glue. Place them randomly, making sure to leave about ⅛" between each tile.

3. Once the glue is dry (I recommend leaving it to dry overnight), spread grout between the tiles with the spackle knife, making sure to get grout in between each and every tile, as well as near the edge of the tabletop.

4. Wet your sponge with cold water, wring it out, and use it to smooth the grout in between the tiles while at the same time wiping off the mirrors.

NOTE: *Your mirrors will have a grout residue when you're done, but don't worry about that. You can clean them off after the grout has dried. Also, don't worry if you don't get grout in every spot right away; you can go over it a second time to get the spots you missed.*

5. Let the grout dry, then tape newspaper over the mirrored mosaic area with masking tape and spray paint the base of the table.

6. After the paint has dried, your table is ready to shine!

DUCT-TAPED SIDE TABLE AND CHAIR

I don't know if your dad tried to fix everything with duct tape when you were growing up, but mine did. Everything that needed some help had a bright strip of silver on it! Well, thank goodness duct tape comes in tons of different colors now, and you can go crazy with it like I did! Have an old side table that could use some stripes? This is the perfect way to get that done quickly without using messy paint. I used a table from Ikea that was a really nice turquoise but had gotten a bit banged up in some areas. I was able to use the turquoise as a stripe in parts of the table.

YOU'LL NEED:

FOR THE DUCT-TAPE TABLE:

- Square end table, with smooth surfaces

- 6 rolls of duct tape, each roll a different color

- Scissors

- Craft knife

HERE'S HOW:

FOR THE DUCT-TAPE TABLE:

1. Starting on the underside of the tabletop, securely attach tape, holding the roll so that the sticky side can be pulled up and over the tabletop. Pull the tape from one end of the table to the other, extending to the underside of the opposite end.

2. Cut off the tape and fold the end piece under the table so it's not visible.

3. Repeat steps 1–2, but use another color of tape to get a striped effect. Continue making stripes, using alternating colors, until the entire tabletop is covered.

4. Apply tape to the legs in vertical strips.

YOU'LL NEED:

FOR THE DUCT-TAPE CHAIR:

- 6 rolls of duct tape, any colors (about 15 yards of each color!)

- Old vinyl chair that needs to be re-covered

- Craft knife

- Scissors

> **OPTIONAL:** *Heavy-duty staple gun*

HERE'S HOW:

FOR THE DUCT-TAPE CHAIR:

1. Starting with one color, tape 4"-long strips onto random places on the cushion of your chair.

> **HINT:** *Don't cover the piping of the chair if it's in good condition.*

2. When you get to the edges of the chair, where the piping is, use your craft knife and carefully cut the tape into the shape of the cushion, or curve, so that it fits in nicely.

3. With another color, repeat steps 1–2.

4. Use all of the colors until a patchwork pattern starts to emerge.

5. For the arms, start your stripes on the inside of the chair, below the cushion line, and tape all the way around the arm, until you get to the underside of the chair.

6. Overlap the colors, so you have different-size stripes and get a pattern you like.

> **DON'T WORRY:** *If you don't like your pattern. You can always remove the tape and add more as you work, so your design is not set in stone!*

> **SUGGESTION:** *Add staples on the underside of the chair, to keep the tape in place, if you find that it's not sticking.*

7. Sit back and relax in your new chair!

FAUX INLAID MARBLE TILE TABLE

This table is superclassy, and supereasy to make!

- Round tabletop, any size (My table's diameter was 41".)

- 6 of each of the following kinds of peel-and-stick tile from a hardware store (24 tiles in total): green marble, black marble, brown stone, beige stone

- Yardstick

- Ruler

- Sharpie pen, fine point, any color

- Craft paper

- Elmer's Tinted Wood Filler, in red (This comes in a tube and is very easy to use.)

- Cutting knife

- Sponge

- Bucket of water

HERE'S HOW:

1. Draw two lines onto your tabletop: one from top to bottom and another from left to right, dividing the surface into four equal parts. Label these lines 1 and 2.

2. Now draw two more lines: one from the top left "corner" to the bottom right and another from the top right "corner" to the bottom left. Label these two lines 3 and 4. Your table will now look like a pie, cut into eight equal pieces.

3. Starting from the center of the table, where all the lines intersect, measure 5" along every line, toward the perimeter, marking your measurements with your Sharpie.

4. Starting at the perimeter of the table, connect the ends of lines 1 and 2 to the 5" marks of lines 3 and 4. Your result will be a four-pointed star, made up of eight triangles.

5. Again starting at the perimeter of the table, connect the ends of lines 3 and 4 to the 5" marks of lines 1 and 2, stopping where they intersect with the sides of the star drawn in step 4.

6. You've created eight triangles along the perimeter of the table (formed by the outside lines of the stars you've made). Halve these triangles so that you create sixteen little triangles.

7. Follow the photo and pattern to decide which of these triangles will be brown marble and which will be beige marble.

8. With a piece of craft paper, create a pattern for each tile, then cut out the shape from the tile and stick it to the area. (Some areas are bigger than what you can cover with one piece, so you will have to piece two different tiles together to fill your shape.)

HINT: *To cut the tile, score the tile with your cutting knife and snap it into pieces along the scored line. Use the straight edges of the tile as much as you can. For the curved outer edges, trim with a cutting knife, and score the tile, just like you did the straight edges.*

9. When you have finished filling in the sections with the beige and brown tiles, it's time to add the black and green tiles onto the rest of the table (using craft paper patterns),

alternating colors, and using the scoring method, as with the outer triangles.

DON'T WORRY: *If your pieces don't perfectly fit together. You can fill the cracks with carpenter's wood fill.*

10. After all the triangles are set, carefully fill in all the spaces in between the tiles with the wood fill. (Don't forget to go all the way around the edges, too.)

11. While the wood fill is still wet, smooth it out with a wet sponge and wipe off the excess. It will leave a residue on the tiles, but that will wipe off easily after the fill dries.

12. Time to dine King Henry style.

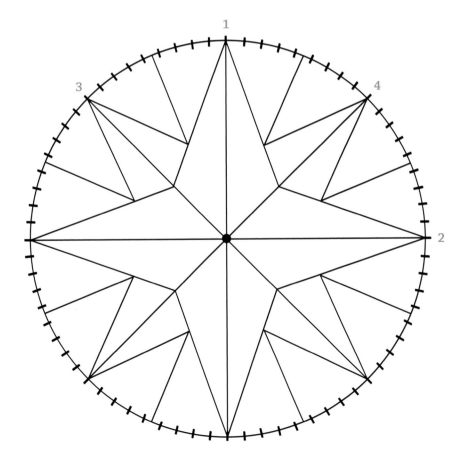

I love working with the inexpensive Parsons style of table from Ikea. They are the perfect size, and you can do anything to them, glue anything on them, and it doesn't matter if you mess up, because they cost less than fifteen dollars. I like that very much.

YOU'LL NEED:

- Parsons table
- Enough dominoes to cover your table
- Medium-grit sandpaper
- Elmer's wood glue

HERE'S HOW:

1. Sand the surface of the table to ensure an even finish, and wipe off the dust.

SUGGESTION: *To make sure you have enough dominoes to finish your project, lay them out on the table how you want them placed before you start gluing. (I left a big square, which I painted black to match the black of the legs, in the middle of my table.) Don't just start gluing, because you could end up with a big mess and dominoes hanging over one end. Trust me on this one.*

2. Spread a few dabs of glue below one domino at a time, and start gluing them down.

HINT: *This will take a few hours because it takes time for the glue to set, but it's well worth it for the result.*

I'm always attracted to the beautiful thousand-dollar Queen Anne pedestal tables in antique stores. Since it's not really in my budget to buy a table every time I see one I like, I thought it would be fun to make one out of papier-mâché. Queen Anne tables don't usually have aprons, but I decided, Why not add one for a bit of whimsy? I was surprised at how sturdy my table turned out, and I love the way it looks. And guess what? It only cost a few dollars to make!

YOU'LL NEED:

- 3 cardboard boxes
- Lots of newspaper, in 1"-wide strips
- Papier-mâché goop and mush (See the recipes on pages 282–3.)
- Black spray paint (either high gloss or flat, any variety)
- Krylon Acrylic Clear Coat
- Black-and-white images
- Craft knife
- Masking tape
- Elmer's glue
- Level
- Fine-grit sandpaper

HERE'S HOW:

CUTTING YOUR PATTERNS FROM THE CARDBOARD:

1. **Tabletop:** Cut three 16"-diameter circles out of cardboard, then stack them and tape them together along the edges.

2. **Apron:** Cut a 45" × 4" apron. (The long, flat edge will be connected to the underside of the tabletop, with the zigzag edge hanging down.)

3. **Pedestal:** Cut a rectangle measuring 10" × 23".

4. **Feet:** Cut three feet, each made up of a layer of three pieces (that's nine of the same pattern, total), taped together.

5. Score your apron piece every inch on one side, and then cut a zigzag along that edge.

6. Tape the ends of your apron to form a circle, then glue it to the underside of the tabletop. Add some masking tape to keep it in place.

7. Score your pedestal, lengthwise, every 1". Bend the cardboard into a long tube, overlapping the edges by 1" and taping the tube in place with masking tape.

8. Glue and tape each foot onto your pedestal. They should be 3" apart and even all the way around.

> **HINT:** *Don't attach your pedestal and feet to the tabletop yet. It's easier to work on the two pieces separately, and then glue them together later.*

COVERING THE PIECES IN PAPIER-MÂCHÉ:

1. Dip the strips of newspaper into your papier-mâché goop and cover your tabletop and base. Do a thin layer of paper first, and let the whole thing dry.

> **WARNING:** *If the table gets too wet, it could start to warp. Start off slowly, and after your first layer dries, go to town! If it does start to warp, put some weights, such as rocks or cans, on it overnight, and it'll straighten out.*

2. Once you've covered your pedestal and table-top with a few layers of papier-mâché mush, center and attach the base to the underside of the tabletop with glue and masking tape.

3. Secure the top to the base with more papier-mâché.

4. Use your level to make sure the tabletop sits on the base properly, without leaning to one side. Prop it up, weigh it down on one side—do whatever you have to do to make sure it dries evenly!

5. When the papier-mâché has dried, sand the whole table.

6. Paint the table with the Krylon spray paint.

7. Decoupage your images to the table by using a mixture of one part Elmer's glue and one part water. Paint the glue mixture onto the back of your images and adhere them to the table, and then paint over the images with the same glue mixture.

8. Let the glue dry, then spray the Krylon Acrylic Clear Coat all over the table, to protect it and give it a nice finish.

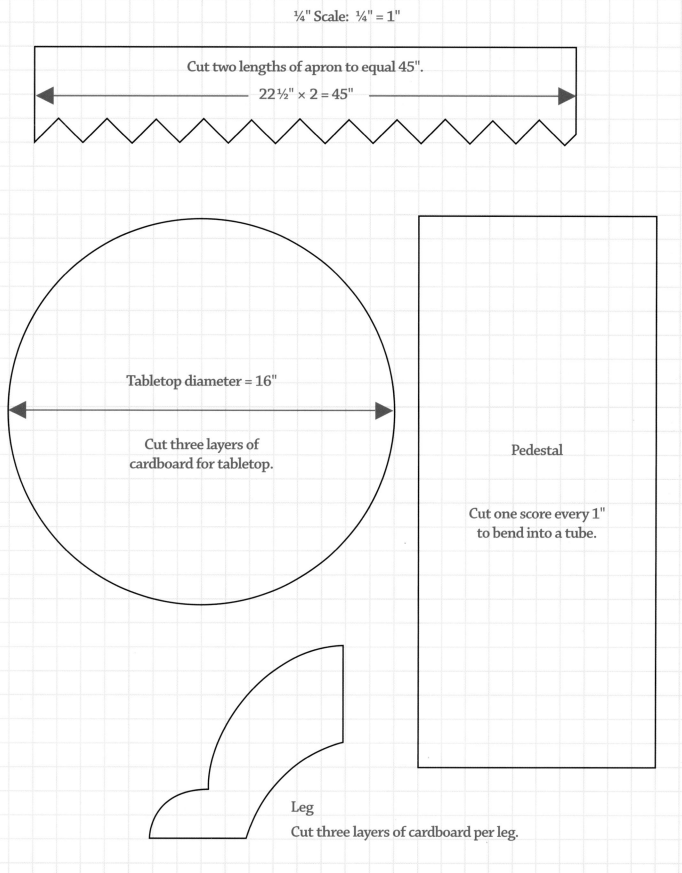

¼" Scale: ¼" = 1"

Cut two lengths of apron to equal 45".

22½" × 2 = 45"

Tabletop diameter = 16"

Cut three layers of
cardboard for tabletop.

Pedestal

Cut one score every 1"
to bend into a tube.

Leg

Cut three layers of cardboard per leg.

DISHING IT OUT

Recently I was shopping—not really buying, but, you know, browsing. In the home-goods department, I found some dishes that were fantastic, and like I always do, I flipped the plates over to see how much they cost. At that moment I realized that dishes are darn expensive. A hundred bucks for a plate! I would have to give up food for a year just to have these dishes on my table. It just wasn't worth it to me. I will admit, I bought a cup and saucer, and I save them for those special times when I'm alone and my new magazines have arrived. For entertaining and decorating, I came up with some easy, fun ideas you can use to make your table one to remember. My punk plates have been featured on several TV shows, and they always get tons of attention. Use photos of your family to spruce up your plates if you want something extra-special. Just remember, being creative is about the process as much as it is about the end result. Creating something to make your environment more beautiful—like enhancing a table with fantastic, personalized dishes—will improve the quality of your life in more ways than you can comprehend.

FASHION PLATES

Beautiful, decorative plates to hang on your walls are functional art, and nothing breaks up a wall or cluster of objects like a big, beautiful circle. These fashion plates are perfect for serving up some attitude or a selection of wrapped hard candies. They aren't for eating off of, but you can find out how to make those on the following pages!

- Plates, in different sizes and colors

- Black-and-white decorative prints

- Color copies of fashion figures

- Clear, oil-based polyurethane

- Elmer's glue

- 1"-wide flat art brush

- 2"-wide paintbrush

- Scissors

- Cup of water

HERE'S HOW:

1. Trim your black-and-white print to fit the entire plate. If your plate is bigger than your print, then make a copy of the print and piece it together, to fill the plate. (It's fine!)

2. Cut out your fashion image for the center of your plate, making sure it fits.

3. Use the 1"-wide art brush to glue the black-and-white print to the face of the plate, using an Elmer's glue mixture of 1 tablespoon of glue and 1 teaspoon of water. (You can always add more glue if the consistency is too thin or if you would like a bit more tack.)

4. Apply a layer of the glue mixture to the back of your fashion image, then apply it onto the black-and-white print.

5. When the glue is dry, cut off any edges that are sticking out from around the edge of the plate.

6. Paint the plate with a thin coat of polyurethane and let it dry. Apply two more coats.

7. Serve up some attitude by hanging your masterpiece on the wall.

COLORFUL LACE GLASS PLATES

You will be working only on the backs of these glass plates, so they are fine for food use. Just be careful to hand wash them!

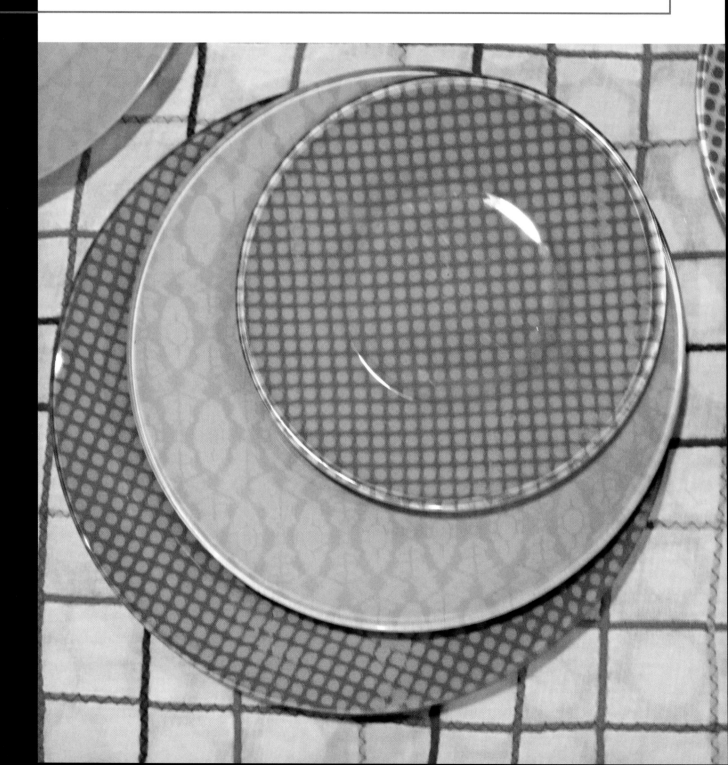

YOU'LL NEED:

- Glass plates in any size you like (Mine varied in size.)

- 1 yard of nylon athletic fabric or polyester lace to use as a stencil

- Krylon Spray Adhesive

- Several different colors of spray paint (I used Krylon Satin colors for this project. They are deep, rich, and bright, and look wonderful together, and I like the way they dry on the back of the plate.)

- Krylon Acrylic Crystal Clear

HERE'S HOW:

1. Wash a plate and dry it thoroughly.

2. Cut out a piece of the athletic fabric or lace big enough to cover the back of the plate.

3. Place the plate facedown on some newspaper, and secure the fabric to the plate with the Krylon Spray Adhesive.

4. Spray your first color over the fabric. Make sure you hit every spot.

5. Give the paint about five minutes to dry a bit, and then remove the fabric by carefully peeling it off the back of the plate. (Because Krylon Spray Adhesive takes awhile to dry, the fabric can be easily removed.) You will be left with a relief design of the fabric.

6. After the paint dries completely (I'd say about fifteen minutes), spray it with a second color of paint and let it dry.

7. When the second color is dry, coat the back of the plate with the Krylon Acrylic Crystal Clear.

8. Give it at least two more coats of Krylon Acrylic Crystal Clear, letting it dry between coats.

9. There you have it! A way to have fantastic, personalized plates without having to spend a hundred bucks!

> **SUGGESTION:** *Spray a light coat of the second color and let dry for a few minutes, then spray again. It will make a better finish.*

PUNK PLATES

My punk plates have been featured on several TV shows, and they always get the most attention of all my dishes. These are food-safe, but remember to hand wash them afterward.

YOU'LL NEED:

- Glass plates in a size you like (Mine were about 5" in diameter.)
- Color copies of a skull that will fit on the plates that you're using.

> **SUGGESTION:** *Use the Internet to find a skull illustration.*

- ½ yard of nylon athletic fabric or polyester lace to use as a stencil

- Elmer's glue
- Krylon Spray Adhesive
- 1"-wide paintbrush
- Several different colors of spray paint (I used Krylon Satin colors for this project. They are deep, rich, and bright, and look wonderful together. I also like the way they dry on the back of the plate.)
- Krylon Acrylic Crystal Clear

HERE'S HOW:

1. Wash a plate and dry it thoroughly.

2. Cut out your skull image.

3. Water down your Elmer's glue a very tiny bit so it's easier to spread. I use one part water to two parts glue.

4. Paint the glue mixture on the face of the image and adhere it to the back of your plate so that you can see it through the front of the plate.

5. Let the image dry, making sure that it's completely stuck to the back of the plate.

6. Complete steps 2–8 from the colorful lace glass plates project on page 129.

7. Rock out with your new flatware.

SILHOUETTE PLATES

Do you want to impress your family and friends with your talent, while feeding them? This is the way to do it. Either hanging on the wall or sitting on the dinner table, these plates are sure to impress. Not only that, they are just darn fun to make. (And the paint is on the backs of the plates, so you can eat off of them!)

YOU'LL NEED:

- Glass plates, in any size

- Black acrylic paint, any brand

- White spray paint (or a color you like), any brand

- Flat artist brushes about ¾"–1" wide

- Minwax Polycrylic Protective Finish

- Shot of a loved one's profile, or an image you like (See page 9 for instructions on how to make a silhouette.)

> **SUGGESTION:** *Dover Books has several great collections of silhouettes. Just take a look at their online catalog and see what you find.*

- Sharpie marker, fine tip, in black

HERE'S HOW:

1. Enlarge your profile image on a copy machine so it's big enough to cover your plate.

2. Cut out the profile, and trace it onto the back of the plate, using the Sharpie marker.

3. Fill in the tracing with the black acrylic paint, using your artist brushes. (This will take several coats.)

4. To see if you've missed any spots, hold the plate up to the light.

5. Once you've filled in the silhouette and the paint has dried, spray the back of the plate with white spray paint.

6. After the paint is dry, apply three coats of Minwax Polycrylic Protective Finish to the back of the plate, letting it dry at least a half hour between each coat.

7. Either hang your plate on the wall using a plate hanger (available at most hardware stores), or use it for spaghetti. It's up to you!

DELICIOUS DECOUPAGE PLATES

I love these decoupage plates, and my friends do too. I pull them out every time I entertain. The only problem is, sometimes my guests get distracted and try to read the flatware.

YOU'LL NEED:

- Clear glass plates, with smooth backs, in different sizes
- Pages from a book (Make sure they're thin. Paperback books are great for this.)
- Image you like (for the center of your plate)
- Clear, oil-based polyurethane
- Elmer's glue
- 1"-wide flat art brush
- 2"-wide paintbrush
- Scissors
- Cup of water

HERE'S HOW:

1. Cut out the image you want for the center of your plate.

2. Coat it with watered-down Elmer's glue (about a 1:1 ratio), with the art brush.

> **HINT:** *Add more water to the Elmer's glue, if it's too tacky, so it's easier to spread on your image.*

3. Stick the image to the back of the plate so you can see it from the front.

4. Cut the book pages into 2" × 2" squares.

5. Glue them onto the back of the plate with the watered-down Elmer's glue, covering the entire back of the plate.

6. After the glue has dried, cut off the edges that are sticking out.

7. With the 2"-wide paintbrush, paint the back of the plate with a thin coat of polyurethane, and let it dry.

8. Repeat step 7 two more times, making sure to let the polyurethane dry between each coat.

9. After the last coat of polyurethane has dried, you're ready to serve up some dinner!

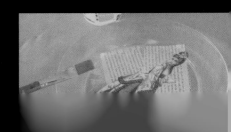

I MADE THIS FOR YOU . . .
SO YOU BETTER LOVE IT!

Every Christmas I get something handmade from my nephews. Last year, my nephew Eli gave me hand-drawn flip books, made from Post-it notepads, featuring little men jumping up and down as the pages rushed one by one through my fingers. They are among my most treasured possessions. (He also gave me some Top Ramen noodles. I still can't figure that one out, but I ate them anyway and told him they were delicious.) The fact is, I would always rather receive a handmade gift from someone than something store-bought. When someone actually takes the time to show their love for you by making something by hand, it's special. You can do this for your friends and family by taking some ideas from this chapter. The variations are endless. Prepare to be appreciated for the creative person you are!

GLASS-FLOWER BROOCHES

For some reason, these remind me of old campaign buttons. I like them because they have a turn-of-the-century feel. Not only can they be used as buttons, but also they would be wonderful as magnets (just substitute the pin back with a small self-stick magnet). Put any image you want inside. (Vintage prints are my favorite.)

YOU'LL NEED:

- Large glass chips, in different colors
- Images that fit onto the backs of the chips
- Self-stick felt
- 1"-long pin backs (from the jewelry section of any craft store, such as Michaels)
- Hot-glue gun and glue sticks
- Elmer's glue
- Various silk flowers

HERE'S HOW:

1. Trim your image so it's the same size as the glass chip.

2. Glue the image to the back of the glass chip so that you can see it from the front.

3. Take apart your flowers by separating the plastic petals from the stems and the faux centers.

4. When the glue on the glass chip is dry, you'll create a flower with the chip as the flower's center. Use Elmer's glue to attach the plastic petals to the back of the chip.

5. When the glue is dry, cut a circle from the felt that's the same size as the glass chip, and stick it to the back of the glass chip, over the petals.

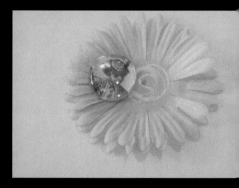

6. With the hot-glue gun, add your pin back to the felt, and you're ready to show off that bling!

URBAN CORSAGE

There's nothing more beautiful than wearing a flower on your wrist. This is a modern way to do it—with flair and just a bit of rebellion! Best of all, you can use the craft scraps from your other projects to make them.

YOU'LL NEED:

- 2 pieces of 11" × 3" fabric (Edges that fray are the best!)
- Buttons
- Rhinestones
- Faux flowers and leaves
- Ultsasuede
- Hot-glue gun and glue sticks
- Different colors of thread
- Sewing machine (with zigzag-stitch capabilities)

HERE'S HOW:

1. Place your fabric pieces on top of each other and zigzag stitch them all around, about ½" in from all four sides. One piece of fabric will serve as the outside, or top, and the other fabric will be the inside part. Think of it as a fat watch band, with a button closure rather than a small buckle.

2. Arrange your leaves next, zigzag stitching them on the cuff.

SUGGESTION: *The more random the placement, the better, so go wild.*

3. Take your faux flower apart by removing the plastic pieces that keep it together, and zigzag stitch it onto the center of your cuff, over the leaves.

4. Cut out hearts (or any shape you like. I'm a huge fan of hearts, because it's wearing your heart on your sleeve) and zigzag stitch them around your flower.

5. Stitch three buttons in a row on one side of your flower, as in the photo, for various wrist sizes.

6. Wrap the cuff around your wrist to determine where your buttonhole is going to be placed, mark the placement, and then stitch one in with the sewing machine.

DON'T WORRY: *If you don't have a buttonhole setting on your machine, you can just cut a slit and stitch the edges of the cut. Remember, on this corsage, the rattier-looking, the better!*

7. With the hot-glue gun, add rhinestones to the center of the flower and around the cuff.

8. Now accessorize a simple outfit, like jeans and a T-shirt, with your corsage, and show it off!

LAMINATED LUGGAGE TAGS

This luggage tag is unique, terrific, and easy to make. I think I've made one for everyone I know!

YOU'LL NEED:

- Map (or a piece of a map), at least 8½" × 11"
- Hole puncher
- Key rings
- Stapler
- Permanent marker, any color
- Access to a laminating machine

HERE'S HOW:

1. Make color copies of your map, and have it laminated.

> **SUGGESTION:** *If someone you know is going on a trip, make the tags from a map of the place they are visiting.*

2. Cut a 3" × 11" piece from the laminated map.

3. Make a 1" fold at one end and staple it in its center. Your map pattern should be on the outside, and you will write your, or your friend's, address on the inside.

4. Fold the other end about 4½", so it slips into the stapled edge (just like a book of matches.)

5. Punch a hole on the stapled side of the tag.

6. Thread your key ring through the hole.

7. Fill out the address information on the blank part of your tag, and attach to your luggage. Have a great trip!

FLOWER HAIR PINS AND FLOWER HAIR BANDS

The two things I can't live without in my craft room are faux flowers and glitter glue. I'll put glitter glue on anything. So these flower hair pins and hair bands were a natural progression for me when making small gifts for my friends.

YOU'LL NEED:

- Rubber hair bands or large bobby pins
- Amazing Goop craft glue
- Needle and thread
- Faux flower
- Glitter glue

HERE'S HOW:

FOR THE HAIR PINS:

1. Remove the flower from the stem, making sure to leave the little plastic nubbin that holds the flower together.

2. Add some glue to the closed end of your bobby pin, and push it into the small hole at the base of your flower, where the stem used to be.

3. Once the bobby pin is in place and the glue is dry, add glitter glue around the top edges of the flower petals.

4. After the glue dries, you can surprise your friend with this pretty present.

FOR THE HAIR BANDS:

1. Remove the flower from the stem, making sure to leave the little plastic nubbin that holds the flower together. Its base is what you will be passing your needle through.

2. Apply glitter glue to the top edges of your flower petals, and let the glue dry.

3. Take one or two hair bands (mine were flimsy, so I used two), and, with needle and thread, sew them to the plastic base of the flower.

4. Add a dot of the Amazing Goop craft glue to the base, where you sewed the hair bands, to give it a little more strength.

5. After the glue dries, gift it to a friend!

PHOTOGRAPHIC TABLE NAPKINS

I'm not a huge fan of paper napkins, so I like to make up as many different varieties of table napkins as I can. This version happens to be one of my favorites because I get to have dinner with my favorite people whenever I use them, even if I'm dining alone.

YOU'LL NEED:

- Photos (to print from your computer)
- Avery T-shirt Transfers
- Iron and ironing board
- Plain men's handkerchiefs, in white

HERE'S HOW:

1. Print your images (I like mine to be small, about 2" × 2" squares) onto a sheet of your Avery T-shirt Transfers.

2. Cut out the images from the transfers, and iron them onto the corners of the handkerchiefs with a very hot iron.

3. It's that simple, and will make dinner so much more special.

MAKE SURE: *To follow the instructions on the transfers package about the iron's setting, as the transfers can vary.*

ULTRASUEDE SCARF

This is a scarf that serves many purposes. You can wear it to jazz up an outfit, or you can decorate your home with it. Why shouldn't a chair or window treatment be adorned with a beautiful scarf? Experiment and see what happens!

YOU'LL NEED:

- 1 yard of Ultrasuede, in beige or brown
- Sewing machine (with zigzag and straight stitch capabilities)
- Pinking shears
- Scissors
- Craft paper (to make your leaf patterns)
- Thread, in a color that is darker or lighter than your Ultrasuede

> **SUGGESTION:** *Use dark thread for light-colored Ultrasuede and light thread for dark-colored Ultrasuede.*

HERE'S HOW:

1. Make a few different leaf patterns from craft paper, ranging in length about 3"–6". You can use the pattern below as a guide.

2. You'll need about fifty leaves. Cut some leaves with regular scissors and others with pinking shears.

3. Using the straight stitch on your sewing machine, sew on veins and midribs to the leaves, to add some contrast.

4. Sew random leaves together, apex to base, using a zigzag stitch and dropping the feed dog. (The feed dog is the little square of teeth under your presser foot that moves the fabric along as you sew. If you drop the feed dog, the fabric will stay in place and you will be able to tack the leaves together easily.)

> **HINT:** *Arrange the leaves slightly askew. This way, they will look like they just fell from a tree.*

5. When you have sewn about thirty-five leaves together in a line, lay out the scarf, to see if there are places that might need to be filled in with the remaining leaves.

6. Wear your creation out on the town, or use it to decorate a window treatment. Heck, even hang it over the edge of a chair. It's beautiful!

Actual Size (But feel free to improvise!)

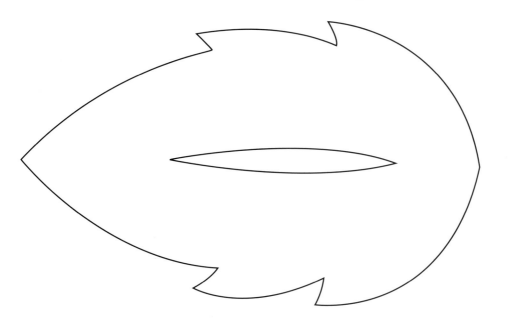

ULTRASUEDE ART CASE

I find this is the chicest way to carry around my art supplies, and the case actually inspires me to make beautiful art.

YOU'LL NEED:

- ½ yard of Ultrasuede, any color
- Thread, in a color that exactly matches the Ultrasuede
- Straight pins
- Chalk pencil
- Ruler
- Sewing machine (with straight-stitch capability)
- 6" × 8" drawing pad or sketchpad that is bound at the top (try Strathmore's products)
- Brushes and pencils to fill the case

1. Cut a 13" × 16" rectangle from your Ultrasuede.

2. Cut two ½" × 14" strands of Ultrasuede (for the ties).

3. Fold up the 13" side of your rectangle 7" and keep in place with a straight pin. You will now have a rectangle that is 13" × 9". The pinned-up 7" is now double-layered Ultrasuede, which will form your pocket.

4. With a ruler, measure the center of the pocket and lightly draw a chalk line from the top to bottom. This should be at 6½".

5. Tuck your ties 1" inside the fold, right in the center of each side edge of your case, between the layers of the Ultrasuede.

6. Sew closed the sides of the double layer of Ultrasuede, making sure to back tack (stitch back and forth) on the parts where there will be tension: where the two pieces of Ultrasuede meet and where the ties are tucked into the sides.

7. Stitch a line down the center of the pocket, along the chalk line, from top to bottom. Make sure to back tack where the two pieces of Ultrasuede meet. (This divides your case in half. The left-hand side will be for the pad, and the right is for the pencils and brushes.

8. On the right-hand side of the pocket, draw vertical chalk lines every ½", starting from the center of the pouch and moving to the right edge, to create long, slim pockets for your brushes and pencils.

9. Stitch your slim pockets along the chalk lines, starting from the open side (at the top), going down toward the fold (making sure to back tack!).

10. Slip in your pad, pencils, and brushes, fold it in half, tie it up, and you're ready to go create!

ULTRASUEDE iPOD CASE/WARHOL iPOD CASE

Protect your iPod in style with this fabulous, fun project. I'm sure you've seen iPod cases everywhere, but I assure you, this one will stand out in a crowd.

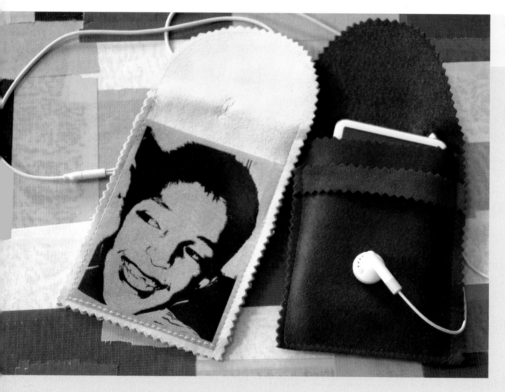

YOU'LL NEED:

- ⅛ yard of Ultrasuede, in any color
- Thread, in a color that matches the Ultrasuede
- Straight pins
- Sewing machine
- Pinking shears
- Scissors
- Craft paper

FOR THE WARHOL iPOD CASE:

- 1 Avery T-shirt Transfer of a 3" × 4" image
- Iron and ironing board

HINT: *You can have these printed at a place like Kinkos or Staples, or you can do this at home.*

NOTE: *Fits standard 2 ½" × 4" iPod.*

HINT: *Choose a light color of Ultrasuede so the image shows up.*

FOR THE ULTRASUEDE iPOD CASE:

1. Draw a 4" × 13" rectangle, and then round one end into a half circle (this curved end will be your flap) onto craft paper. The strap will be a ¾" × 4" rectangle. Cut out both patterns.

2. Trace your patterns onto the Ultrasuede, and cut them out, using your straight-edge scissors.

3. Trim both long edges of the strap with the pinking shears.

4. Fold up one end of your rectangle to you create a 5"-high pocket, and pin in place.

5. Pin the strap 3½" up from the folded end.

6. Stitch around the entire case, including the curved flap, catching the sides of the strap as you sew up the sides. Leave a ⅜" outside border.

> **SUGGESTION:** *Go back and forth with the sewing machine over the edges of the mouth of the case and the strap to make it sturdy. This is called "back tacking."*

7. After the case is stitched, carefully cut around the edges with the pinking shears, to get a decorative edge.

8. Insert your iPod and note where your earphones plug in, then cut a small hole so that it's easy to plug in the earphones and fold down your flap. If you want to stitch around the hole, that's great. (You don't have to, though. Ultrasuede won't fray.)

9. Enjoy your tunes!

FOR THE WARHOL iPOD CASE:

1. Follow steps 1–8 above.

2. Carefully iron your image onto the front or back of the case, and rock out!

LAMINATED JEWELRY

Jewelry is one of the most beautiful ways we adorn ourselves, and let's face it, the real stuff is expensive! This is a kitschy way to make some beautiful jewels that are just plain fun to wear. Pair them with a T-shirt and jeans, or pull them out for a glam costume party.

YOU'LL NEED:

- Magazine or catalog photos of jewelry
- Access to a laminating machine
- Self-stick Velcro circles
- Earring wires
- Jewelry pin backs
- Scissors

- Large safety pin
- Amazing Goop craft glue
- Needle-nose pliers

OPTIONAL: *Small jump rings (little wire rings)*

HERE'S HOW:

FOR THE BROOCH:

1. Make a color copy of the photo you'd like to use for your brooch, then have it laminated.

2. Cut out the image.

3. Glue the pin back to the back of the photo with the Amazing Goop glue.

FOR THE BRACELET:

1. Make a color copy of the photo you'd like to use for your bracelet. You may have to measure around your wrist so you know how much you need to enlarge or shrink the image.

2. Laminate your bracelet image.

3. Cut out the image.

4. Add Velcro dots on the underside of each end of the bracelet to use as a clasp.

FOR THE EARRINGS:

1. Make a color copy of the photo you'd like to use for your earrings, and then have it laminated.

2. Cut out the image.

3. Poke a hole in the top of each "jewel" with the large safety pin.

4. With the needle-nose pliers, bend the earring wires open to loop the laminated jewels on, then bend them back into place.

HINT: *If you want a double dangler, you can attach two different laminated images together, by making a hole at the bottom of each earring, looping on a jump ring and an attached image, and securing the jump ring closed with needle-nose pliers.*

PERSONALIZED PHOTO PAJAMAS/BOXER SHORTS

My best friend and her husband sleep in boxer shorts every night, and their little dog jumps into bed with them. Cute, right? I got to thinking, Why not make a personalized pair of boxers (or cotton pajamas) for them? It's something they can use, and at the same time, it's a thoughtful gift.

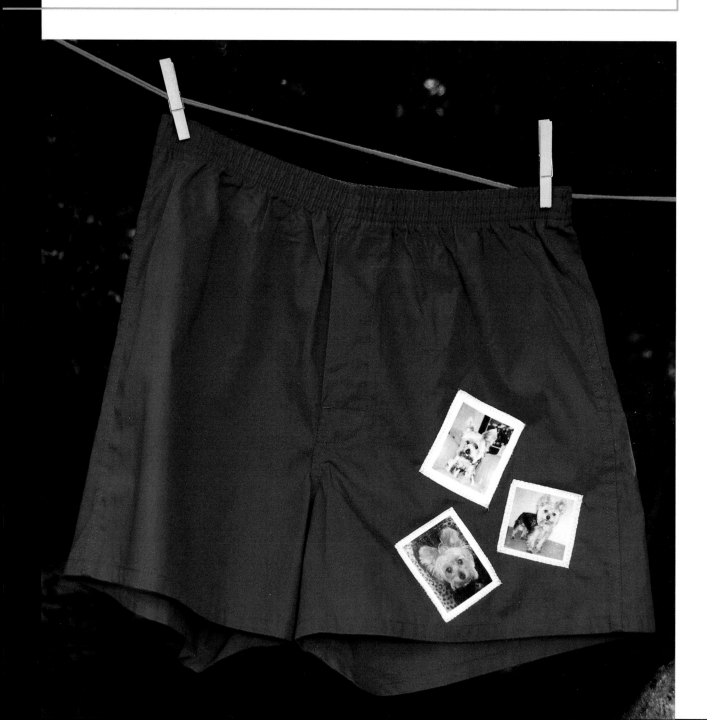

YOU'LL NEED:

- Pair of boxer shorts or pajama bottoms

> **SUGGESTION:** *Feel free to use a pajama top or even a nice, simple cotton robe.*

- Avery T-shirt Transfers
- ¼ yard of white cotton (an old T-shirt will do)
- Iron and ironing board
- Sewing machine (with zigzag-stitch capabilities)
- Thread, any color
- Scissors
- Straight pins

HERE'S HOW:

1. Print your photos at about 2" × 3" onto an Avery T-shirt Transfer.

2. Following the instructions on the transfers package, iron your heat transfers onto the white cotton.

3. Cut out your photo from the fabric, leaving a ¼" border.

4. Pin the photo to the leg of the boxers (or pajama leg or pajama top), to hold it in place while you sew.

5. Sew the cotton to the clothing by stitching all the way around the photo, using a zigzag stitch, making sure to go over the edges of the fabric. Voilà, you're done!

> **SUGGESTION:** *If you are making this for a loved one, use a photo of yourself, and pack the pajamas in his or her suitcase, as a surprise the next time he or she goes on a business trip.*

COPPER-SCOURING-PAD WINE SOCK

This project makes such a great gift. The copper is a festive color and texture, and who doesn't like getting wine?

YOU'LL NEED:

- Copper dishpan scrubber, any brand
- Curling ribbon
- Scissors

HERE'S HOW:

1. Unroll the copper scrubber, so it's the shape of a tube.

2. Close the hole on one end by twisting or wrapping some ribbon around the end. This will be the bottom of your wine sock.

3. Place a wine bottle through the open end.

4. Roll the copper tube up to the neck of the bottle. Tie some ribbon at the top to hold the copper in place, and curl the ribbon with scissors.

5. Your wine sock'll be a hit at the next party you go to!

LAMINATED BOOKMARKS

Say you are hosting the monthly book club party, and you want to make it special. Here is your answer (two answers, actually): Make the invite a bookmark that either includes all the necessary information or reflects the theme of the book you are reading!

YOU'LL NEED:

- Several photos, images, paint chips (from the hardware store), pages from a book, or loteria cards (used in a Mexican card game. See page 308 for more info on these colorful cards.)
- 8" ribbon, any color
- Hole puncher
- Glue stick
- Very thin cardboard

HERE'S HOW:

1. Cut a piece of cardboard into the size and shape you'd like your bookmark to be. (You can make these any size you like, but I like a wide bookmark, so mine are about 2½" × 6".)

2. Arrange the photos, images, paint chips, book pages, or loteria cards on your cardboard and glue them down. (I made the bookmark with photos of myself for my mom, so she always has me around!)

3. Take your bookmarks to a copy shop and have them laminated. You can get several done onto a page, so lay them out wisely. Lamination sheets come in 8½" × 11" or 11" × 17".

> **NOTE:** *Make sure to add your invitation information before you laminate or just include an invitation with the bookmark so it's not dated.*

4. Punch a hole about ½" from the top of your bookmark.

5. Tie the ribbon through the hole. (Or tie several ribbons through the hole to give a fringe effect.)

6. Pass out these bookmarks and prepare to be thanked!

STICKY BACK FOAM STAMPS AND WRAP-IT-UP WRAPPING PAPER

I already told you how much I love giving and receiving homemade presents. Why not make the entire gift amazing by making your own wrapping paper too? It's easy, it's beautiful, and you can make a card to match while you're at it.

YOU'LL NEED:

- Roll of butcher paper or craft paper (I like the look of craft paper because the brown is a nice rich color.)

- Sticky Back Foam Sheets, in any color

- Small blocks of wood, any shape

- Large ink pads, in any color

- Graphic design that you like

SUGGESTION: *Try anything from a simple flower to a sophisticated tile design for your graphic design.*

- Scissors

OPTIONAL: *Glitter glue*

HERE'S HOW:

1. Trace your graphic design onto the Sticky Back Foam, cut it out, and apply it to the first layer of foam.

> **HINT:** *Cut out a square of the Sticky Back Foam to the size of the wood block, and apply it. This will give your stamp some extra cushion.*

> **DON'T WORRY:** *If you don't like your design. Just peel it off and try something else! You'll be surprised how terrific a few simple shapes will look once they are stamped onto some large sheets of paper.*

2. Once you are happy with your design, press it onto the ink pad and give it a whirl on a piece of scrap paper.

3. If you like it, start filling up your craft/butcher paper with the design, until you have covered your "wrapping paper."

> **SUGGESTION:** *Outline your stamped design with glitter glue for an extra-special effect.*

4. Once you get the hang of it, try stamping your design onto a simple piece of colored card stock, to finish off your presentation. I promise, your gift will be special from the outside in!

POPSICLE-STICK SEWING BASKET

This looks much more difficult to make than it actually is. It's much less time-consuming than you might think. I made mine on a little card table while watching *The Color Purple*. By the time the movie was over, I was bawling (you know the part, where they see each other at the end, after a bazillion years. So sad!) and I was pretty much done with the project. Altogether, it was a really good night of crafting and a movie.

YOU'LL NEED:

- 400 Popsicle sticks
- Small 1" × 1" wood cube
- Scissors
- Pencil
- Ruler
- Newspaper spread or craft paper
- Elmer's glue

HERE'S HOW:

1. Make an octagon by first folding your newspaper/craft paper in half, lengthwise, then in half again, widthwise.

2. Lay the square on the table with the folded corner of the paper pointing toward you (where the two folds meet), like a diamond.

3. Fold the paper in half by bringing the left corner over to the right corner. You'll have a triangle, with the long side on your left and the open ends on the right.

4. Starting from corner closest to you, measure up and mark 5½" on each side of the triangle.

5. Connect the dots with the help of a ruler, and cut along the line.

6. Unfold the paper, and you will have an octagon.

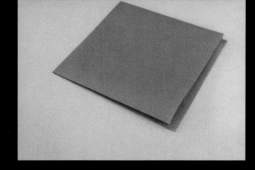

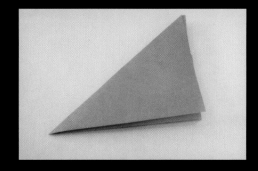

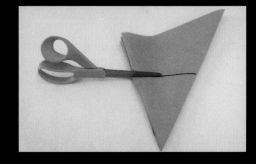

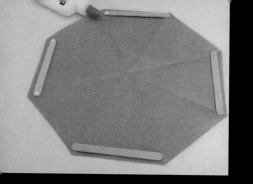

7. Lay down your octagon and place four Popsicle sticks on every other side, nearly flush with the edges of the paper.

8. Dab glue on each end of the sticks and lay four more down over the first stick, end to end, slightly overlapping. This is your base.

9. Keep gluing your Popsicle sticks, alternately spaced, until you are about twenty-two Popsicle sticks high. This is about 3½".

10. For the next five layers, you will start to move your sticks inward about ⅛" per layer. You will start to notice that the mouth is narrowing.

11. Skip the glue on the twenty-eighth layer because we are now going to start making our lid. Pile your sticks as you would for your twenty-eighth layer, as if you were still creating the base.

12. On your twenty-ninth layer, start to use the glue again, being careful not to shift your sticks.

13. Keep inching in ⅛" at a time until you have another twelve layers of Popsicle sticks.

14. Remove the lid (layers twenty-eight to forty-one) from the base.

15. Add a layer of sticks in a straight line across the center of the lid.

16. Glue your wood cube onto the center of the lid, for a handle.

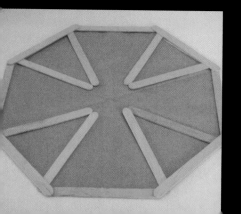

17. Finishing the bottom of your basket is easy. Glue Popsicle sticks, starting from the edge of the basket, toward the center of the base, and following the folds of your octagon.

18. When the glue is dry, adhere another long line of Popsicle sticks, side by side, across the bottom.

19. Repeat this process, except going in the opposite direction.

20. Add more sticks to cover up any holes.

21. Let the glue dry, and fill the basket with yarn, sewing supplies, or bags of buttons.

FAN-TASTIC SUMMER FAN

Fans were found in King Tut's tomb, and have been a part of history ever since. Fans have been a luxury item, a necessity, and a form of advertising. The decline of the fan began in the early 1900s, which is when it became more of an advertising tool rather than an accessory. However, they are still popular in Spain, where they're used in dance and in everyday life.

YOU'LL NEED:

- Cardboard from a heavy mailing envelope (I like to use the free priority-mail envelops from the post office, but don't tell anyone!)

- 2 images (For the pattern I've provided, you'll need images that are at least 6" × 6").

- Wide tongue depressor (Michaels, an arts and crafts store, has these in a variety of colors.)

- Elmer's glue

- Scissors

- Spray mount, any brand

- Paper, in a color that complements your images

- Decorative-edge scissors (Fiscar has amazing scissors with decorative edges!)

- Gold spray paint, any brand

1. Trace the large fan pattern below (the outside line) onto cardboard, cut it out, and spray paint it gold. Repeat.

2. Trace the small fan pattern below (the middle line) onto your colored paper, and cut it out with your decorative-edge scissors. (I chose green here, but it will depend on your image and what matches.) Repeat.

3. Cut out your two images, then spray mount them to the two decorative-edge paper-fan shapes.

4. Spray mount the decorative-edge paper fans (with images attached) onto the gold cardboard fans.

5. With the Elmer's glue, trap the tongue depressor in between the cardboard fans for a handle, and put your new fan underneath a book until it dries. What a great way to stay cool!

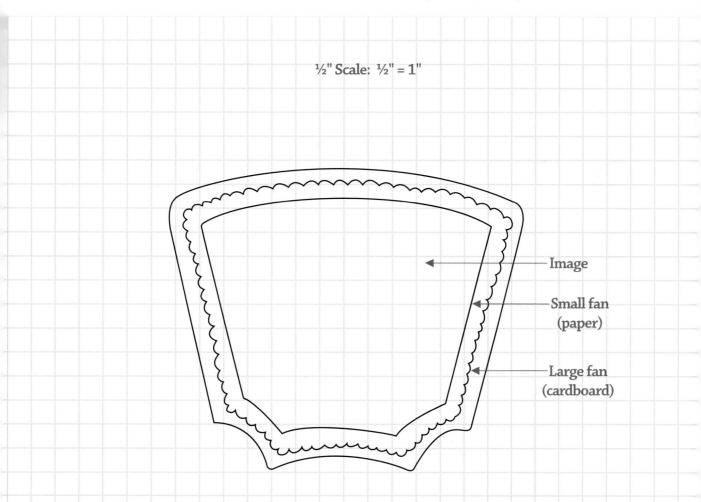

½" Scale: ½" = 1"

Image

Small fan
(paper)

Large fan
(cardboard)

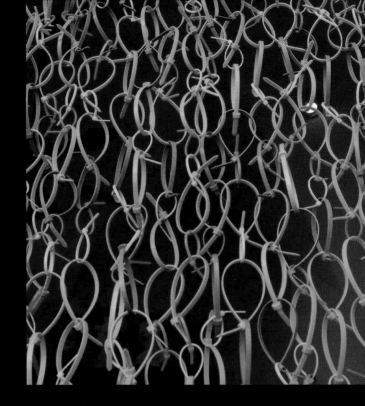

I SAW IT IN THE WINDOW

I f you live in a beautiful area and enjoy the views you have from your home, forgo window treatments! If you are like me and live in a city and can see your neighbor running around in a sloppy bathrobe at all hours, then it's time to block that scary view with a terrific window treatment. Fabric drapes are great for warming a room, but who wants something that everyone else has? The following projects are perfect for small windows or places that need just a little more help. The fishnet window treatment is great for letting in the light and can be used for more than just a window; it's great for draping over a headboard. The felt-leaf treatment could be made with squares or different-colored circles for a more whimsical look. Any way you look at it, these window treatment techniques will make your home as special as you are and improve your views at the same time!

FISHNET WINDOW TREATMENT

Ultrasuede is an amazing fabric that can be used for almost anything. It's great for upholstery and pillows, but I wanted to find a way to use it for a window treatment. The problem was finding a way to use it so the light would come through. Simple cuts in the fabric solved that dilemma and resulted in a very unique curtain.

YOU'LL NEED:

- 1½ yards of Ultrasuede (This will make three 20"-wide panels (Ultrasuede is 60" wide) that are 7' long, once your pieces are cut.)

- Curtain rod rings with clips

- Scissors

- Ruler

- Craft knife (I like Olfa knives.)

- Cutting board

- Sharpie marker

HERE'S HOW:

1. Cut your Ultrasuede in half lengthwise into three 20"-wide panels.

2. With one panel of the Ultrasuede laid flat, use your ruler to measure 1" from the top edge and 1" from the left-hand side, and mark that point with the Sharpie.

3. From the point you've just made, draw three horizontal lines across the fabric. Each line should be 5" long with a 1½" space in between.

4. Next, you will draw four horizontal lines from the first set of lines you've made. This second set should be 1" below the first set, and the lines should be 4¼" long with a 1" space in between. (See the first photo below.)

5. Continue drawing these two sets of lines, alternating between the two, for the entire length of the Ultrasuede.

6. After all the lines have been drawn, cut them against a cutting board, using a craft knife.

7. After your lines have been cut, clip the top part of the panel, and hang from a rod.

8. Repeat this process for the next two panels. Easy!

> **TIP:** *I prefer using two panels as a curtain accent rather than hanging three panels together, but it's up to you. Smaller cuts closer together make a very dramatic statement too.*

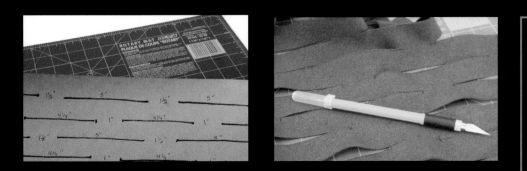

LAMINATED WINDOW SHADE

This is the perfect way to dress up a simple window. It's like art on the wall, and these shades are so easy to make, you will want to hang them all over your home!

YOU'LL NEED:

- An image you would like to have for your window
- A plastic, pull-down shade from a hardware store (These are inexpensive and can be easily cut to size.)
- Household Goop glue
- Double-sided tape
- Access to a copy center with a laminating machine

HERE'S HOW:

1. Go to a copy center and have them supersize your image to the size of your window. (They can enlarge any image to 24" × 36".)

2. Laminate your image.

3. Unroll the plastic shade and cut it off near the top, leaving just a few inches of the plastic, onto which you will attach your laminated image.

4. Glue your shade image onto the plastic strip of the shade with Household Goop glue (it's strong and will keep your new shade in place).

5. Remove the wooden rod from the cut-up shade, which weighs the shade down and keeps it straight, and attach it to your laminated shade.

6. Admire your handiwork and block out that ugly view!

> **DON'T WORRY:** *If your window is greater than 24". You can simply attach your laminated image to the existing shade by applying double-sided tape all the way around the back of the image and sticking it on the old shade. Just make sure it's centered properly, and work on a flat surface so that your image is perfectly placed on the plastic.*

SCARF WINDOW TREATMENT

Lately I've been finding "pashmina" scarves all over, for very little money (sometimes even for six bucks on the street in New York), and I decided that they would make amazing window treatments. There's not too much work involved, other than finding six scarves that match and for a really good price. Try discount stores and street vendors who will give you a great deal for buying more than one at a time.

YOU'LL NEED:

- 6 scarves, in the same pattern or in matching colors (My scarves were 5' long—not enough to reach the floor, but enough to cover the window.)
- 20 clip rings (for hanging the scarves)

HERE'S HOW:

1. Starting at the end of one scarf, attach a clip ring every few inches, making sure they're evenly spaced. (I usually leave about 6" between clips. The length of the scarf should be perpendicular to the floor.)

2. When you get to the end of the scarf, attach the end of another scarf to the last clip. This way, there are not gaps in between your new drapes.

3. Continue clipping on scarves, and when you're done, thread the curtain rod through the rings.

4. That's it, folks. Enjoy the beauty and simplicity of your new drapes.

FELT-LEAF WINDOW TREATMENT

There are projects I always encourage others to do in front of the television, and this is one of them. You are going to have to cut out about, say, five hundred leaves, to make 6' × 8' strands. It's definitely a task to do while watching a miniseries! And while you're sewing, keep that TV on, and it will go much faster.

YOU'LL NEED:

- Felt fabric on the bolt (usually comes 60" wide)
- Sewing machine

NOTE: *One yard of felt will make a strand of leaves that measures about 30' in length and 3" wide, so plan accordingly when you buy your felt. Measure your window and figure out how many strands you will need to cover it properly. You should be able to figure out how much fabric you'll need from that.*

- Scissors
- Thread, in a color that complements your felt

SUGGESTION: *If you are using green leaves, use brown or white thread, so it makes a nice contrast. If you are using brown leaves, use yellow or white thread. Make sure that the thread pops a bit, to give your leaves some nice detail.*

1. Cut out your leaves. Go crazy with the sizes and appearance. I make them 1"–5" in length and 1½"–3" wide.

2. Once you have cut out your leaves, straight stitch right down the center of your first leaf, with the sewing machine, starting at one tip and ending at the other.

3. When you get to the end of the leaf, try to add another leaf under the feet of the sewing machine, tip first, so that the two leaves touch and are sewn together.

> **DON'T WORRY:** *If there is a space of just thread in between the leaves. It gives a nice, organic feel to the strands.*

4. Keep sewing leaves until you get a strand that best fits your window. This will serve as a model for the rest of your strands. Make as many strands as you need to cover your window.

5. Hang the strands somewhere you'll enjoy them!

> **NOTE:** *You can hang them from clip rings or over a long twig, or tack each strand up separately with thumbtacks. These are all great ways to hang your felt-leaf window treatment.*

CABLE-TIE DOOR BEADS

This project is absolutely perfect for a kids' room or to put up whenever you have a party. You'll need some patience for this project. (I did this while watching TV one night, but you could do it with a bunch of friends.)

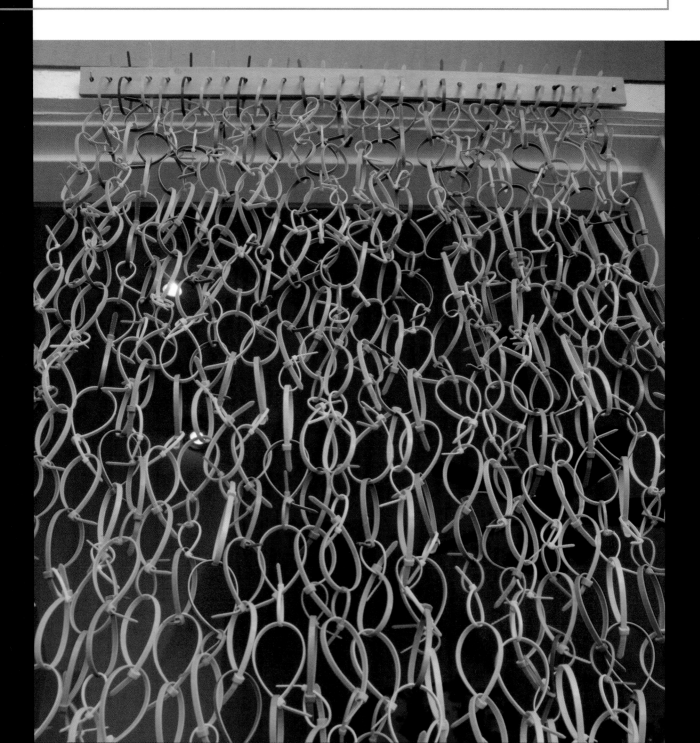

YOU'LL NEED:

- 1,500 multicolor cable ties, various sizes (I found these at Home Depot. They come in jars of five hundred!)

- 1 yardstick, or a 1"–2" × 36" piece of wood

- Drill and ¼" diameter drill bit

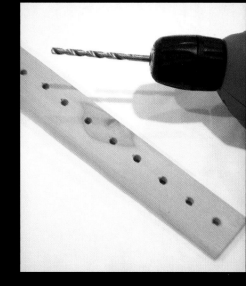

HERE'S HOW:

1. Drill thirty-six holes down the center of your piece of wood. They should be 1" apart from one another.

2. Make a loop with one of the larger-sized ties.

3. Loop your next cable tie through the first one, creating a chain.

4. Keep looping cable ties until you reach your desired chain length.

> **DON'T WORRY:** *If your chain is too long. You can cut it or tighten the ties, so it shortens.*

5. Attach the cable-tie chain to the wood by looping a tie through the hole, then fastening it to the first loop of the chain. Attach all thirty-six strands to the wood.

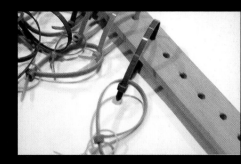

6. Hang your new creation above a doorway, and enjoy!

LAMINATED PAPER-DOLL WINDOW TREATMENT

This is such a charming project. Hang your paper dolls in your window and watch them dance!

YOU'LL NEED:

- Paper dolls

- Ornament hooks, or a roll of thin wire that you can easily cut

- Wire cutters, if you are using wire

- Large needle or small hole puncher

- Tape or tension rod (from which to hang the dolls)

- Sharp scissors with Teflon blade (Fiskars makes scissors great for cutting sticky things. The goo won't get on your scissors!)

- Access to a laminating machine and color copier

1. Measure your window so you know how many dolls you will need. Five dolls make about a 30" strand.

2. Decide which paper dolls you'd like to use for your window treatment. Pick ones with outfits that match your room's decor!

3. Arrange the dolls on a piece of paper. Try to get at least three on a page (for when you color-copy them). Make as many color copies as you need.

4. Have the pages laminated, then cut out each doll. (This is going to take some time, so pick a movie and sit down for a while and enjoy the process!)

5. Make a small hole with the needle or hole puncher at the top and bottom of each doll.

6. Hook the dolls onto the ornament hooks, and attach them to form strands.

7. Hang the strands from your tension rod, or simply tape them to the top of your window frame. (They are light enough that a little bit of tape will do the trick.)

8. The dolls are ready to light up any room!

I'LL BE IN THE BEDROOM
(WINK, WINK!)

You spend a third of your life in the bedroom. So if you live to be ninety-nine, you will have spent thirty-three years in there! Your bedroom should be a place that is filled with everything that makes you feel good. The hangers in your closet should be special. Your bed should be beautiful, and your blankets should be comfortable and inviting. The following projects can be used in many different ways. For example, the room divider could be a headboard, or a way to hide that pile of clothes you always seem to have in the corner. It's all up to you and your imagination. Making your room a special place, so those thirty-three years are something to remember, is a worthwhile investment.

ROPE-FRONT DRESSER

I've said it before and I'll say it again: If I see a piece of furniture on the side of the road that needs some sprucing up, I will pull over, haul it home, and figure out what to do with it to give it another life. This dresser had been sitting in my house for months before I finally decided it was crying out for some rope to cover up some of its flaws.

YOU'LL NEED:

- Dresser that needs some sprucing
- 60 yards of ¼"-thick rope
- Hot-glue gun and a lot of glue sticks
- Scissors

HERE'S HOW:

1. Starting at a back corner of the dresser top, glue the rope down along its perimeter, about 5" of rope at a time.

2. Glue rope around the narrow outside edge of the dresser top, starting and ending at the back.

3. Pull out each drawer, then attach rope along the perimeter of the drawer's front, about 5" at a time. Keep gluing the rope around the face of the drawer, moving toward the center and covering the whole front of the drawer.

4. Repeat step 3 for the rest of your drawers.

5. If you feel that the whole dresser should be covered with rope, then continue the process of gluing rope around the perimeter and working the rope inward. (I decided that I should quit while I was ahead.)

6. After the glue has dried, replace your drawers and enjoy your masterpiece!

HINT: *Rope can contain small splinters, so wear cotton gloves to do this project if you have sensitive hands.*

FABRIC PANEL ROOM DIVIDER

This is such a cool way to cover up your home office, separate a room, or add a headboard, and it's so easy to custom-make your own to match your decor.

YOU'LL NEED:

- JT21 staple gun
- 3 wood-framed 1½' × 5' painter's canvases
- 6 yards of fabric, any type
- 4 2"-long brass hinges
- Drill and Phillips-head drill bit
- Pencil
- Pushpins or thumbtacks
- Iron and ironing board

SUGGESTION: *In case you choose a fabric with a repeat in the pattern, as in the fabric pictured, make sure you take your tape measure to the store with you so that you buy enough fabric to properly center your pattern.*

HERE'S HOW:

FOR EACH PANEL:

1. Follow steps 1–9 from the fabric wall panels project on pages 25–6.

FOR THE HINGES:

1. Place two of the canvases back-to-back, right side up.

2. Measure 1' down from the top of one canvas. This is where one hinge will be placed. Lay a hinge over the 1' mark, and mark the holes on both frames.

3. Repeat step 2, except you'll measure 1' from the bottom.

4. Screw the hinges into place with the drill. You will now have two attached panels.

5. Stand the panels up and place your third panel onto the left-hand side.

6. Repeat steps 1–4, attaching the third and middle panels to each other. You're ready to enjoy your privacy!

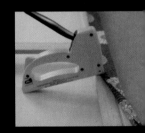

PAPER- AND FABRIC-COVERED HANGERS

Waste not, want not. Rules to live by! My dry cleaner always gives me wire hangers, and I feel terrible throwing them away. I figure there are some clothes that are fine to keep on wire hangers, so why not make a cool paper or fabric cover for them and spruce up a closet! I think these are perfect for lingerie (not that I wear it!).

YOU'LL NEED:

FOR THE PAPER-COVERED HANGERS:

- Images, extra wallpaper that matches your room, or photos of yourself or friends

- Hangers

- Scissors

- Glue stick, any brand

- Access to a copy machine

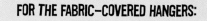

FOR THE FABRIC-COVERED HANGERS:

- 1 yard of fabric, to cover about four to five hangers (If you are using plastic hangers, find a fabric that matches; if you have hangers with a wire swivel hook, you can use any fabric.)

- Hangers

- Sewing machine

- Scissors

- Thread, in a color matching the fabric

- Straight pins

- Fabric marker/chalk

FOR THE PAPER-COVERED HANGERS:

1. Cut out your image so that it fits in the center of the hanger and can be copied onto an 11" × 17" piece of paper.

2. Copy your image so that it is centered in the top half of an 11" × 17" piece of paper.

3. Lay a hanger flat onto a tabletop, then center your image on top of the hanger. Press down on the paper, along edges of the hanger, to make a light impression on the paper.

4. Fold the paper around the hanger, toward its back, and cut off the excess paper.

5. Glue the folds together with a glue stick.

6. Trim off any excess, so the paper sits evenly on the hanger. Now, get hung up!

FOR THE FABRIC-COVERED HANGERS:

1. Fold your fabric in half, then place your hanger onto it.

> **WARNING:** *You will need two layers of fabric per hanger.*

2. Trace the hanger onto the fabric, leaving a 4" border.

3. Cut out the pattern from the fabric.

4. Make sure both layers are facing inside out, then pin all the way around with straight pins.

5. With a ½" seam allowance, sew the left and right sides of the fabric, leaving the bottom open. Keep a small ¼" space at the top of the pattern, for the hook to go through.

6. Turn the fabric right side out.

7. Slip the hanger inside, threading the hook through the hole.

8. Make a ½" fold at the bottom, into the hanger cover, and pin across the edge.

9. Sew along the edge of the folds, enclosing the hanger inside. It's that easy!

ELEGANT MENSWEAR THROW

I always love soft men's woolens. I like to wear them because they keep me warm and they are elegant. I also enjoy the way men's fabrics look when incorporated in home decor. The following project is a wonderful way to make a simple throw for your home. It will look fantastic draped over the edge of a sofa or on the end of your bed, and it requires little sewing.

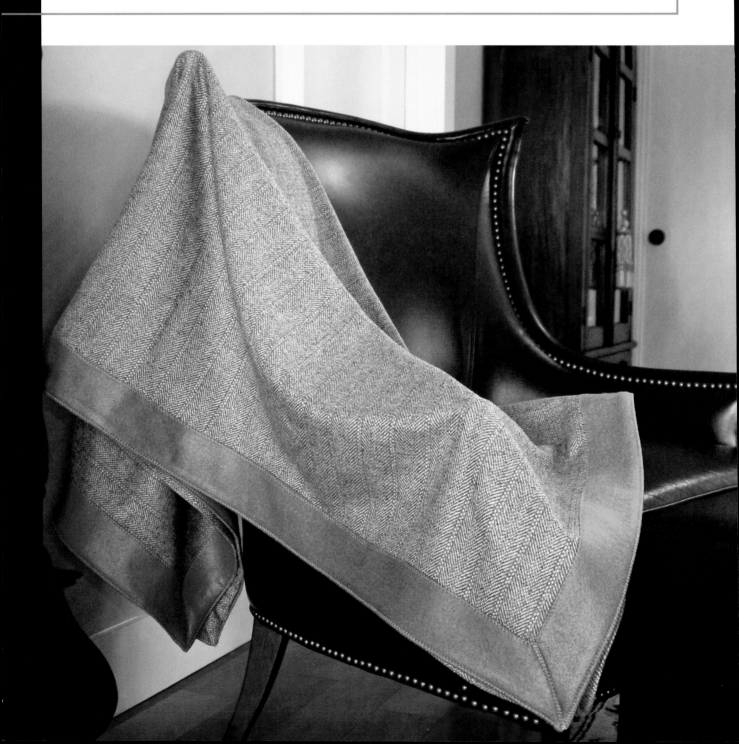

YOU'LL NEED:

- 2 yards of men's woolen fabric, approximately 54" × 60" and looks the same on both sides

  > **SUGGESTION:** *Try the remnant section of your local fabric stores for great deals.*

- 2 yards of felt (It should be the same width as your woolen fabric.)

- Sewing machine (with zigzag stitch capabilities)
- Thread, in a color matching your fabric
- Scissors
- Iron and ironing board
- Long ruler
- Straight pins
- Tailor's chalk, or pencil

> **NOTE:** *The felt and the fabric should be the same width because you will need uninterrupted strips of felt to sew along the edges of your blanket, so it looks professional and home worthy. If you get the same yardage of felt, you will not have to piece your strips together for your blanket. Don't worry; felt's cheap!*

HERE'S HOW:

1. Cut four 3½"-wide strips of felt for the edges of your throw. Measure these out with your long ruler and tailor's chalk, so they are straight and professional.

2. Make sure that your 2 yards of wool are square at the corners. If it's not, trim the edges so that they are.

3. Trim off the fuzzy edges of the selvage edge also.

> **NOTE:** *The selvage edge of the fabric is the fuzzy edge with small holes that runs lengthwise along the fabric. It's usually about ½" wide and is missing the printing on printed fabrics.*

4. Pin the strips of felt along the edges of your woolen fabric, cutting off any excess.

5. At the corners of the throw, cut the felt at a 45-degree angle, so that they are mitered. (Mitered is when the corners meet at an angle, like on a picture frame.)

6. After the felt has been pinned down, use your sewing machine to zigzag stitch (on your widest setting) the edges of the throw, on the wool side of the fabric, making sure you are catching the border of the wool and the felt together.

7. Zigzag the edge of the felt to the throw on the edge that's closer to the center of the blanket.

8. Zigzag stitch at the corners, at a diagonal.

9. Iron on low heat, and you're done!

MEXICAN HEADBOARD

I had a bed that was just plain boring, so I headed over to the lumberyard and found some scrolled shelf brackets and was able to make a headboard that's absolutely fantastic. You can use this technique on a mirror, too, with amazing results.

- Headboard

- 2 18"-long wooden scroll shelf brackets

- 2 10"-long wooden scroll shelf brackets

- 10 1½" wood screws

- Drill and screw drill bit and ⅛" diameter drill bit

- Sharpie marker

- Elmer's wood glue

- Oil-based paint, any color (I chose turquoise for my Mexican-inspired room)

HERE'S HOW:

1. Find the center of your headboard, and mark its location along the top edge with the Sharpie.

2. Place your two 18"-long wooden scrolls atop the headboard, flush together, on the center of the headboard.

3. Drill a hole through the bracket and into the headboard to mark your screw's placement.

4. Glue the brackets to the headboard with wood glue, and then secure them with wood screws.

5. After your center pieces are in, place the 10"-long brackets. Place the smaller brackets on each side of the larger brackets to create your design, and then attach.

6. Paint the bed with the oil-based paint, to get a nice high-gloss finish.

7. Sleep like a king . . . or queen.

I'VE BEEN FELT UP

Felt is one of those fabrics from our childhood that we *always* used for craft projects. I admit that I gave it up for years, because it reminded me of awful turkey hand puppets and bad Halloween costumes. One day, while walking through Michaels craft store, I came across the holy grail of felt: sticky felt, in colors that were unique and pieces large enough for even the biggest of projects. So I bought some and just kept it in a closet for a while. Then all craft broke loose, and I got inspired. Why not take those simple techniques from childhood and kick them up a notch? You can do anything with felt—from window treatments to dressing up a simple skirt, shirt, or pillow by cutting out interesting shapes and applying them. Sticky felt is even great for covering the bottom of your vases, so they don't scratch your tabletops! Any way you look at it, felt is fantastic—it doesn't fray, it's soft, it holds its color, and it's easy to cut into different shapes. Go out and get some and see what happens. Get felt up, like I did! It's wonderful!

FELT TABLECLOTH OR THROW AND FELT APPLIQUÉ PILLOWS

I love these projects and will use them for years to come. You will too!

YOU'LL NEED:

- Sewing machine, with zigzag stitch capability
- Spools of thread, in colors that match your felt
- Krylon Spray Adhesive
- Scissors

FOR THE TABLECLOTH OR THROW:

- 2 yards of medium to heavy fabric, 60" wide
- 1 yard each of five different colors of felt

FOR THE PILLOWS:

- 1 yard of medium to heavy fabric, 60" wide
- ¼ yard each of felt, in two colors
- Thread, in a color that matches your pillow fabric
- Sewing needle
- Pillow stuffing (I buy inexpensive pillows, rip them open, and use the stuffing.)

> **DON'T WORRY:** *If you don't have a sewing machine and really want to make this project. You might try using the sticky felt they sell at craft stores. It's a stiffer fabric, but it looks just as good. Simply cut out your shapes from the sticky felt and apply them to the fabric. It will give you the look you are going for. Just be careful to spot clean!*

> **SUGGESTION:** *For your medium to heavy fabric, try poplin, heavy muslin, or cotton pique.*

HERE'S HOW:

FOR THE TABLECLOTH OR THROW:

1. Cut out your shapes from the felt. Position them any way you like on your fabric. Feel free to improvise!

> **HINT:** *If this is for your sofa, place the fabric on the sofa, then start pinning. If it's for a table, do the same, so you have an idea of what it will look like when it's done.*

> **SUGGESTION:** *If you do want to make a large tablecloth, you may need to sew pieces of fabric together. Appliqué the smaller piece first, because it will be easier to maneuver around the sewing machine. Add on your other side pieces later to make it larger. You can do that by using a simple zigzag stitch.*

2. Spray the adhesive onto the back of each felt piece, and put them in place. This will make it very easy to sew them onto the fabric.

3. Sew the pieces onto the fabric with the zigzag stitch.

FOR *THE* PILLOWS:

1. Cut two 18" × 18" squares from the fabric you're using for your pillow.

> **NOTE:** *If you would like to make your own pattern, draw it out on craft paper.*

2. Follow steps 1–3 from the felt tablecloth or throw instructions on page 191.

3. Pin the pieces of the pillows together, with the shapes on the inside, and sew around the edges with a straight stitch and a ½" seam allowance. Leave a 6"-wide hole on one side, so that you can fill the pillow with stuffing.

4. Turn the pillow right side out, then fill with stuffing.

5. Sew the hole closed using a needle and thread.

FELT SLEEPING MASK

Pamper yourself with these fun sleeping masks! And don't forget to take one with you on long flights, to make your fellow passengers jealous.

YOU'LL NEED:

- Felt scraps, in three different colors
- Sewing machine
- Brightly colored thread
- 1 yard of ¼"-wide satin ribbon
- 2 buttons, in colors matching your fabric
- Scissors
- Pinking shears
- Needle and thread

HERE'S HOW:

1. Cut out the base of your mask from the felt. (Shown in green in the photo above.)

2. Repeat step 1, except use pinking shears and another color of felt. (Shown in blue.)

3. Repeat step 1 with the flowers and leaves, with plain scissors.

> **SUGGESTION:** *It's okay to experiment here. Try differently shaped flowers and leaves!*

4. Sandwich your ribbon horizontally between the two layers of the sleeping mask, toward the top edge.

5. Zigzag stitch around the mask, making sure to catch the ribbon on the sides. Go back and forth over the ribbon with the sewing machine, to ensure that the ribbon stays put and the stitches stay intact.

6. With your needle and thread, stitch on your leaves, and then the flower, covering the stitches with buttons.

7. Nice work! Now you can hit the sack in style.

FELT CREATURES

These little guys are great gifts for kids (ages five and up!), and they make fantastic dog toys.

YOU'LL NEED:

- 2 9" × 12" squares of felt, two different colors
- Needle
- Thread, in a color that complements your fabric
- 3 buttons (at least two of them the same size, for the eyes)
- Pillow stuffing (I buy inexpensive pillows, rip them open, and use the stuffing.)

- Scissors

> **SUGGESTION:** *Try pinking shears for the ears!*

- ¼ yard of yarn or ribbon (to make a tiny scarf)

> **OPTIONAL:** *Sewing machine*

HERE'S HOW:

1. Pin two layers of felt together and cut out your creature using the patterns below. Use your imagination! (Don't forget its ears!)

2. Determine which color will be the front of the creature. Take a scrap of the fabric you're using for the back and cut out two small ears (they should be smaller than the creature's ears.)

3. Either hand stitch, or with your sewing machine, attach the small ears to the larger ears of the piece of felt you're using for the front, making sure the small ears are centered.

4. Working with the same piece of felt, sew buttons for the eyes and nose, and sew the little ear pieces onto the creature's ears.

5. Add eyelashes, a heart, or a weird shape that you like to your creature, using your sewing needle and thread. The shapes can also be added on with a sewing machine.

6. With a ¼" seam allowance, start sewing the two creature layers together, starting at the outside edge of one leg and working your way around the perimeter.

> **IMPORTANT:** *You are not turning the creature inside out after you sew it, like you would a pillow.*

7. When you get to the head, sandwich the ear pieces in between the two layers and stitch over them as you go around the head.

8. Leave a 1½" hole on one side of your creature. Stuff the creature with pillow stuffing, and stitch the hole closed.

> **SUGGESTION:** *Do some extra stitches here since these will be tugged on by children and immature adults.*

9. Tie your ribbon into a bow, or just a knot, depending on how stylish your creature is, around the creature's neck.

10. Happy hugging!

½" Scale: ½" = 1"

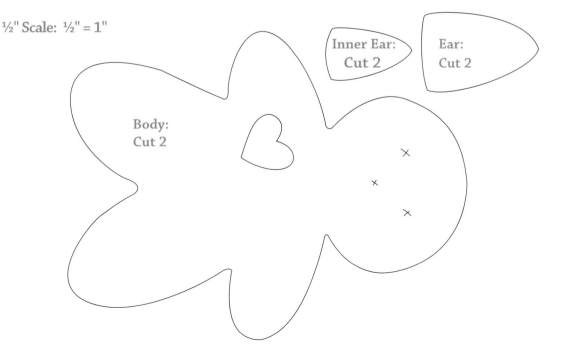

Body: Cut 2

Inner Ear: Cut 2

Ear: Cut 2

LET ME ENTERTAIN YOU

(WITH KITSCHY KITCHEN KRAFTS)

When I was growing up, my mom had this wonderful cabinet filled with dishes, napkins, coasters, and trays that she would use for parties. Sometimes for no reason she would bring out the fancy dishes to make a midweek meal something special. Fabric dinner napkins, nice dishes, and real plates instead of paper turned an everyday dinner into a celebration. I always knew that one day, no matter what, I would have the same kind of party cabinet in my house. I love to gather a few people together and entertain. Just having some coffee in the afternoon with a friend can become an event and something to look forward to, and adding a personal touch to your partyware will make it extra special. The projects in this section are sure to inspire you to entertain, so pull out the fancy dishes and napkins, make some cookies, put on a pot of coffee, and call over the gang. You'll be glad you did.

FABRIC-COVERED SALT-AND-PEPPER SHAKERS

What I really like about these is that you can use large jars and almost never have to fill your salt-and-pepper shakers. And they make great gifts!

YOU'LL NEED:

- Glass jars, any size, with screw-on metal lids
- ¼ yard of cotton fabric, in a great print
- Minwax Polycrylic Protective Finish
- 1"-wide flat artist's brush
- Scissors
- Small nail and hammer
- Medium-grit sandpaper
- Spray paint, in a color that matches your fabric, any brand
- Measuring tape

1. Measure the circumference of your jar.

2. Measure the height of your jar from the base to the lid's lip.

3. Cut out any pattern you'd like, based on the measurement of the jar's height and circumference, from your fabric.

4. Cut small ¼"-long slits every ½" along the edges of the fabric with your scissors, at the parts where the fabric will meet the tops and bottoms of the jars, where they curve. (This'll make it easier to stick the fabric to the jar, and makes for a cleaner look.)

5. Paint your jars with the Minwax Polycrylic Protective Finish, which will be the glue to which your fabric sticks.

6. Apply your fabric to the jar, then apply more Minwax, so the cloth looks wet.

7. Overlap the slits of fabric with the curved parts of the jars, so it's completely covered.

8. After the fabric dries, use your hammer and small nail to tap holes into the metal lid. You can either put tons of holes in randomly, like I did, or you can tap holes in the shape of an *S* for the salt and in the shape of a *P* for the pepper.

9. Sand the lids on both sides.

10. Spray two coats of spray paint onto the lids, waiting ten minutes in between each coat.

11. Let the lids dry completely.

12. Fill the jars with your salt and pepper, screw on the lids, and season away!

TRAY, TRAY JOLIE

I will only serve my snacks on beautiful trays. That way, even a bowl of plain potato chips looks fancy! But that's only one reason I have a collection of fancy trays in my kitchen. The other reason is that I like to eat in bed, and I'm always making a mess, so I needed some great trays, in case I spill. These are four fun options for trays that would fit in with any decor. Enjoy!

YOU'LL NEED:

FOR THE MIRROR TRAY:

- 14" × 24" × ½" piece of plywood
- Approximately 150–200 round mirror tiles
- 2 drawer handles, with screws
- 3 sheets of sticky felt
- Drill and ⅜" diameter drill bit
- Jigsaw, with a scroll blade (a thin blade that makes it easy to cut curvy edges)
- Elmer's wood glue
- Medium-grit sandpaper
- Latex tile grout
- Spackle knife
- Sponge
- Big bucket of water
- Scissors
- Paint for the edges, any color
- ¼"-wide paintbrush
- Pencil

> **OPTIONAL:** *Large dinner plate, to use as a stencil*

FOR THE MIRROR TRAY:

1. With your pencil, trace the shape you want your tray to be onto your plywood. (Try intersecting three circles, using a dinner plate as a stencil.)

2. Cut out your shape with the jigsaw.

3. Mark where your handles are going to be with your pencil, so you don't apply a mirror to those places on the plywood.

4. Cover a 4"× 4" area with wood glue and apply your mirror tiles, keeping them about ⅛" apart. Keep working with small 4" × 4" areas until the tray is covered.

5. Once the glue is dry, apply tile grout with a spackle knife.

DON'T WORRY: *If you miss a spot. You can fill it in later with more grout.*

---

6. As you are applying your grout, wipe off the excess as you go. You will have a little film on the mirrors, but that will easily wipe off.

7. When your grout is dry, sand all the way around the edges of the tray, making sure not to scratch the mirror tiles.

8. Drill holes where your handles will be attached.

9. Insert your screws up from the bottom of the tray. On the top side, screw on the handles until they're tight.

10. Paint the edges of the tray in a color of your choice. (I chose gold for my edges.)

11. I like to apply sticky felt to the bottom of the tray, so that it doesn't scratch my tabletops when I put it down. Three sheets of felt would be enough to cover this tray. Just lay out the felt pieces side by side, trace the tray's shape onto your felt, cut it out, and apply.

YOU'LL NEED:

FOR THE INLAID MARBLE TRAY:

- 2 black-and-white faux-marble self-adhesive floor tiles

- 2 green-and-white faux-marble self-adhesive floor tiles

- 12" × 18" × ½" piece of plywood

- 2 drawer handles, with screws

- Latex tile grout

- Sponge

- Cutting knife

- Big bucket of water

- Black acrylic paint, any brand

- Small artist's brush

- Drill and ⅜" diameter drill bit

- Ruler

- Sharpie marker, fine point

- 2 sheets of sticky felt

- Elmer's wood fill, in a color that closely matches your wood

HERE'S HOW:

FOR THE INLAID MARBLE TRAY:

1. Use the pattern on page 203 to make your tile pieces for your tray.

2. Trace the patterns onto the tile, using your permanent marker.

3. Cut the pattern out of the tile by scoring the tile with a ruler, using your cutting knife, and breaking it along the scored cuts. (Use the straight edges of the tile as much as you can.)

4. Apply the tile pieces onto the tray (try to keep your pattern centered).

> **DON'T WORRY:** *If your pieces do not fit perfectly together. You can fill the cracks later with carpenter's wood fill. In fact, I think it looks better if it's not perfect.*

5. After all your tile pieces are adhered to the tray, carefully fill in the spaces in between the tile with latex tile grout, including the edges.

6. While the grout is still wet, smooth out the edges and wipe off the excess with a wet sponge. (It may leave a residue on the tiles, but that can be easily removed after it dries.)

7. Paint the sides of the tray with black acrylic paint.

8. Place your handles on the sides of the tray and mark where the holes will be with the permanent marker.

9. Drill the holes for your handles.

10. Insert your screws up from the bottom of the tray, then attach the handles on the top side, screwing them on until they're tight.

11. Cover the bottom with sticky felt to protect your tabletops.

¼" **Scale:** ¼" = 1"

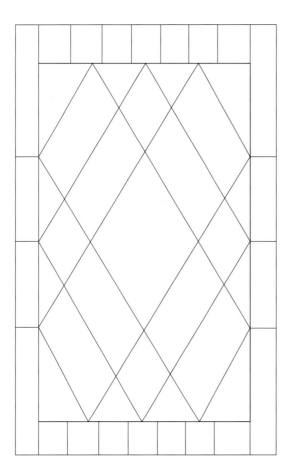

YOU'LL NEED:

FOR THE LOTERIA TRAY:

- 11" × 14" × ⅛" piece of Plexiglas

- 11" × 19" × ½" piece of plywood

- 15 loteria cards

- 1 yard of nylon athletic fabric

TIP: *If you can't get athletic fabric, lace—or any-*
thing that you can use as a stencil to apply a
design to the wood—will work as well.)

- Drill and ⅜" diameter drill bit (for the handles)
  and a ⅛" diameter drill bit (for the Plexiglas)

- Small hammer

- 25–30 thin ⅜" brad nails

- Krylon Spray Adhesive

- Krylon H2O spray paint, in two bright colors
  (Krylon makes a great environmentally
  conscious latex spray paint called H2O. It's
  really good paint, it comes in great colors,
  and you can use it on practically anything.)

- Krylon Acrylic Crystal Clear

- 2 drawer handles, with screws and bolts

- 3 sheets of sticky felt

- Pencil

FOR *THE* LOTERIA TRAY:

1. Place your handles on the plywood, about 1½" from the edge on each side, and mark where your screw holes will be.

2. Drill the holes for the handles' screws, using the ⅜" diameter drill bit.

3. Spray the plywood with your base paint color, and let it dry. (I used light green.)

4. Lay the athletic fabric over the tray, then spray it with your second paint color. The athletic fabric will work as a stencil and give you a beautiful relief.

5. When the paint is dry, spray the backs of the loteria cards with spray adhesive, then apply them to the center of the tray.

6. Spray the tray with a coat of Krylon Acrylic Crystal Clear, which will preserve the tray and give it a nice finish.

7. Using the ⅛" diameter drill bit, drill holes every 2" around the edges of the Plexiglas.

8. Lay the Plexiglas onto the center of the tray, so that it covers the loteria cards but not the screw holes for the handles, and gently tap in the brad nails along the perimeter.

9. Insert your screws up from the bottom of the tray, then attach the handles on the top side, screwing them in until they're tight.

10. Add sticky felt to the back of the tray to keep it from scratching your tabletops.

YOU'LL NEED:

FOR *THE* KITCHEN ART TRAY:

- Wooden picture frame, at least 12" × 14"
- 2 cabinet door handles
- Gold spray paint, any brand
- Images, black-and-white or color (or both!)
- Elmer's glue
- ½"–1"-wide flat artist's brush
- Small cup of water
- Enough sticky felt to cover the back of the tray
- Household Goop glue
- Drill and ¼" diameter drill bit

FOR THE KITCHEN ART TRAY:

1. Remove the glass from your frame.

2. Cut out the images you'd like and arrange them on the glass.

3. Thin the Elmer's glue with just a bit of water, so it's easier to spread.

4. Paint the front of your image with the glue, using the artist's brush, and adhere it to the glass, so that you see it through the glass.

5. When the glue dries, clean the glass around the image, then spray the entire back of the glass, along with the image, with a light coat of gold spray paint.

6. Let the paint dry. Repeat step 5 until the back is completely covered with spray paint.

7. Flip the glass over and admire your work for a moment. Then mark where the screws for your handles will be placed.

8. Drill holes for the screws, then attach your handles.

9. Put a small amount of glue around the inside of the frame, where the glass sits, so that there is a seal between the frame and the glass when you replace your glass.

> **NOTE:** *This will keep moisture and crumbs from getting underneath the frame of your tray.*

10. Place the glass back into the frame.

11. Add another thin layer of glue around the inside of the frame, once the glass is in place, to give it some extra strength. (Remember, it's all about being *home worthy*!)

12. Trim your Ultrasuede to fit the back of the tray, and then glue it on with the Household Goop glue.

13. After the glue dries, flip over the tray and serve up some style!

THREE-TIERED TRAY

Want to wow your guests at a party? Here is a surefire way to make your table amazing, and all it takes are some dishes that you may already have and a little glue. Put this tiered tray in the middle of your table and see how your presentation comes to life.

YOU'LL NEED:

- 3 glass plates, one in each of these sizes: small, medium, and large

- 2 wineglasses

> **SUGGESTION:** *Feel free to mix and match plates and wineglasses. Head to the dish department at the thrift store, and experiment. Chances are you'll find what you need for less than five dollars, like I did.*

- E6000 glue

HERE'S HOW:

1. Wash and dry your dishes so they are free of dirt.

2. Stack your dishes so you can see how they will fit together, with the large plate on the bottom, then a glass, then the medium plate, then a glass, then the small plate.

3. Glue the base of your first glass to the center of the large plate.

> **CAREFUL:** *With the glue. Use a cotton swab to get it on evenly!*

4. Center the medium plate on the first glass, then glue its base to the glass.

5. Align the second glass over the first glass, then glue it to the top of the medium plate.

6. Center the small plate over the second glass, then glue it on top, making it the top tier.

7. Let the glue dry overnight, then fill with fruit, candies, or tarts, and enjoy.

WOODEN CREATURE COASTERS

These will protect your tables, and they're great conversation pieces. Kids love them too!

YOU'LL NEED:

- 4" × 4" pieces of ¼"-thick plywood
- Gold spray paint, any brand
- Black-and-white images, reduced/enlarged to fit onto the squares
- Medium-grit sandpaper
- 4" × 4" squares of sticky felt, in any dark color
- Clear, oil-based polyurethane
- Scissors
- Elmer's glue

HERE'S HOW:

1. Sand your 4" × 4" wood squares so they have a nice smooth finish all the way around.

2. Cut out your images. (If you don't like sea creatures, try buildings or silhouettes, or whatever turns you on!)

3. Spray paint the fronts and backs of the wood squares with the gold spray paint, and let them dry.

4. Spread a thin layer of Elmer's glue on the backs of the images, and adhere to the wood squares.

5. When the glue is dry, coat the coasters with the clear polyurethane and let them dry overnight (or as long as it takes. Depending on the weather, sometimes it can take longer! Damp climates will lengthen the time of paints to dry, whereas arid climates can cut the time in half.)

6. Attach the sticky felt to the bottoms of the coasters.

7. Serve up some attitude!

KID–ART NAPKINS

What better way to show children how important they are than to prominently display the fruits of their creativity in your home? I love these napkins because they remind me of afternoons spent with my nieces and nephews, making cookies and craft projects. (Which is more fun than watching TV, don't you think?)

YOU'LL NEED:

- Men's handkerchiefs (1 per child)
- Crayola Fabric Crayons
- Copy paper, any size
- Iron and ironing board
- Cardboard

HERE'S HOW:

1. Have the kids use the Crayola Fabric Colors to draw a self-portrait or a picture of their pet (or whatever they'd like), about 4" × 4" in size.

> **HINT:** *Draw a 4" × 4" square on the paper for them, and tell them to keep their drawing in the lines.*

2. Ask each kid to make several drawings, then let them pick the one they like best.

3. With the iron set on high heat, iron the drawings onto the handkerchiefs. Begin by placing a piece of cardboard on your ironing board to protect the cloth. Place the drawing faceup on top of the cardboard, then the handkerchief facedown on the drawing, and iron.

4. Make sure you wash these masterpieces on the gentle cycle, then hang them to dry, to keep them vibrant for years to come.

BATHROOM-TILE COASTERS

I love tile. Broken tiles, square tiles, Moroccan tiles, glass tiles . . . I'm a tile freak! Give me some tile and I'll figure out something amazing to do with it. These projects falls into the "Look what I made you for your birthday/housewarming/ Christmas gift" category. And you can coast right through the projects . . . get it?

YOU'LL NEED:

- 4" × 4" white ceramic bathroom tiles
- Sticky felt, enough to cover all your tiles
- Krylon Color Creations Crystal Clear Top Coat

FOR THE LACE TILE COASTERS:

- Lace
- Black spray paint, any brand

FOR THE BLACK–AND–WHITE IMAGE TILE COASTERS:

- Black spray paint, any brand
- Black-and-white images
- Scissors
- Elmer's glue or Krylon Spray Adhesive
- 1"-wide brush (if you are using glue to adhere your images)
- Cup of water (if you are using glue to adhere your images)

FOR THE GOLD TILE COASTERS:

- Gold spray paint, any brand
- Color or black-and-white images
- Scissors
- Elmer's glue, or Krylon Spray Adhesive
- 1"-wide brush (if you are using glue to adhere your images)
- Cup of water (if you are using glue to adhere your images)

HERE'S HOW:

FOR THE LACE TILE COASTERS:

1. Lay your tiles side by side, then lay the lace over the white tiles and secure the fabric down, so it doesn't move. (You can hold down the edges with rocks, or any sort of weight that you don't mind getting spray paint on.)

2. Lightly spray the black spray paint over the lace.

3. Let the paint dry for one minute, then remove the lace.

> **HINT:** *Practice spray painting on some plain paper, just to get the hang of it before you start painting your tiles.*

4. When the paint is fully dry, coat the tile in several layers of Krylon Color Creations Crystal Clear Top Coat. Make sure to let each layer dry in between applications.

5. Cut out 4" × 4" pieces of sticky felt, and stick to the backs of the tiles. (This will prevent the coaster from scratching your tabletop.) Trim around the edges if necessary.

6. Now it's time to coast through the evening in style!

FOR THE BLACK–AND–WHITE IMAGE TILE COASTERS:

1. Carefully cut out your images, making sure they fit onto your tiles (one for each tile).

2. Lightly spray the black spray paint onto the tile, making sure you get a nice, even coat. Let the paint dry.

3. Either water down some Elmer's glue (a 1:1 ratio) and, with the brush, spread it over the backs of the images, or spray the backs of the images with Krylon Spray Adhesive.

4. Attach the images to your tiles.

5. Lightly spray your images and the surrounding tile with a thin layer of Krylon Color Creations Crystal Clear Top Coat.

6. After the first coat is dry, apply three more layers, making sure to let each layer dry in between applications.

7. Cut your sticky felt to the size of your tiles (4" × 4" per tile) and attach it to the backs of your tiles, so that they won't scratch your tables.

8. Now serve up those drinks and enjoy the evening!

FOR THE GOLD TILE COASTERS:

1. Follow steps 1–8 for the black-and-white image tile coasters, except spray paint the tiles gold instead of black.

RUBBER-STAMPED PAPER NAPKINS

This is an easy project, but wow, does it make a difference at a simple dinner party at home!

YOU'LL NEED:

• Paper napkins

• Rubber stamps (FancifulsInc.com has an amazing selection.)

• Waterproof ink, in any color (I like the graphic look of black on white.)

OPTIONAL: *Ribbon, in any color*

HERE'S HOW:

1. Ink your stamps, and apply them to your napkins.

2. Make a whole stack, so you have them for several occasions.

3. For an easy and great gift, tie a ribbon around a stack and give them to a friend!

LAMINATED PLACE MATS AND NAPKIN RINGS

These place mats and napkin rings will add flair to any table! They use basically the same materials, so once you get the gist of the process, go nuts and get creative!

YOU'LL NEED:

- Several images, photos, pages from a book, paint chips (from the hardware store), or loteria cards (depending on the style of place mat you choose)

- Ribbon, any color

- Hole puncher

- Glue stick, any brand

- Krylon Spray Adhesive

- Scissors

- Copy paper, any colors, as many sheets as you want (You'll need pretty big sheets.)

- Access to a laminating machine

FOR THE PAINT-CHIP PLACE MAT:

1. Trim a piece of paper so that it measures 10½" × 13½". This will be your base paper on which you will apply your art.

2. Cut out several paint chips and use a glue stick to attach them to your base paper. Be creative with the pattern!

3. Take your art to a copy shop (I like Staples) and have it laminated.

4. Cut around the edges of the mat, so that you have a ¼" border of the clear lamination.

5. Finally, a place mat to match *any* color dishes!

FOR THE BOOK-PAGE PLACE MAT:

1. Trim a piece of paper so that it measures 10½" × 13½". (This will be your base paper on which you will apply your art.)

2. Cut out several book pages and use the Krylon Spray Adhesive to stick them to the base paper in a random order.

3. Cut out an image and use the Krylon Spray Adhesive to glue it onto the book pages, so that you'll be able to see it after you have placed a plate on top of the mat.

4. Take your artwork to a copy shop, such as Staples, and have it laminated.

5. Cut around the edges of the mat, so that you have a ¼" border of the clear lamination.

6. Hey, why not use some poems and take turns reading them to each other at the dinner table?!

FOR THE PHOTO PLACE MAT:

1. Trim a piece of paper so that it measures 10½" × 13½". (This will be your base paper on which you will apply your art.)

2. Either print out several photos (as many as you'd like) from your computer, or use photos you've already developed, and apply them to your base paper with a glue stick.

3. Take your artwork to a copy shop, such as Staples, and have it laminated.

4. Cut around the edges of the mat, so that you have a ¼" border of the clear lamination.

5. This is such a great way to have dinner with friends and family—even if you're dining alone.

> **SUGGESTION:** *If you are having a special dinner for someone, or hosting a birthday party, it's a great idea to use lots of photos of the guest of honor for the place mats. You can give them away as favors at the end of the night.*

FOR THE LOTERIA PLACE MAT:

1. Trim a piece of paper so that it measures 10½" × 13½". (This will be your base paper on which you will apply your art.)

2. Make color copies of your loteria cards, then cut out the cards and then lay them out in a pattern you like.

3. With a glue stick, apply them to the base paper until it's completely covered.

4. Take your artwork to a copy shop, like Staples, and have it laminated.

5. Cut around the edges of the mat, so that you have a ¼" border of the clear lamination.

6. This place mat will make even the blandest meal seem delicious!

FOR THE NAPKIN RINGS:

1. Trim your images, photos, book pages, paint chips, or loteria cards to about 1½" × 8", and glue them onto a base sheet of paper. Arrange them as you'd like them to appear on the rings.

2. Take your artwork to a copy shop, such as Staples, and have it laminated.

> **HINT:** You can get tons of napkin rings on one sheet of lamination, so go crazy!

3. Cut out 1½" × 8" strips from the laminated sheet and, with a hole puncher, make a hole about ⅓" from the edges on both ends of the strip.

4. Cut the ribbon into 6"-long pieces, and thread one strand of ribbon through the holes and tie a knot, to form the ring.

5. Just slip your napkin through the ring!

DOMINO MAGNETS

Dress up your fridge with these easy-to-make magnets.

YOU'LL NEED:

- Dominoes (look around for thinner dominoes, or the light wooden ones. Some can be too heavy.)
- Self-stick magnet sheets (These come in all sizes.)
- Teflon scissors (They're specially made to cut items covered with adhesive.)

HERE'S HOW:

1. Trace your dominoes onto the self-stick magnet sheets.

2. Cut out the domino shapes from the magnet sheets with some Teflon scissors.

3. Stick magnets to your dominoes.

4. Stick a note on the refrigerator to remind yourself to pat yourself on the back!

GLASS-CHIP MAGNETS

Even boring reminders will look beautiful stuck to the fridge with glass-chip magnets!

YOU'LL NEED:

- Large, round glass chips (which can be found at any dollar store or craft store)

- Images sized to fit onto the chips (Use photos, black-and-white copies from a book, or an alphabet so you can spell things out.)

- ½" magnetic disks

- Elmer's glue

- ½"-wide flat artist's brush

- Scissors

- Household Goop glue

- X-Acto knife

HERE'S HOW:

1. Cut your images into circles that are the same size as the glass chips.

2. Water down your Elmer's glue a bit (a 1:1 ratio) to make it spread more easily. Use your brush to paint over the fronts of the images.

3. Apply the images to the backs of the chips, so that you can see them from the front.

4. Let the glue dry, then cover the back of the images with the Elmer's glue mixture, to ensure that the images stay adhered to the glass.

5. Carefully scrape off any glue that gets on the glass with an X-Acto knife.

6. Attach your magnet disks to the backs of the images, using Household Goop glue.

7. Go decorate the fridge, and have a snack while you're at it!

CHEESE BOARDS

Let's face it. We all love cheese, and we all need a cheese board! This project is fun, is easy to do, and can add some whimsy to your kitchen without much effort. Cheese boards also double as trays when not covered in fromage. (By the way, if you just use a more durable wood for this project, you can make a cutting board for your kitchen by following the very same instructions.)

YOU'LL NEED:

- 1"-thick plywood (A quarter of a sheet should be enough to make about four cheese boards.)

> **NOTE:** *Plywood comes in standard-size sheets of 4' × 8', in various thicknesses and qualities. A quarter of a sheet is 4' × 2', and a good size for this project.*

- Jigsaw, with a scroll blade

- Large pieces of paper, for your patterns

- Pencil

- Medium-grit sandpaper

- Drill and ½" diameter drill bit

- Mineral oil (to keep your board in great shape and prevent the wood from cracking)

HERE'S HOW:

1. Draw your design onto the paper. (Or use one of the patterns on page 222.)

> **TIP:** *Try different shapes that fit your lifestyle, or make one for a friend as a present. For example, I made a violin shape for a musician friend, and a boot for a fashion-designer friend. You can truly do anything, and it's a gift that is always appreciated.*

2. Trace your design onto the wood.

3. Carefully cut out the pattern with your jigsaw.

> **HINT:** *Use the drill to make holes at the corners and the sharp angles of your cheese-board shape, so that you can insert your jigsaw blade and make more intricate cuts as you saw around your wood.*

4. Drill a hole into one end of the board, so that you can hang it on the wall if you want to.

5. Sand the entire board on all sides—front and back—so there are no splinters.

6. Rub the board with oil until you get a very nice finish.

7. Use this at your next party and say cheese!

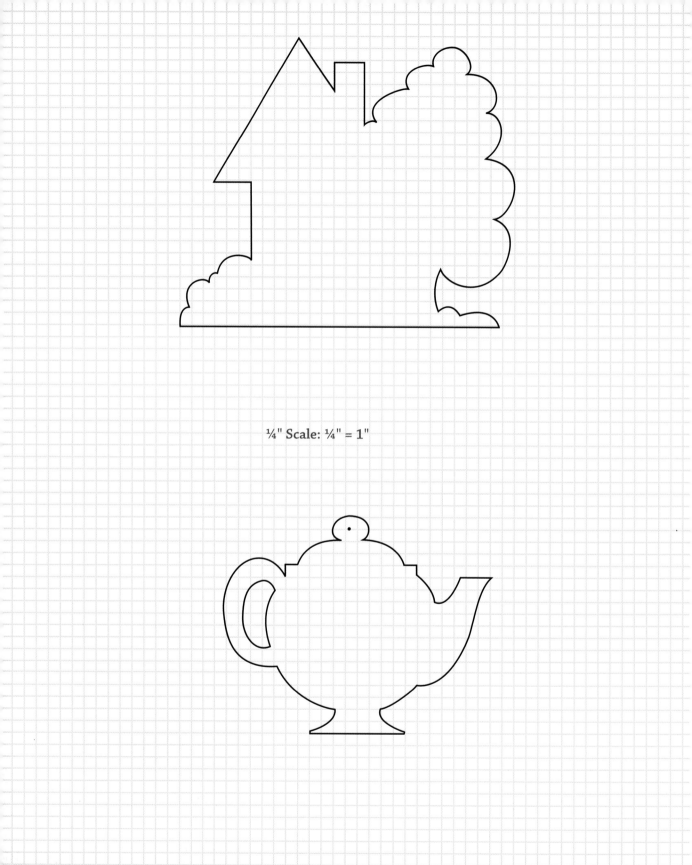

¼" Scale: ¼" = 1"

Ultrasuede doesn't fray at the edges, and it's washable, so you can throw these lovely coasters into the washing machine, and they will come out looking as good as new. But my favorite thing about these coasters is that I can toss them randomly across a table, and it'll look like a lawn in autumn.

YOU'LL NEED:

- 1 yard of Ultrasuede, any color

- Thread, in a contrasting color to your Ultrasuede

- Sewing machine, with decorative-stitches capabilities

- Pinking shears or regular scissors

HERE'S HOW:

1. Use the leaf patterns on page 147 (or make one of your own) to trace and cut out leaves from the Ultrasuede with pinking shears.

2. Using the decorative stitches on your sewing machine, start sewing from the center of the leaves' bases to the tips.

3. Starting from the center line of stitches, sew outward to the edges of the leaves, every ¼" to ½" or so, to make your leaves' veins.

DON'T WORRY: *If you don't have decorative stitches on your sewing machine. You can use a straight stitch and make several stitches, or even use the zigzag setting. Just experiment and have fun!*

MIRROR, MIRROR, ON THE WALL

've lived in a five-hundred-square foot apartment for almost fifteen years, and although I love it, I have to tell you, if it weren't for the mirrors on the walls, I would have gone crazy. All interior designers know that the best way to make a room feel bigger is to add a mirror. My favorite place to hang one is across from a window, so that it increases the light and doubles the view. A mirror can be used in place of a piece of art, and if you make an amazing mirror, it can *double* as a piece of art. In case you're afraid your friends will think you're a narcissist for having a big mirror or two in your apartment, well . . . I've never understood why people think you are vain if you have mirrors in your home. I happen to like the way I look, and if I take a glance at my bum on the way into the kitchen, just to make sure it's still perky, so be it! It's my business and no one else's.

WOOD-SCRAP BLOCK MIRROR

I hate to waste anything, so this wood-frame mirror was a great way to use the small scraps of wood left over from my larger projects.

YOU'LL NEED:

- 12" × 12" beveled mirror tile
- 2' × 2' × ½" piece of plywood
- Scraps of wood, as many as possible, no bigger than 3" × 3"
- Elmer's wood glue
- Medium-grit sandpaper

- Krylon Acrylic Crystal Clear
- Newspaper
- Masking tape
- Self-leveling OOK saw-tooth steel hanger
- Hammer

HERE'S HOW:

1. Glue your beveled mirror tile in the exact center of the 2' × 2' piece of wood.

2. Sand your small wood pieces and glue them around the edges of the mirror.

> **HINT:** *Put the glue on the piece of wood, then place the piece onto the frame instead of spreading the glue on the frame and then attaching the wood. This way, if there are empty spots that you cannot fill with a wood block, you won't have glue on the mirror base*

> **DON'T WORRY:** *If some of the base wood shows. It will add dimension.*

3. Keep applying wood scraps until you have covered the plywood surrounding the mirror.

4. When the glue is dry, cover your mirror by taping some newspaper over it with masking tape. Make sure to leave the wood exposed.

5. Spray the wood with the Krylon Acrylic Crystal Clear.

6. Nail the steel hanger to the back of the plywood with a hammer, so you can hang your new mirror on the wall and enjoy the view!

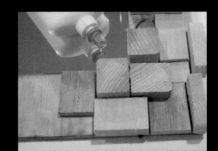

LINOLEUM-TILE MIRROR

Most linoleum looks pretty awful. But I've found that if used out of context (i.e., not on a kitchen floor), it's not bad. I appreciate the design of this linoleum much more when it's used on a mirror than I would if I had to walk on it. Use linoleum on side tables or picture frames, or even put a square of it outdoors on the patio as an accent piece. Please, just don't put it in your kitchen!

YOU'LL NEED:

- 2 1' × 1' mirror tiles
- 22" × 34" × ½" piece of plywood
- 1 yard of linoleum
- Craft knife
- Mirror adhesive, any brand
- Elmer's wood glue
- Ruler
- Sharpie marker, fine point

1. Center your mirror tiles onto the wood and trace a line around them, using your Sharpie. There should be a 5" border of wood all the way around the mirrors.

2. Remove the mirrors and apply a generous amount of mirror adhesive inside of the area you traced, then place your mirrors onto the glue.

3. While the glue is drying, cut out two 5" × 34" strips and two 5" × 22" strips from the linoleum.

4. Place one of the longer strips of linoleum next to the mirror, and, with the Sharpie and ruler, draw lines onto the linoleum, going from the corners of the mirror to the corners of the wood frame. This will mark where you'll cut the linoleum pieces so they all fit together without overlapping.

5. Remove the linoleum and cut along its line with your craft knife, to create your mitered edges.

6. Repeat steps 4–5 for the remaining three pieces of linoleum.

7. Glue the linoleum to the plywood with the Elmer's wood glue.

8. Cut out two ½" × 22" strips and two ½" × 34" strips from the linoleum and adhere them to the sides of the plywood.

9. Finally, a use for linoleum that actually looks great!

JAPANESE HAND MIRROR

You see hand mirrors all the time in salons, and you might even use one at home to check out the back of your hair, but they're usually boring, plain plastic with nondescript handles. I think we should do something to make hand mirrors chic again. To that end, here is my version of a Japanese hand mirror.

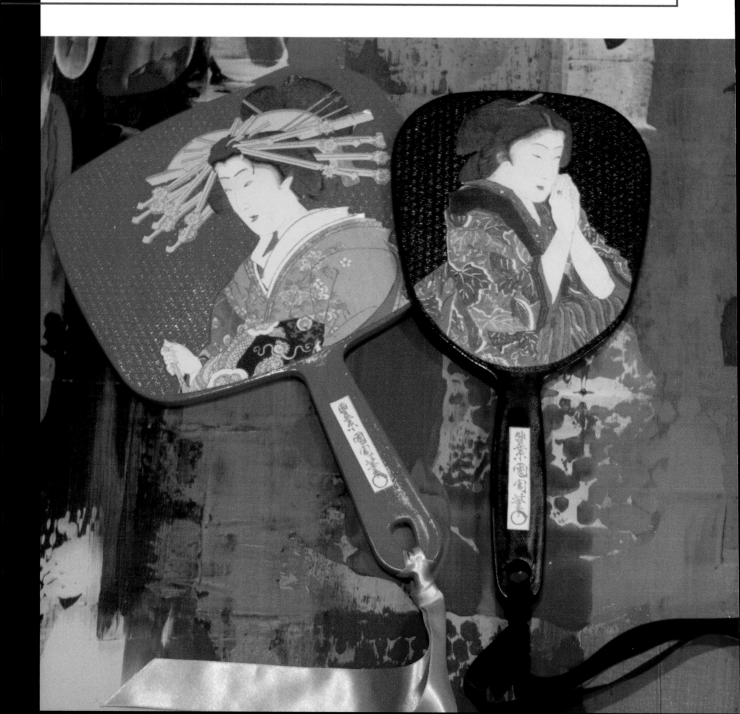

- Hand mirror, with smooth flat back (You can get these at the grocery store in the cosmetics aisle, or in discount stores.)

- Color copy of a Japanese geisha (or another image that you like) that will fit the back of the mirror

- Color copy of any small image, for the handle

- Hot-glue gun and glue sticks

- Krylon Spray Adhesive

- Krylon Acrylic Crystal Clear

- Scissors

OPTIONAL: *½ yard of fuzzy trim, about ¼" wide (for the outside edges), and ½ yard of ribbon (if there is a hole in the handle and you want to hang it)*

HERE'S HOW:

1. Cut out your image so that it fits the back of your mirror.

SUGGESTION: *I found an antique photo of my grandmother, and copied it to use on one of my mirrors. Try it with your own vintage photos!*

2. Use Krylon Spray Adhesive to stick your image to the back of the mirror.

3. When your image is on securely, lightly spray the back of the mirror with the Krylon Acrylic Crystal Clear to protect it.

4. Cut out your smaller image, for the handle, and apply it by using Krylon Spray Adhesive, following with a coat of Krylon Acrylic Crystal Clear to protect it.

SUGGESTION: *Using the hot-glue gun, carefully attach the trim around the edge of the mirror. If you want to hang your mirror from a hook, thread the ribbon through the handle's hole and tie the ends.*

5. Now take a look at your beautiful self!

MAGNOLIA BATHROOM MIRROR

This is a gorgeous alternative to boring old bathroom mirrors, which are usually so plain.

YOU'LL NEED:

- Round mirror
- 2' × 4' × ¼" piece of plywood (¼ of a standard whole sheet of plywood)
- Elmer's wood glue
- Household Goop glue
- Large paper, to draw your pattern on
- Acrylic paint, in two colors of brown (I used Liquitex's burnt umber for the dark outer part and their raw sienna for the lighter inner part.)
- Jigsaw, with a scroll blade
- Medium-grit sandpaper
- Krylon 18KT Gold Leafing Pen
- Paintbrushes, any type
- Krylon Acrylic Crystal Clear
- Self-leveling OOK saw-tooth steel hanger
- Hammer
- Cups filled with water
- Pencil

HERE'S HOW:

1. Trace the patterns on page 233 onto the plywood. You will need one base and four petals.

2. Cut out your shapes with the jigsaw.

3. Water down your raw sienna paint with some water (squirt 5" of paint and mix with ½ cup of water), then use the mixture as a stain, to color wash your petals.

4. Water down the burnt umber paint and color wash the mirror's base, until you get your desired color.

5. Once the paint is dry, glue the petals to the mirror's base with Elmer's wood glue.

6. After the glue is dry, center your saw-tooth hook behind one of the leaves toward the top, and attach it.

7. With your Krylon 18KT Gold Leafing Pen, draw your accents onto the wood. Take your time and draw them out lightly in pencil first, if you have to.

8. Coat the mirror with three layers of Krylon Acrylic Crystal Clear, being sure to let each layer dry in between applications.

9. Position your mirror onto the base, centering it among the four small petals, then lightly mark where the edges of the mirror are, so you know where to glue it down.

10. Use a generous amount of Household Goop glue to attach the mirror to the petals.

11. Let the glue dry overnight, then go dress up your bathroom!

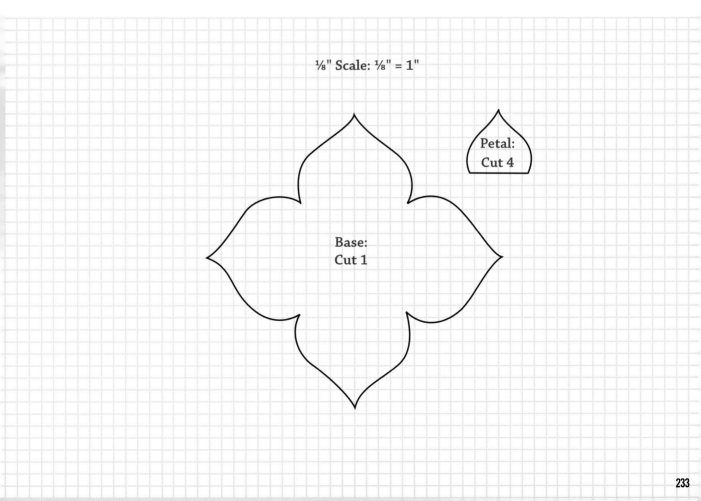

⅛" Scale: ⅛" = 1"

Petal: Cut 4

Base: Cut 1

CLOTHESPIN MIRROR

I love using wooden clothespins for projects. It's amazing what you can do with those cheap little pieces of wood, and everything always turns out looking great.

YOU'LL NEED:

- 500 wooden clothespins
- 3 bevel-edged mirror tiles, each 12" × 12"
- 2' × 4' × ½" piece of plywood
- Elmer's wood glue
- Household Goop glue
- Pencil

OPTIONAL: *Stain, in any color*

HERE'S HOW:

1. Center the bevel-edged mirror tiles onto the plywood, then draw a line around them with your pencil.

2. Glue the mirrors into place with a generous amount of the Household Goop glue, making sure to apply glue to all the mirrors' edges.

3. Take apart your clothespins by removing the metal pieces.

4. Starting at the top left edge of the top mirror, overlap three clothespins end to end, and glue them down with the Elmer's wood glue by placing one flat onto the board next to the mirror and extending toward the edge of the plywood. Overlap the second clothespin onto the first by 1", then the third overlapping the second by 1".

5. Once you have covered the area above the top mirror, start gluing the clothespins down the sides of the mirror, repeating step 4.

6. After you've glued down all the clothespins, give the glue a chance to dry.

7. Once the glue has dried, turn the mirror on its side, and add a row of glue all the way around the edges, where the clothespins meet the plywood, to ensure that they stay put.

8. If you want your mirror to match your decor, stain the clothespins, or leave it raw. Either way, it will look beautiful!

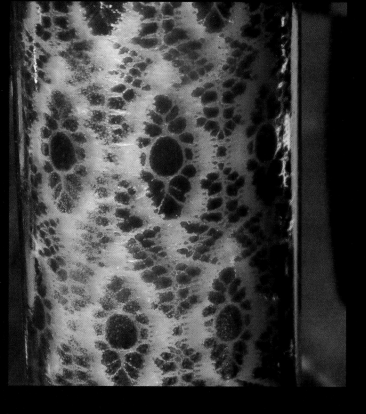

MORE STUFF TO DUST

My great-aunt Jenny had a house where all the bric-a-brac in the world went to die. I have no idea how she kept it all dusted. I would spend hours looking at every little ceramic dog, doll, and clown. When I got older I realized we were definitely from the same family, as I have collected, created, and received as gifts tons of objects that make my home into a little museum. I display my fancy match containers, candleholders, vases, and bushels of fake flowers like a professional set designer. When I get tired of something, off it goes to my storage closet until it's rediscovered a year later to make a grand comeback. Remember, it's the little things that make for a comfortable (and unique) home.

HARLEQUIN FLEUR-DE-LIS MINISHELVES

I like wood projects that don't have to be nailed together. I'm finding in my crafts that Elmer's wood glue is darn strong, and when used properly, it bonds wood even better than nails! These little shelves are perfect for holding candles.

YOU'LL NEED:

- 12" × 24" piece of birch plywood (This will make two shelves.)
- Jigsaw, with a scroll blade
- Elmer's wood glue
- Medium- and fine-grit sandpaper
- White, black, rust, warm yellow, and gold latex paint, any brand
- Ruler
- Pencil
- Masking tape
- Selection of artist's brushes (½" flat and different-size bristles)
- Drill and ¼" diameter drill bit
- Krylon Acrylic Crystal Clear
- Nail
- Hammer

HERE'S HOW:

1. Use a pencil to trace the patterns on page 239 onto your wood.

2. Cut out the shapes using your jigsaw and scroll blade.

3. Drill a hole into the top of your piece, so you can hang it when it's done.

4. Sand each piece with the medium-grit sandpaper, then with the fine-grit sandpaper.

5. With the ruler and pencil, draw a harlequin pattern onto the wood pieces by making lines about 1½" apart in opposite, slanting directions to create diamonds.

6. Paint the base piece with the latex paints, painting every other diamond shape white, and the remaining shapes alternating warm yellow and rust.

7. Paint stripes onto the shelf pieces, making every other stripe white and the remaining stripes alternating warm yellow and rust.

8. With a fine-bristled brush, go around the edges of each shelf piece with black paint.

9. Draw your fleur-de-lis design over your painted harlequin base with a pencil.

SUGGESTION: *Cut a fleur-de-lis out of a vertically folded piece of paper first to use as a pattern.*

---

10. Outline your fleur-de-lis with black paint, then fill it in with gold paint.

11. Paint black dots in between each diamond.

12. After the paint is dry, use wood glue to attach the shelving pieces, so they are perpendicular to the base piece, using masking tape to hold them in place while they dry.

13. After the glue is dry, cover the shelves in two coats of Krylon Acrylic Crystal Clear, letting each layer dry in between application.

14. Hang your shelf from a nail using the hole you drilled at the top, and give your knickknacks a home!

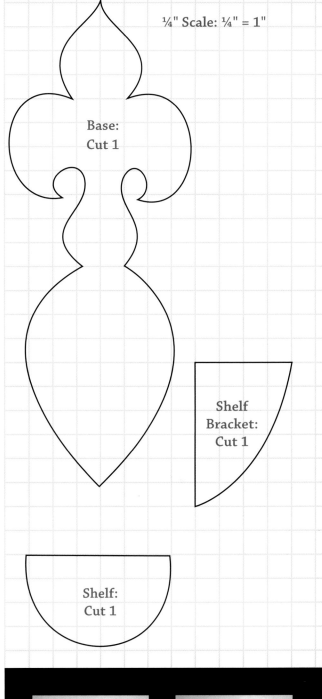

¼" Scale: ¼" = 1"

Base: Cut 1

Shelf Bracket: Cut 1

Shelf: Cut 1

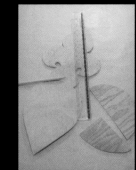

FABRIC-COVERED MATCH CONTAINERS

These are swellegant and are the perfect little containers to keep on the table for whenever you feel like lighting candles. Place a few of these around the house in matching fabrics and you will never be short of a light.

YOU'LL NEED:

- Small glass containers, 2½"–3" high
- Cotton fabric with a small print
- Large boxes of wooden matches with the strike paper on the sides
- Minwax Polycrylic Protective Finish
- 1"-wide flat artist's brush
- Elmer's glue
- Scissors
- Pencil
- Measuring tape

HERE'S HOW:

1. Measure the circumference and height of your glass.

2. Cut your fabric to this size (a rectangle).

3. Paint your glass with the Minwax Polycrylic Protective Finish.

4. Wrap your fabric around the glass.

5. Paint over the fabric with the Minwax so it looks wet, and then let the fabric dry.

6. Cut the strike strips (the rough brown side of the matchbox, where you strike your match) off the sides of the matchbox and tape them together into one large strip of strike cardboard.

7. Trace the bottom of your glass onto the strike strip.

8. Cut out the circle, then glue it onto the bottom of the jar.

9. When the glue is dry, fill the glass with matches, red tips up.

LACE CANDLEHOLDER

If you buy large prayer candles and want to make them a bit more decorative, this is the perfect project for you. You can also take any small jar or juice glass and use this technique to make it into a wonderful candleholder.

YOU'LL NEED:

- Candle that is surrounded by glass, or some glass containers

- Black spray paint, or any other color, any brand

- Krylon Spray Adhesive

- ¼ yard of lace

- Scissors

HERE'S HOW:

1. Measure the circumference and height of your glass.

2. Cut a piece of lace to match this size. Make sure to trim the edges, so it fits over the glass perfectly.

3. Spray the lace with Krylon Spray Adhesive. Be generous, or else the lace won't stick to the glass (two coats of the adhesive should be enough).

4. Stick your lace to the glass and let the glue dry.

5. Lightly spray the glass with the black spray paint.

6. Keep spraying the glass lightly, until you've covered all the glass that's not covered by the lace.

7. Let the paint dry for about fifteen minutes, then remove the lace.

> **SUGGESTION:** *If you want to take your candleholder to the next level, add some glitter glue or rhinestones to make it shine.*

COLORED-PENCIL VASE

These rock, plain and simple. Every time I hit the discount store, I make sure to pick up the ninety-nine-cent packages of colored pencils, just for inspiration. I can't resist. And it paid off when I came up with the idea for this project. This vase is great to put in a kid's room, but it can even be chic on a table full of flowers. It's up to you to use the vase artistically, so it reaches its full potential.

YOU'LL NEED:

• Tons of colored pencils

HINT: *If you want to make the short vase, you need thirty-three pencils, and for the tall vase, sixty-six pencils.*

• Hot-glue gun and glue sticks
• Old soup or bean cans (You'll need two cans for the large vase.)
• 1 yard of ¼"-wide ribbon, any color (I used red and black for mine.)

HERE'S HOW:

FOR THE SMALL VASE:

1. Figure out how to arrange the colors around the cans. (I like to put them in rainbow formation.) Usually they will look great in the order that they are presented in the package, but you could go crazy and see what happens, too.

2. Draw vertical lines from the bottom of the can to the top, so you can make sure that you glue your pencils on straight. (Make sure to take the pencils' width into consideration!) If the pencils are glued on crooked, then you'll have to rip them all off and start again.

3. Put a line of glue down the line you drew (that rhymes!) and apply your first pencil with the tip (the end that could be sharpened to a point) down, flush with the bottom of the can.

4. Keep gluing pencils around the can, making sure to place your pencils straight up and down and flush with the bottom. The pencils will be longer than your can, so have the excess of the pencil extending above the mouth of the can.

5. When you've surrounded the can with pencils, wrap ribbon around the can's bottom, holding it in place by applying dabs of hot glue to the tips of the pencils (whether they're presharpened or not). After you've encircled the bottom of the can with the ribbon, wind it up, so there's about 1" of ribbon covering the pencils.

FOR THE LARGE VASE:

1. Glue the base of one can to the base of another can.

2. Follow steps 1–5 above, except that for this project you will glue the pencils with the tips pointing toward the center of the vase, where the cans meet.

3. Wrap the ribbon enough times around the center of the vase to cover the points of the pencils (again, they might not be sharpened), using dabs of hot glue all the way around the can to keep the ribbon in place.

4. Now everything you put in these vases will look exciting and colorful.

TILE MATCHBOX DRAWERS

My grandma had one of these, and I loved playing with it. She kept her earrings in it, but I liked it because it was made of matchboxes. (What little kid doesn't enjoy playing with matches?) I think this is a nice craft to revive—Look out, moms!

YOU'LL NEED:

- 2 4" × 4" ceramic bathroom tiles, any color

- Spray paint, any color (if the tiles are in a shade you don't like)

- Image, black-and-white or color

- 6 small 1½" × 2" boxes of matches

- 6 ballpoint pins

- 1"-wide brush (if you are using glue to adhere your images)

- Krylon Color Creations Crystal Clear Top Coat

- Elmer's glue or Krylon Spray Adhesive

- Scissors

- Cup of water

HERE'S HOW:

1. Follow steps 1–6 on page 211-2 for the bathroom tile coasters with images. Make one of these for the top part of your drawer. The other tile can be either left plain or spray painted. This will be the bottom part of the drawer.

2. Use plenty of Elmer's glue to sandwich the six small matchboxes in between the two bathroom tiles into two rows of three "drawers."

3. After the glue is dry, push your ballpoint pins into the center of each box, to create your drawer handles.

> **TIP:** *Dab some glue onto the sharp edges of the pins once they're in, to keep them from poking you when you take out your matches.*

4. Add a small amount of glue onto the inside of each drawer, to keep the pins in place.

5. Place your drawer on the table and let the sparks fly, or fill it with your favorite earrings and treasures.

WINEGLASS CANDLEHOLDERS OR VASES

The next time you are in the housewares section of your favorite haunt, start experimenting with different glassware, to see if you can put a couple of glasses together to make a candleholder or vase. Sometimes I find wineglasses and tumblers for ninety-nine cents, and with just a bit of glue, they can be turned into something amazing.

Decorate a dinner table with a cluster of these, and watch how dramatic your evening becomes.

YOU'LL NEED:

- 2 drinking glasses (per candleholder or vase)

- E6000 glue

- Candles, small enough to fit into one of the glasses, or flowers (depending on what you are planning to put into your creations)

HERE'S HOW:

1. Glue the base of one glass to the base of the other glass with the E6000, then let the adhesive dry.

2. Fill the top glass with candles or flowers.

3. Marvel at your thriftiness!

WOODEN DISPLAY STANDS

We all have little things that we've collected throughout the years, and although they are special, they aren't always displayed properly. This project is an excellent way to show off even the smallest treasure. From a seashell to a small mask to a small faux bird, these elegant stands do justice to anything you want to put on top of them. Best of all, they are supereasy to make. For this project I chose seashells in honor of my mom, who loves them.

YOU'LL NEED:

- Hardwood rosettes, one for each treasure you want to display, about 5" × 5" (Rosettes are decorative wood squares that are traditionally used on the corners of window and door moldings.)

- Wooden dowels, ³⁄₁₆" in diameter (or around that size)

- Elmer's wood glue

- Household Goop glue

- Craft knife

- Drill and drill bit that's the size of your dowels (For example, if your dowels are ³⁄₁₆", then get a drill bit that is also ³⁄₁₆".)

HERE'S HOW:

1. Find the center of your hardwood rosette, and drill straight down into it from the top, about ½".

2. Check to make sure the dowel will fit inside the hole you've just drilled. If not, then you may need to use a slightly larger bit size.

3. Fill the hole with wood glue and insert your dowel.

4. Using your craft knife, cut your dowel down to size.

> **TIP:** *Don't cut your dowels until you have decided how long you would like them to be. Heavier objects work well on shorter dowels and smaller objects work well on longer dowels. It's all up to you and your taste. (When figuring out how long your dowels will be, don't forget the ½" hole you'll be drilling!)*

5. Use Household Goop glue to attach your item to the top of the dowel, then let the glue dry.

6. Now every piece of your collection will look museum quality.

> **SUGGESTION:** *Use these stands to display dolls' heads or small carved figurines.*

BEAUTIFIED MATCHBOXES

Fill even the smallest gestures with beauty. In my home, I try to choose items that reflect my personality, especially the items I use every day. If it's a knife, I want it to have a terrific handle. If it's a napkin, I want to love looking at the pattern. So I decided I would be thoughtful about even something as small as my matchboxes. Some of them are completely covered with images and surrounded by glitter glue, while others are spray painted and have cut-out images applied to them. These are so easy to make, and they look beautiful sitting on any table. Also, friends love getting a personalized set of these as gifts.

YOU'LL NEED:

- Small and large matchboxes (depending on what you want to make)

- Blue painter's tape

- Gold spray paint

- Images, any size

- Scissors

- Krylon Spray Adhesive

- Krylon Acrylic Crystal Clear

OPTIONAL: *Glitter glue, for some embellishment*

FOR THE SPRAY-PAINTED MATCHBOX:

1. Cover the strike strip, where you strike your match, with the blue painter's tape.

2. Cover the matchbox on all sides with the gold spray paint.

3. Cut out an image, then spray the back of it with Krylon Spray Adhesive. Attach it to the top of the matchbox.

4. Spray the entire box with Krylon Acrylic Crystal Clear.

FOR THE COMPLETELY COVERED MATCHBOX:

1. Cover the strike strip, where you strike your match, with the blue painter's tape.

2. Cut out an image that will be one side, preferably the top, of your matchbox.

3. Spray the back of the image with Krylon Spray Adhesive, then attach it to the box.

4. If you want, make a line of glitter glue around the edges of the image, to give it a frame, then let the glue dry.

> **SUGGESTION:** *Some images will look great if you embellish them with the glitter glue, like my image of Ganesh. I covered the gems with glitter, and I think it looks great.*

5. Coat with Krylon Acrylic Crystal Clear and let the layer dry.

6. No one will be able to match your ability to light up a room!

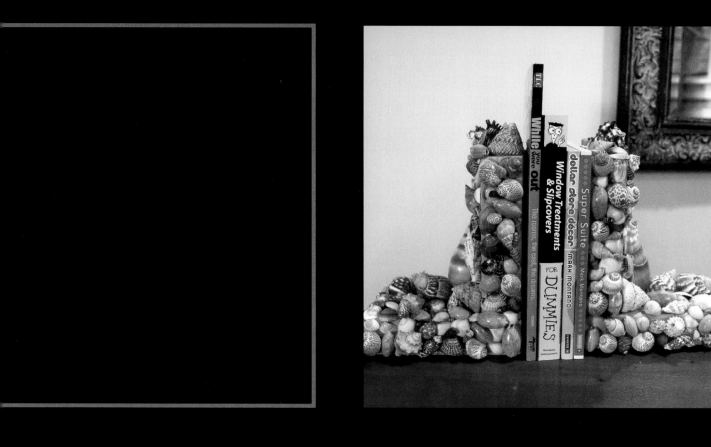

NATURE CALLS

don't know about you, but I am forever picking up seashells from the beach and beautiful pieces of wood, pebbles, leaves, and flowers each time I take a walk. Whatever nature leaves behind, I gather like a squirrel preparing for the winter. You'd think just once I could lie on the beach and do nothing for a few minutes! Instead, I'm there with a basket, gathering whatever I can find for my next crafting adventure.

Nothing is more beautiful than something found in nature (especially when you're walking down a trail and find a hundred-dollar bill! But that's not the point here. . . .), and few things say "comfortable" and "organic" like flowers, leaves, wood, and seashells. Gather them up and use them in your projects. You'll be surprised how wonderful they look and what fantastic projects you can invent.

SEASHELL-ENCRUSTED BOOKENDS

We all have books and we all need bookends. Liven up your bookshelves with these seashell bookends, and enjoy a beach read in your home!

YOU'LL NEED:

- 4 pieces of 2×4, each 6" long
- Seashells, different sizes
- Medium-grit sandpaper
- Elmer's wood glue
- Household Goop glue
- 1 sheet of sticky felt
- 1 sheet of Sticky Back Foam Sheets, any color
- Krylon Acrylic Crystal Clear

HERE'S HOW:

1. Use Elmer's wood glue to attach two 2×4 pieces to form an L shape, with the vertical part of the L sitting on the horizontal part. Repeat with the other two pieces of wood.

2. After the glue is dry, start applying the seashells to the outsides of the L, making sure not to glue them to the bottoms of the bookend or to the sides that touch the books.

3. After the glue on the seashells is dry, fill in gaps with smaller seashells.

4. Cut the Sticky Back Foam to the size of the bottom of your bookends and apply. (This will give them some grip and keep them from slipping.)

5. Cut the sticky felt to the size of the sides that touch the books, and adhere. (This will make sure your books aren't damaged or scratched.)

6. Coat your new bookends with Krylon Acrylic Crystal Clear.

7. Now your bookshelves will be as beautiful as the stories they hold.

SEASHELL CANDLEHOLDER OR VASE

This project took me a day and a half to complete, but I like the results. Take it from me: Do not use hot glue. The shells will fall off, and you will be frustrated!

YOU'LL NEED:

- Loads of seashells
- Glass vase, any size
- Amazing Goop craft glue or E6000 glue
- Scotch tape

OPTIONAL: *Krylon Frosted Glass Finish paint, in white, for the inside of the vase (I tried it and liked the way it looked for this project.)*

HERE'S HOW:

1. Lay your vase on its side. (You can prop your vase up with some seashells so it doesn't roll around while you work.)

2. Before you start gluing, hold each seashell to the vase, so you can see where to apply the glue to the shell (otherwise you will waste a lot of glue).

3. Put glue wherever the shell will touch the vase, and then attach it.

HINT: *If the shell starts to slip before the glue dries, put a piece of tape over it to hold it in place.*

4. Adhere a whole column of shells from the bottom of the vase to the top, and let the glue dry for an hour or so.

5. Once the glue has dried, turn the vase just a little and, working next to the first column, add another column (or as many as you can, so long as they don't start slipping off). The first row will help the second stay in place.

6. Repeat step 5 until the entire vase is covered. Now go show off your vase!

SEASHELL MAIL HOLDER

Aren't you tired of putting your mail into a pile on the counter? I know I am. This project is a chic and interesting way to clean up the clutter.

YOU'LL NEED:

- Seashells, various sizes
- ¼ sheet of 2' × 4' × ¼" birch plywood
- Jigsaw, with a scroll blade
- Drill and ½" diameter drill bit
- Elmer's wood glue
- Elmer's glue
- Medium-grit sandpaper
- Silver spray paint
- Faux pearl beads
- Nail
- Hammer

HERE'S HOW:

1. Use the pattern on page 255 to trace the base design onto the plywood.

2. Trace the box pieces onto the plywood

3. Use the jigsaw to cut out your shapes.

4. Drill holes at the points in the pattern.

5. Fit your jigsaw blade into the holes, then cut out the shapes.

6. Sand all the pieces.

7. Glue the box pieces together with Elmer's wood glue, using the picture as a guide.

8. After the glue is dry, attach the box to the base piece with Elmer's wood glue.

9. After the Elmer's glue is dry, artfully glue on the seashells.

SUGGESTION: *Echo the design of the seashells on each side to achieve symmetry.*

11. After all the glue has dried, spray the mail holder with silver spray paint, then let the paint dry.

10. After the mail holder is covered in shells, glue the pearl beads onto different areas. (I went to town on this project!)

12. Hang your mail holder on a nail through the center hole, and kiss those piles on your countertop good-bye!

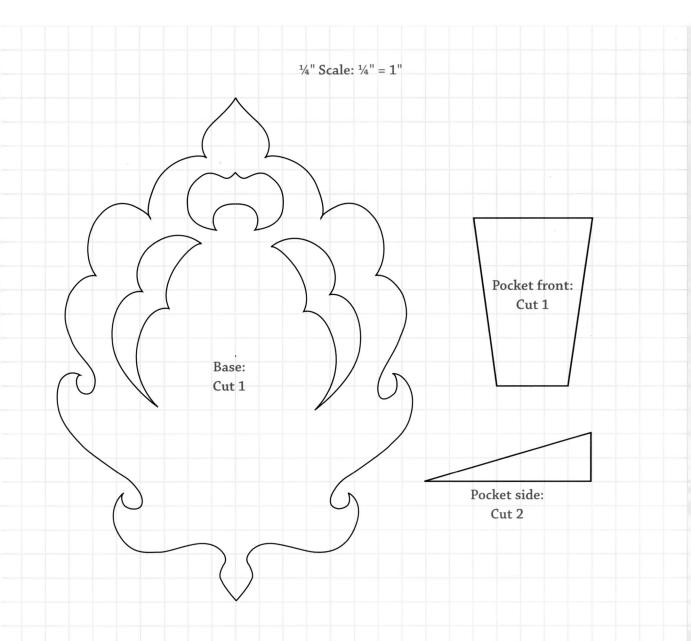

¼" **Scale: ¼" = 1"**

Base:
Cut 1

Pocket front:
Cut 1

Pocket side:
Cut 2

BRANCH INCENSE BURNER

I've recently been spending a lot of time outside, and I wanted to use an incense burner for insect repellent. The problem is that I can never find a burner that is beautiful enough to be part of my outdoor decor, so I decided to take matters into my own hands and use a bit of nature for this project. I put this creation right in the middle of my outdoor dinner table. It's attractive, and it keeps the bugs away.

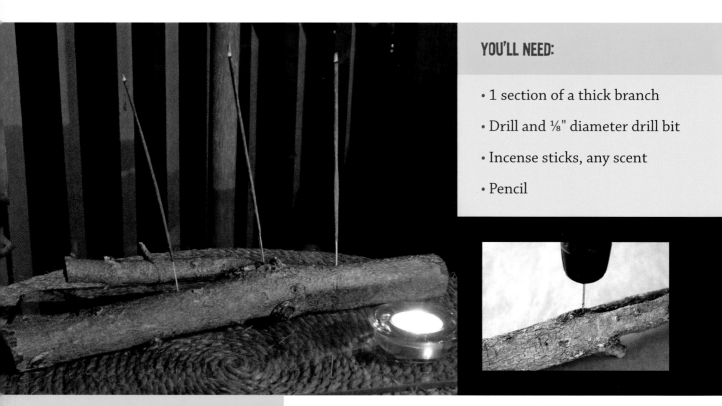

YOU'LL NEED:

- 1 section of a thick branch
- Drill and ⅛" diameter drill bit
- Incense sticks, any scent
- Pencil

HERE'S HOW:

1. Place your branch on the table in a way that it will not move or wobble.

2. Mark with a pencil where you would like your incense sticks to be. (I put three holes in mine, but you can put as many as five in yours.)

3. Drill 1" holes into your branch, using your pencil marks as guides.

4. Insert your incense sticks and light. Now, how easy was that?!

TRAPPED AND PRESSED FLOWER–AND–LEAF ART

This is a terrific way to display your pressed flowers and leaves, and framing something this way makes it automatically match your room, because you get to see the wall behind the work you're framing.

YOU'LL NEED:

- 2 frames of equal size and with the same size glass

HINT: *Buy one nice frame for your project and another cheap frame from the dollar store for the extra piece of glass.*

- Pressed flowers and leaves

HERE'S HOW:

1. Remove the glass from one frame, and clean it carefully. (You won't need the rest of the frame and the backing.)

2. Remove the cardboard and paper from the back of the other frame, leaving only the glass and the actual frame. (The glass from the other frame will serve as the back of this frame.) Clean the glass carefully.

3. Place your pressed leaves and flowers onto the glass that will be the back of the frame.

4. Place the other piece of glass over the backing glass, to keep the leaves and flowers in place.

5. Place both pieces of glass into the frame and bend the small metal stays onto the back of the frame to keep both glasses in place.

NOTE: *You are basically replacing the cardboard of one frame with the glass from another, and making a see-through frame. Pretty easy, don't you think?*

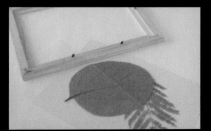

FAMILY TREE

The next time you are walking down the street after a windstorm, or just hanging out in your backyard, pick up some twigs and branches and let your imagination soar. I use them for everything—from chandeliers to jewelry holders. They are free and beautiful and available in abundance.

YOU'LL NEED:

- 1 small branch, with many different limbs jutting off of it

- Small photographs

- Cardstock, any color

- Ornament hooks, or small-gauge wire that you can bend into hooks

- Large sewing needle

- Small square of scrap wood, about 4" × 5"

- Drill and drill bit in the diameter of the base of your branch (Mine was ¼".)

- Elmer's glue

1. Mount your photos on cardstock using Elmer's glue. (For this project I chose green cardstock, but you can use any color, or not use cardstock at all.)

2. Drill a hole into the center of your piece of scrap wood.

3. Fill the hole with glue and insert your branch.

4. While the glue dries, poke small holes at the tops of your photos, using the needle, and then thread the wire hooks through the holes.

5. After the glue is dry, hook the photos onto the limbs of the branch.

> **SUGGESTION:** *If you don't want to hang photos, then just hang a few necklaces and earrings, and keep it on your dressing table. It's a great way to keep things organized and show off your favorite pieces.*

FLOWER–AND–LEAF PRESS

I always see these in stores, and I decided I would make one for my mom, who has the most amazing garden. Before getting started, I thought a lot about whether to use blotter paper or newspaper, and I think that newspaper is the way to go. In addition to adding a cool visual element, it's also a great way to make this project more cost effective (it's already inexpensive to make), and why go out and buy something you don't really need when you already have a perfect substitute around the house? I also made my project a standard size, 8½" × 11", so that it's easy to find paper that fits into your book as well.

YOU'LL NEED:

- Belt, with a slide buckle or D rings (so that it's easy to tighten)

- 2 pieces of 8½" × 11" × ½" plywood

- Medium-grit sandpaper

- Jigsaw, with a scroll blade

- Drill and ¼" diameter drill bit

- 12–16 sheets of newspaper, cut to 8½" × 11"

- 6–8 pieces of 8½" × 11" corrugated cardboard

- White 8½" × 11" printer paper

- Flowers and leaves (to dry and press)

HERE'S HOW:

1. Sand your plywood.

2. Drill about twenty holes in any design you like all the way through one of the pieces of plywood. This will allow moisture in the leaves and flowers to escape more easily.

3. Gather the leaves and flowers you want to press. Work fast, because the sooner you get them drying, the more color they retain.

4. Start to layer your papers onto the plywood without the holes: First the wood, then cardboard, newspaper, printer paper, flowers, printer paper, newspaper, cardboard.

5. Repeat step 4 for all your flowers and leaves.

6. Place the wood with the holes on top and tighten the belt around all of the layers.

> **HINT:** *The color retention of your flowers will be better if you put the flowers between sheets of paper, and then change just the newspaper layer every couple of days. The flowers will turn brown if they don't dry quickly enough.*

7. Make sure to leave some flowers in your garden to enjoy.

POE-TREE

This project is perfect for adding a touch of class and personality to any room, filling up a dark, uninteresting corner, and making something wonderful out of a book you're done reading but not ready to part with.

YOU'LL NEED:

- Discarded book
- Branches, all different sizes
- Planter or decorative pot
- Plaster of Paris
- Moss
- Clothespins
- Scissors
- Elmer's glue
- Krylon Acrylic Crystal Clear

HERE'S HOW:

1. Take six of your larger branches and tie them together, to make the trunk. (Don't worry if your branches aren't very tall. You will be able to extend them by gluing on branches to make your tree the size that you want.)

2. Fill your decorative pot with plaster of Paris, place your trunk into the plaster while it's wet, then let the plaster dry. This will be the base of your tree.

3. With clothespins and Elmer's glue, attach branches to the trunk's branches, to make the tree the size and height that you want.

4. Cut leaf shapes from the pages of your book. (I like simple leaves that are tapered, but you can use any shape you like.)

5. To attach the leaves to the tree, dab some Elmer's glue onto the ends of the leaves and wrap them around the branches.

6. Use Elmer's glue to attach leaves to the ones you've already wrapped around the branch. Do this along each branch, until you get the fullness that you want.

> **HINT:** *If you need more branches, just add them. If you don't like the shape, just break off a branch and glue it somewhere else. The leaves will cover your glue and clothespins.*

7. When you are done gluing on the leaves, cover the plaster of Paris in the planter with moss, to give it a nice, finished look.

8. Spray the tree with Krylon Acrylic Crystal Clear. This will protect the project and give it a long life!

OUTDOORSY

After living in a busy, concrete city for twenty years, I finally have a yard. In fact, I have a front yard *and* a backyard! It's like having another two thousand square feet of living space, and I love it. Now my goal is to make the outdoors as comfortable as the indoors, and these projects are just the beginning: They're sturdy, hold up under bad weather, and are far more attractive than most of the furniture and decorations you can purchase for outdoor spaces. Use the techniques in this chapter, but make the projects your own. I guarantee you will be just as proud of your outdoor space as you are of your living room.

POPLAR OUTDOOR RUG

I have had a ton of different rugs outside my back door, and they usually end up looking terrible after only a few weeks. They either get bleached by the sun or get filthy. I decided the best way to make an outdoor rug that would look good as it aged was to make one out of wood slats, and this is what I came up with. The sun can bleach it, the rain can warp it, and with every passing day, it just looks more beautiful.

YOU'LL NEED:

• 24 24" × 2" × ¼" thick poplar slats

• Drill and ¼" diameter drill bit

• 5 yards of strong twine

1. Drill a hole 1½" from the ends of each side of the slats, making sure the holes are centered.

2. Line up your slats side by side, so you can see how your rug will come together.

3. Beginning with the top hole of the slat on the farthest left, thread the twine through the hole until you have 1¼ yards of twine on the top and bottom of the slat.

4. Tie a knot so that it sits between the slat you've threaded and the slat to the right.

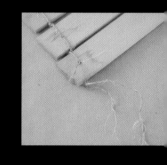

5. Thread the bottom part of your twine through the top hole of the slat on the right, from the underside, then thread the other end of the twine through the hole from the topside.

6. Tie a knot so that it sits between the second slat and the third slat.

7. Repeat steps 5–6 until you get to the end of the top row.

8. Repeat steps 3–7 for the holes at the bottoms of the slats.

9. Any way you step on it, this rug's got style!

OUTDOOR CHANDELIER

Being outdoors at night is magical when there are candles all around and the air is cool. This outdoor chandelier is the perfect way to make your outdoor space the most chic spot in town.

1. Attach your plant hangers, using the holes provided, to each side of the block of wood with your eight ½"-long screws and drill.

2. Attach your eye screws to the center of the top and bottom of the block of wood.

3. Paint the wood, screws, and hangers with spray paint.

4. Wrap the chain around the neck of one glass jar, to create a tight choker.

5. Attach the links together at the end of the chain, so that it fits around the neck of the jar nicely and doesn't slip off. You can adjust your chain length by loosening a link with your pliers and unhooking extra links.

6. Attach a 20" length of chain to opposite sides of the choker that you just created, to form a handle from which to hang your glass jar.

7. Create chain chokers and handles for three more jars.

8. For the last jar, repeat steps 4–6, except make the handle 26".

9. Attach one side of the handle on the last jar to the choker, thread the other side through the bottom eye screw, and attach to the other side of the choker.

10. Attach a length of chain, the length depending on where you want to hang your chandelier, to the top eye screw.

11. Hang your four jars from the end hooks of the plant hangers.

12. Fill your jars with candles, and light up the night.

OUTDOOR BENCH

I had to enlist my friend Matt to help me with this one. This project was more work than I thought it would be, but in the end it was well worth the effort. I've been taking naps on it almost every afternoon.

YOU'LL NEED:

- 6 pieces of 4×4 post that are 18" long

- 2 sheets of 4' × 8' × ¾" birch plywood

- Table saw

- Heavy-duty jigsaw, with a scroll blade

- Electric sander

- 3 sheets of 36"-wide, 5'-long craft paper

- Drill with ⅛" diameter drill bit and Phillips-head drill bit

- 45 3"-long Phillips-head wood screws

- Paint or wood stain, any color

1. Cut a 34" × 80" rectangle out of one sheet of the plywood. This will be the seat of the bench.

2. With your drill and drill bit, make starter holes in the plywood seat where the four corner legs will be placed.

3. Place the 4×4 legs under the seat and, using your drill and Phillips-head screws, put the screws in the starter holes and attach them with the wood screws.

4. To create the two center legs, repeat steps 2–3 with the remailing two 4×4 posts, attaching one at the center of each long side.

5. You're halfway there. Not so bad, right? Cut the second sheet of plywood into a 80" × 48" piece to create the back of the bench.

> **NOTE:** *The bench's back will rest on the ground to give the piece extra strength.*

6. Using the pattern at the top of page 272, draw the bench's back on the craft paper, making sure that the point in the middle is 48" high and dips down a bit on the sides. Only draw half of the design, then flip your pattern over and trace the other half so it's a mirror image on both sides.

7. Trace out your pattern onto the bench's back and cut it out with the heavy-duty jigsaw. (Take your time; I broke many jigsaw blades on this project by going too fast!)

8. When you've cut the pattern from the back plywood, screw it to the seat of the bench by using the drill to put screws into the back three legs and the seat. Use about eight screws across the back and two screws on each leg.

9. Using the pattern on page 272, draw the design for the arms and cut them out from the scrap wood left from what you've cut so far. The arms rest on the seat of the bench and do not extend all the way to the ground.

10. Use the drill to screw the arm pieces to the bench's back (from the back) and seat (from the bottom).

11. Sand the entire structure, then stain or paint it in the way that makes your day.

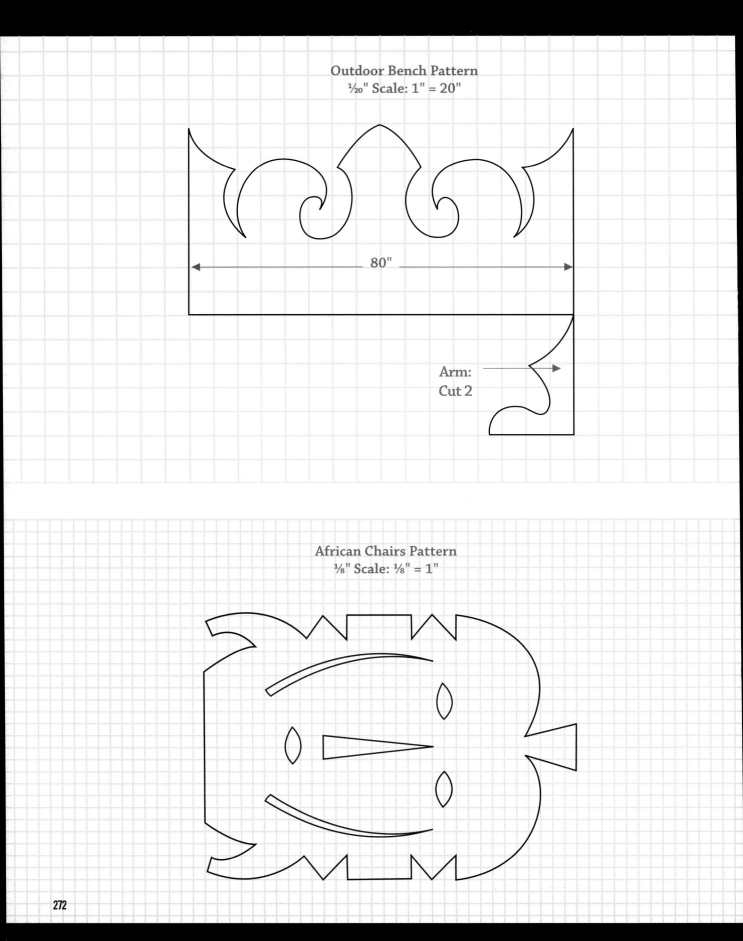

Outdoor Bench Pattern
¹⁄₂₀" Scale: 1" = 20"

80"

Arm:
Cut 2

African Chairs Pattern
⅛" Scale: ⅛" = 1"

I was sick of my patio furniture and wanted something amazing that didn't look like everybody else's furniture. Since I had so many mismatched chairs, I thought up this project to make them into a set. I hope you like this project as much as I do.

YOU'LL NEED:

- Sheet of ½"-thick plywood (One chair requires 2' × 4' of plywood, and you can get four chairs out of one 4' × 8' sheet of plywood.)

- Acrylic paint, any colors, any brand (I recommend rust, white, and black.)

- Jigsaw, with a scroll blade

- Drill and ½" diameter drill bit

- Paintbrushes, from art brushes to 2"-wide brushes

- Fine-grit sandpaper

- Household Goop glue

- 20 ¾"–1"-long wood screws

- Large sheets of paper, about 3' × 4'

- Cardboard (A big old box is perfect.)

- Some old chairs

- Twine

- Wood stain, in brown

- Spray paint, for the chairs (if you need to give them a new color)

- Krylon Acrylic Crystal Clear

> **OPTIONAL:** *Dremel Moto-Tool*

1. Prepare your chair. Paint it, if you want to, so that when you are ready to apply the mask, it's ready to go. If you decide to spray paint your chair, make sure to sand it a bit with fine-grit sandpaper to help the paint stick.

2. Now make your mask pattern. Since all chairs are different, you will have to experiment with a large sheet of paper, and use the pattern at the bottom of page 272 as a starting point.

3. Cut out your pattern from old cardboard and hold it up to the back of your chair to see how it will look and fit. (This helps; trust me!)

4. Trace your cardboard pattern onto the plywood, then cut out the shape, using your jigsaw.

5. For the eyes, mouth, nose, and decorative holes, you will need to make holes in the centers of each shape with the drill to help you cut them out.

6. Insert your jigsaw blade into the holes and cut out your shapes.

7. Sand the mask so it's nice and smooth and without splinters.

8. Stain the mask, using a 2"-wide brush. If you used the Dremel Moto-Tool, you will notice that the scratches stand out, and they make the mask look authentic.

9. Paint details onto the mask. (I added dots, stripes—you name it. Just copy mine if you can't think of anything to paint onto the mask, or for inspiration check out the Internet for some images of African masks.)

10. After your mask is dry, wrap the tusks and horns with twine, tie it into a knot so it doesn't unravel, and use Household Goop glue to keep it in place.

11. With your drill and screws, carefully apply the mask to the back of the chair, making sure that it's secure and in a comfortable position.

12. Cover the chair with Krylon Acrylic Crystal Clear for a nice finish, and if you want, add a cushion for comfort!

OPTIONAL: *Take your Dremel Moto-Tool and, with your carving and engraving bits, make scratches on the mask that will complement the design.*

I needed a fire pit for a party—and fast. Here's what I came up with. It worked like a charm and is pretty to look at, too!

CAUTION: *This is an open-flame fire pit, so make sure it's placed in an area that is surrounded by a lot of open space, and, as with all open flames, you must keep an eye on it at all times.*

YOU'LL NEED:

- Terra-cotta hose pot, any size
- Heavy-duty rod-iron plant stand, big enough to comfortably fit your hose pot
- Lid from a tin can, with about 2½" diameter
- Tin snips

HERE'S HOW:

1. Cut two tabs on either side of your tin-can lid, using your tin shears. The lid will be used to cover the hole at the bottom of the hose pot.

2. Place the lid over the hole of the pot, and bend the tabs onto the outside of it, to keep the lid in place.

3. Place your pot onto the plant stand, away from bushes and anything that can catch fire.

4. Add some firewood and light it up!

TOMATO–CAGE CHANDELIER

This is just the most romantic outdoor lighting fixture. I love mine.

YOU'LL NEED:

- 7 small glass jars, with lips
- 1' of ribbon, any color
- Three-ring wire tomato basket
- Spool of small-gauge wire, bendable
- Spool of medium-gauge wire, bendable
- Wire cutters
- Big needle-nose pliers
- 7 tea lights or votive candles

HERE'S HOW:

1. Cut your wire tomato basket above the largest ring. There will be two rings left, with 1' of wire sticking out from the top and bottom. (In the photo, the wires that are curled at the top and bottom are the 1' pieces that will be left after you cut off the bottom ring.)

SUGGESTION: *If you don't want to hang your chandelier from ribbon, you can leave the third ring on to serve as a base, and set your chandelier on the table.*

2. Above the smaller ring, which is the top of the chandelier, gather the three wires and wrap them with the small-gauge wire. (Just follow the photo. It's easy!)

3. Curl the ends of the top three wires into a curlicue design by grabbing the end with the big needle-nose pliers and twisting.

4. Curl the ends of the bottom three wires into a curlicue design. These curlicues will serve as hooks from which to hang your candles.

5. When you've finished making the curlicues, you will have your chandelier base. To give it a decorative flair, twist the medium-gauge wire around every strand of wire of the chandelier, so it resembles the twist of a rope.

> **HINT:** *Don't worry about making it perfect. It's wire, and you can fix it later.*

6. Twist two 10" pieces of small-gauge wire together so it looks like a tiny wire rope, and wrap it around the mouth of one of the small glass jars so it is secure.

7. To make the jar handle, twist two more 10" pieces of small-gauge wire together, then hook the ends on opposite sides, onto the wire that is around the mouth of the glass jar.

8. Repeat steps 6–7 for the other six glasses.

9. Twist two 10" pieces of small-gauge wire together, then cut it into 1" pieces. With your needle-nose pliers, twist the pieces into small S shapes, from which the glass jars will hang. A 10" length of wire should give you plenty of room to make four "S" hooks.

10. Put a tea light or votive into each jar, then hang three of your "S" hooks from the center ring and one "S" hook from the top of the chandelier, where all three wires meet.

11. Hang your glass jars with handles from the curled hooks on the bottom row, from the "S" hooks on the middle row, and from the "S" hook at the top.

RECYCLE IT!

What to do with those aluminum cans, old magazines, or piles of newspaper in the corner? What about that ugly chair that you just can't throw away? Personally, I think recycling is the way to go. Manipulating something over and over, so it becomes something new each time, will give you a sense of accomplishment, and hopefully save you a few bucks. Along the way you will have created some wonderful things (and helped keep the planet clean).

My favorite medium is paper. Paper is abundant and there is so much you can do with it—from making papier-mâché to weaving it like fabric. Add a little glue and you have a way to make practically anything you can dream of. Old furniture is fun to work with too—pieces should never be tossed if they're sturdy. Instead, paint them, decoupage them, or glue a million pennies onto them. Never throw anything away! The possibilities are endless, and you will have conversation pieces for years to come.

ROLLED-MAGAZINE BOWL AND BASKET

Need something to do with those stacks of magazines that are just sitting around, taking up space? Get out some glue and scissors, and make something beautiful out of them. You already have everything you need! (By the way, I made mine while watching *Oprah*!)

YOU'LL NEED:

- Stainless-steel bowl, with the mouth wider than the base
- Old magazine
- Hot-glue gun and glue sticks
- Elmer's glue
- Scissors
- Krylon Color Creations Crystal Clear Top Coat

HERE'S HOW:

FOR THE ROLLED-MAGAZINE BOWL:

1. Cut the magazine pages into 3"-wide strips.

2. Taking one corner of a strip, start to roll the strip into a stick shape. With a little bit of glue, tack down the edge of the roll so the finished product looks something like a straw.

3. Make about forty of these sticks, then set aside.

4. Place the bowl onto your workspace, mouth downward, and start to wrap the sticks around the base of the bowl. As you do this, hot-glue the paper sticks together end to end, working your way up in a spiral until you get to the bottom of the bowl.

5. For the bottom of the bowl, add magazine sticks to a small roll, continuing outward until it is the size of your bowl's base. Be sure to glue as you roll on sticks, so it's sturdy. When you finish, attach it to the bottom of the rolled bowl.

6. Remove the magazine bowl, coat it with polyurethane, and let it dry.

NOTE: *Hot glue won't stick to a stainless-steel bowl because it's cool. It will stick to the paper, however, and the magazine straws, which are now joined to one another, should easily come off the bowl when you're finished, after you've applied the glue and the top coat.*

FOR THE ROLLED-MAGAZINE BASKET:

1. Follow steps 1–2 in the directions for making the bowl. (You'll need about 300 sticks!)

2. Flatten the straws. Then, starting from one end of the stick, roll each stick into a circle with a diameter no greater than 1".

3. Glue the "tails" down. You will have to hold them in place for a bit because it takes a few seconds for the glue to set.

HINT: *You will need a few hundred of these circles, so invite some friends over to help. Do it while you are watching a movie!*

4. Once you have enough circles to start with—I'd say about two hundred—place the bowl onto your workspace, mouth downward, and hot glue them, side by side, around the bowl.

5. Continue gluing until the entire bowl is covered except for the bottom.

6. For the bottom, remove the basket and add magazine sticks to a small roll until it is the size of your bowl's base. (Think cinnamon roll!) Be sure to glue as you roll on sticks, so it's sturdy. When you finish, attach it to the inside bottom of the basket and add more glue to ensure that it stays put.

7. You need to make this basket home worthy, and that is going to take applying some Elmer's glue to all the areas where the rolls are touching, on the inside of the basket, and around each coil, so they don't unravel and pop out. (This is going to take a while, so be patient.)

8. After the glue is dry, brush the entire basket with Krylon Color Creations Crystal Clear Top Coat.

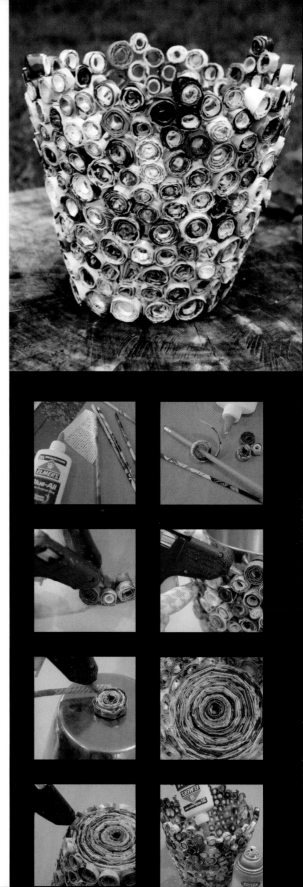

PAPIER-MÂCHÉ RECIPES

I must warn you: Papier-mâché is not for the neat and tidy. It's messy, but it's fantastic, and you will love it if you don't mind getting a little dirty. Tidy people, skip this next part! Messy folks, stick with me. I started making papier-mâché as a child, and as an adult, it's even more fun. I am seriously addicted to it now and have batches of paper mush (to use like clay) and the goop (for dipping) always ready to go. Here are my recipes for both.

NOTE: *If you want to do papier-mâché right, then you have to take your time. Make your paste thick and gooey, and your projects will last. Add some white glue, and your project will be indestructible. Coat it with Krylon Color Creations Crystal Clear Top Coat, and your project will be amazing forever.*

PAPIER-MÂCHÉ MUSH

YOU'LL NEED:

- 18 12" × 23" sheets of newspaper, shredded by a paper shredder or ripped by hand into 2" × 2" pieces

- 6 cups white flour, any brand

- 4 tablespoons salt (It keeps the papier-mâché from molding.)

- 4 ounces white glue, any brand (It's the magic that makes dried papier-mâché so very hard.)

- 6 cups water

- Hand mixer

- 2 large mixing bowls, big enough to hold all the shredded newspaper

NOTE: *This will yield about 2½ quarts of mush, which will make several items.*

1. Soak your shredded paper in a big mixing bowl overnight. Make sure to put in enough water to cover the top of the shreds, so that they get a good soak.

2. In the morning (or whenever you get to it) drain out the water and put your soaked shredded paper into the other mixing bowl.

3. Add the flour, salt, and glue, then, with a mixer (it really helps a lot!), start mixing up your mush. The ingredients will combine to make a gray, mushy paste that will have the consistency of thick, overcooked oatmeal.

DON'T WORRY: *If you don't have a mixer. If you let your paper soak enough, it will break down and make a pretty good mush on its own. Just stick your hands in it and start squishing!*

NOTE: *As you mix, you will have to add more water to your mixture to get it to a good consistency.*

4. Once it's mixed up, you are ready to use it for all those papier-mâché projects!

PAPIER-MÂCHÉ GOOP

YOU'LL NEED:

- 3 cups white flour, any brand

- 1 tablespoon salt

- 2 ounces white glue, any brand

- 3 cups water

- Hand mixer

- Large mixing bowl

HERE'S HOW:

1. Combine the flour, salt, glue, and water into the large mixing bowl, then mix using the hand mixer.

2. Once mixed, the goop will have the consistency of glue. It dries superhard and is great for the papier-mâché projects that you want to last!

3. You are now ready to begin dipping in your strips of newspaper and applying them to your project bases!

PAPIER-MÂCHÉ DAY-OF-THE-DEAD DEVIL

I have long been obsessed with Frida Khalo and Diego Rivera—the clothes they wore, the art they made, and especially the art with which they surrounded themselves. I like Mexican folk art the best, especially the life-size Day-of-the-Dead skeletons and devils. Now, you might be asking yourself, "Who would want a life-size Day-of-the-Dead devil?" Well, my friends, the question is, really, who wouldn't? This is going to take some time, so be prepared! Trust me, it's worth it. Mine looks fantastic in the backyard during a party. Here's how to make it.

YOU'LL NEED:

- Large cardboard pieces, enough to make your devil as high as you'd like

- Large batch of papier-mâché goop (See the recipe on page 283.)

- Very large batch of papier-mâché mush (See the recipe on page 282.)

- Lots of newspaper, in 1"-wide strips

- Several newspapers, enough to pad the devil to your desired size

- Packing tape

- Masking tape

- Paint, either acrylic or latex house paint, any brand and color

- Krylon Color Creations Crystal Clear Top Coat

- Drill and ¼" diameter drill bit

- Craft knife, X-Acto knife, or box cutter

- Ribbon (to hang your arms)

- Pencil

HERE'S HOW:

1. Draw out your devil on cardboard, using the pattern below as a guide.

2. Use packing tape to join large, flat pieces of cardboard together, to create the devil's legs, body, and head. (Mine was nearly 9' tall.)

3. Cut out your devil's arms from other pieces of cardboard. (They will dangle from the body when you're done.)

4. Use the shape of your own foot as a pattern to cut out your devil's feet, then tape them to the ends of the legs.

5. Crumple up dry newspaper, to give the body dimension, and attach it to your devil cutout with the masking tape.

> **NOTE:** *Masking tape is made out of paper, so it's easy to put papier-mâché over it. Packing tape is plastic, and the papier-mâché wouldn't adhere to it as easily.*

6. Dip newspaper strips into the papier-mâché goop and lay them all over the body and the arms. Put a lot of layers onto the body because it's going to have to stand when it's all finished.

7. After the strips are dry, turn over the body and the arms and add some onto the backs.

8. After the strips on the backs are dry, it's time to add the papier-mâché mush. This will give your devil a sturdy quality that will make it withstand being moved around.

9. After the mush dries, which will take about two days, paint the devil's body and the arms.

10. Drill a hole through each shoulder from front to back and drill another hole through each arm from front to back. Tie the arms to the shoulders by stringing ribbon through the holes and tying them together.

11. Cover your new devil with Krylon Color Creations Crystal Clear Top Coat. It will protect it for years to come!

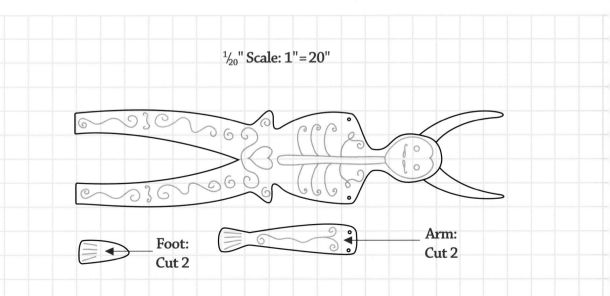

¹⁄₂₀" **Scale: 1"=20"**

Foot:
Cut 2

Arm:
Cut 2

PAPIER-MÂCHÉ FLAPPER-HAT AND WIG HEADS

Why not honor your favorite hat with a wonderful resting place? Your hat will always be ready to go, and the stand will be a work of art, thanks to this project. These are great for a kid's room and even better for an eclectic bedroom setting. Just don't freak out when they stare at you at night or start talking to one another. Mine do it all the time!

Since this is a papier-mâché project, it's going to take some time. So start on a few heads, and while they are drying, work on another project. I like some "instant gratification" projects to be going on at the same time I'm doing projects that take days to finish. Remember, we are making something that is home worthy here, so taking time to make it wonderful is very important.

YOU'LL NEED:

- 12–16-ounce aluminum can (emptied and cleaned) (per head)
- Balloon, any color (per head)
- Papier-mâché goop, enough for your heads (See the recipe on page 283.)
- Papier-mâché mush, enough for your heads (See the recipe on page 282.)
- Masking tape
- 3 faux flowers (per head)
- 5" × 5" wood block (per head)

- Hot-glue gun and glue sticks
- Lots of newspaper, in 1"-wide strips
- Scissors
- Medium-grit sandpaper
- Acrylic paints, any brand
- Set of artist's brushes, with a fine brush to a 1"-thick flat brush
- Pencil
- Krylon Acrylic Crystal Clear

HERE'S HOW:

1. Use masking tape to cover the inside of the can's mouth, to cover sharp edges. (This will keep the balloon from popping when you place it on the can.)

2. Blow up your balloon to a 22"–23" diameter. (That is the size of an average head, if you measure around the forehead.)

3. Place the balloon on the mouth of the can, with the knot inside the can, and tape the balloon and the can together with the masking tape to hold the balloon in place.

4. Dip the newspaper strips into the papier-mâché goop and completely cover the balloon and can.

5. Let the goop dry. Remember, it may take one or two days to completely dry, so be patient.

6. Cover the dry head with your papier-mâché mush, making sure that it's evenly covered all the way around.

NOTE: *If you think your head is hard enough without the mush, or you just can't get the papier-mâché mush process to where you are comfortable with it, that's fine! Just make sure you've covered your head with a lot of goop and that you feel it's strong enough, and skip the mush step. (It took me a while to get into my papier-mâché mush groove.)*

7. When the mush is dry, sand it to smooth out the rough patches.

8. With your scissors, smooth out the base of the head by cutting off any jagged edges.

> **DON'T WORRY:** *If the head is not perfectly smooth. Just get off the big bumps and the prickly edges so you have a nice surface to paint on.*

9. Mix your paints to make your skin tone color, then paint your head.

10. Lightly pencil in the face that you are going to paint.

11. Paint on the face.

12. Let the paint dry, and then protect it with two coats of Krylon Acrylic Crystal Clear, letting each layer dry before applying the next.

13. Glue the head to the wooden base, and attach the flowers around the neck. You're done!

PAPIER-MÂCHÉ BOWL AND VASES

I love the organic shapes of these, and think that at some point in my life I will be making them while lounging in my backyard in a huge caftan. It's a nice alternative to throwing clay pots, which, for the life of me, I cannot seem to do.

YOU'LL NEED:

- 12–16-ounce aluminum cans (emptied and cleaned)

- Metal or plastic bowls, any size

- Papier-mâché goop, enough to cover your vases and bowl (See the recipe on page 283.)

- Papier-mâché mush, enough to cover your vases and bowl (See the recipe on page 282.)

- Plastic wrap (the kind used for keeping food fresh), any brand

- Balloons, any size (large, medium, or the long, skinny balloons mimes use for making animals)

- Masking tape

- Thin cardboard, one piece per double-sphered vase

- Lots of newspaper, in 1"-wide strips

- Scissors or a craft knife

- Medium-grit sandpaper

- Acrylic paint, any color, any brand

- Acrylic paint, in brown or black

- Old rags

- 2"-wide brush

- Krylon Acrylic Crystal Clear

- Cup of water

MAKING THE DIFFERENT SHAPES

THE BOWL: Cover the entire bowl with plastic wrap and apply newspaper strips that have been dipped in papier-mâché goop. After the goop dries, you can pull the papier-mâché bowl off of the metal/plastic bowl. Your papier-mâché bowl will take on the shape of the bowl you are covering.

THE SMALL, SQUAT VASE WITH A NECK: Use masking tape to attach the bottom of the can to the knot of a balloon 8" in diameter. The great thing about this vase is that you can fill the can with water and it won't damage the vase.

THE DOUBLE-SPHERE VASE: Tie the knots of two balloons together and bridge them with a piece of cardboard curved into a cylinder and secured with masking tape, placed so as to cover the knots. You will also create a cardboard ring in which to set your structure, so it can stand.

HERE'S HOW:

1. Dip the newspaper strips into the papier-mâché goop and completely cover your structure. Make sure not to cover the top, since it'll be the opening for your bowl or vase.

2. Let the goop dry. Remember, it may take one or two days to completely dry, so be patient.

3. Cover the structure with papier-mâché mush, making sure that it's evenly applied all the way around.

4. After the mush is dry, sand it to smooth out any rough patches.

DON'T WORRY: *If the structures are not perfectly smooth. Just get off the big bumps and the prickly edges so you have a nice surface to paint on.*

5. Pop the balloon(s) and remove. With your scissors, trim the mouth of the bowl or vase, so it has an even edge. If the scissors don't work for this, use a craft knife, but be careful.

6. Paint the inside with your black or brown acrylic paint.

7. Paint the outside in the color of your choice.

8. After the paint is dry, water down your black or brown paint to make a stain, which you will rub on with old rags, for an antique finish.

9. Spray your creations with several coats of Krylon Acrylic Crystal Clear.

This project is classy and trashy.

YOU'LL NEED:

- Corrugated cardboard pieces
- Papier-mâché goop (See the recipe on page 283.)
- Lots of newspaper, in 1"-wide strips
- Elmer's glue
- Craft knife
- Medium-grit or coarse-grit sandpaper
- Square of sticky felt
- Acrylic paints, in white, gold, black, warm yellow, and rust; any brand
- Artist's brushes, including fine-bristled
- Masking tape
- Blue painter's tape
- Krylon Acrylic Crystal Clear

HERE'S HOW:

1. Draw the four sides and the base pieces, using the patterns on page 292, onto the cardboard, and then cut them out.

2. Tape the side pieces together by generously applying masking tape onto the outside, around the edges where the sides meet. Then do the same for the bottom piece.

3. On the inside of the bin, apply a line of Elmer's glue where the sides meet.

4. After the glue is dry, dip strips of newspaper into papier-mâché goop and cover the can.

5. After the papier-mâché is dry, sand your bin, to get rid of any rough patches.

6. Apply a base coat of white paint.

7. After the base paint is dry, mark your stripes with blue painter's tape.

8. Carefully paint over the tape, making sure to cover it completely with the white base coat.

TIP: *Here's a secret for getting perfect stripes and edges using painter's tape: To get perfect stripes, it's necessary to paint over the tape with the color you are applying it to. For example, your wall is white, and you are going to paint stripes onto the white wall. Once your tape is on the wall, you would paint over it with white (the color you applied the tape to). This will allow the white paint to seep under the edges of the tape and create a barrier layer for the next color, and it keeps the second color from seeping under the tape. Wait about ten minutes before applying each color, then carefully remove the tape. This technique will make sure that your stripes turn out perfect and crisp.*

9. After the paint on the tape is dry, paint the spaces in between the tape with rust, black, and warm yellow paint.

10. Pencil in the fleur-de-lis shapes, then fill them in with gold paint.

11. After the gold paint is dry, outline the fleurs-de-lis with black paint, using a fine-bristled brush.

12. Spray your bin with Krylon Acrylic Crystal Clear after all the paint is dry.

13. Cut your sticky felt to the same size as the bottom of the bin, and apply it.

14. It's time to get trashy!

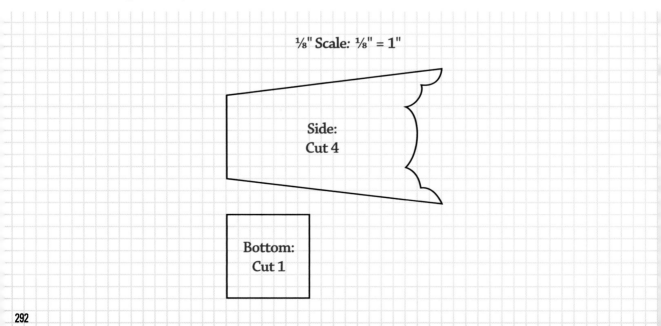

⅛" Scale: ⅛" = 1"

Side:
Cut 4

Bottom:
Cut 1

HOMEMADE DRYER SHEETS

Here's something you may not have known: Dryer sheets are made of fabric softener, like Downy, dried onto a small piece of fabric. It's just the stuff you put in the wash, but in solid form. After doing some research, I learned people have been making their own dryer sheets for a while, and I want to spread the word on this easy way to save a few bucks. If you make your own dryer sheets, one bottle of fabric softener can last you more than a year, and you'll save some big bucks. Not bad if you have a lot of laundry and a tight budget.

YOU'LL NEED:

• 1 yard of cotton fabric, any pattern

• Pinking shears

• Spray bottle

• 1 bottle of fabric softener, any brand

> **OPTIONAL:** *Sewing machine, with zigzag stitch capability (Why? I wanted mine to be pretty.)*

HERE'S HOW:

1. Cut your cotton fabric into 8" × 8" squares.

> **DON'T WORRY:** *If your squares aren't pretty. But if you do want to beautify them, do what I do: Zigzag stitch around the edges to make them look nice and to keep them from fraying.*

2. Fill your spray bottle with fabric softener.

> **SUGGESTION:** *If you have concentrated softener, just mix one part softener and one part water.*

3. When you're ready to do a load of laundry, spray a cotton square six to eight times, and toss it in the dryer.

> **TIP:** *Wash your squares every once in a while to remove buildup of softener. With a little care, these dryer sheets should last for years.*

WOVEN–PAPER CREDIT CARD HOLDER, NOTE CARD, AND WALLET

Want to impress your friends while picking up the tab? Pull out this fantastic recycled credit card holder or wallet, and watch them gasp at your generosity and style. You've saved so much making the credit card holder, you can afford the dinner for your friends!

YOU'LL NEED:

FOR THE CREDIT CARD HOLDER:

- TYVEK envelope (This is a paper made by Dupont that doesn't rip. It's what they make the flexible express mail envelopes out of, at the post office.)

- 10 different brightly colored paint chips (from the hardware store)

- 2 Velcro dots, in white or black

- Scotch tape

- Sewing machine, with zigzag and straight stitch capabilities

- Scissors

HERE'S HOW:

FOR THE CREDIT CARD HOLDER:

1. Cut your paint chips, lengthwise, into ¼"–½"-wide strips. (You want the strips to be as long as you can get them.)

2. Line up the strips side by side, into any color combinations, until you have a row that's 5" wide, and then tape the very tops together, so that they don't move around.

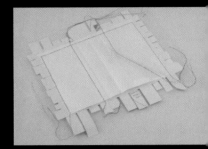

3. Weave the other strips in and out of the 5" row, working from left to right. Push the first horizontal strip up to the top, to meet the tape, and continue adding strips until you get to the bottom, not leaving any space between the rows.

4. Tape all around the very edges on all sides, so the woven strips don't move. You should now have a piece of woven paper that is about 5" × 6".

5. Cut a piece of TYVEK that's 4" × 10½".

6. Fold the paper in half lengthwise, so it's 5¼" × 4", and make a crease. This is the center crease.

7. Unfold the paper and fold the top and bottom halves in to the center crease.

8. Fold the edges that meet at the middle crease under ½". These will be your pockets when you stitch around the entire holder.

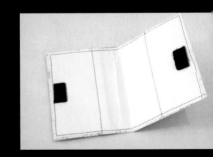

9. Unfold your TYVEK, except for the ½" folds, and zigzag or straight stitch along the ½" folds.

10. Refold the ends that will form the pockets, then place the TYVEK pocket-side up onto the back of your woven paint chips and stitch them together, about ⅛" from the edges. (By doing so, you will have created the pockets.)

11. Trim around the edges, fold in half (pocket side facing inward), center your Velcro dots on the edge of each end, and you're ready to use it!

FOR *THE* NOTE CARD:

- 10 different brightly colored paint chips (from the hardware store)

- Brightly colored cardstock

- Scissors

- Sewing machine

HERE'S HOW:

FOR *THE* NOTE CARD:

1. Follow steps 1–4 from the credit-card holder project on pages 294–5.

2. Cut out a piece of your cardstock that's 6" × 5".

3. Place the cardstock onto the back of your woven paper and stitch around the edges.

4. Trim off the excess paper around your edges, and there you have your note card!

YOU'LL NEED:

FOR *THE* WALLET:

- TYVEK envelope

- 15 different brightly colored, extralong paint chips (from the hardware store)

- Scissors

- 2 Velcro dots, in white or black

- Sewing machine

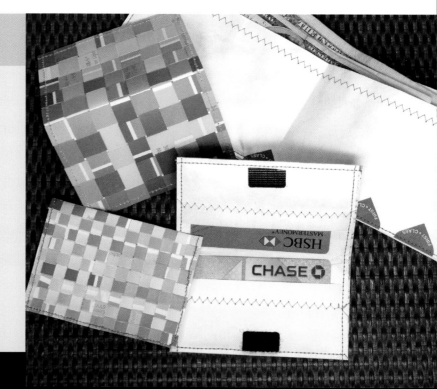

HERE'S HOW:

FOR THE WALLET:

1. Follow steps 1–4 from the credit card holder project, except that you should have a piece of woven paper that is about 5" × 11".

2. Beginning at the folded edge of your TYVEK envelope, cut out a strip that is 3½" × 9", so when it's unfolded, it's actually 7" × 9" with a crease, lengthwise, along the center.

3. Unfold the strip and fold the one long side ½" under, toward the crease.

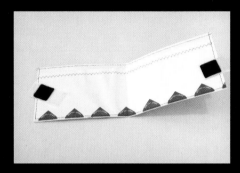

4. Stitch all the way across the 9" side.

5. Refold the TYVEK and center it onto the back of the 5" × 11" woven paper, stitched side facing up.

6. Stitch together the woven strips and the TYVEK, all the way around the outside edges. Leave a ¼" border outside of your stitches.

NOTE: *You are creating a long pocket, which will hold your cash.*

---

7. Trim the edges all the way around so they are perfectly straight.

8. Fold in half, like a wallet folds, center Velcro dots on the edge of the three sides, and fill with money!

CRAFT-PAPER FEATHERS

Need a quick centerpiece for a dinner party? How about just a great alternative to a traditional flower arrangement? Feathers are a cool, interesting way to go. Recently I went to buy some ostrich feathers for a centerpiece and realized that I was about to break the bank. I thought, Why not just try to make something that has the same feel? This project is what I came up with, and I actually like it just as much as the real thing. I hope you do too.

YOU'LL NEED:

- Roll of craft paper
- Scissors
- Elmer's glue

- 20-gauge wire
- Wire cutters
- Transparent tape

1. Cut a piece of craft paper to 7" × 18", then fold it in half lengthwise.

2. With the paper still folded, trace out half of a feather (rounded at the top and tapered to a point at the bottom) and cut it out. Unfold it to check your shape.

3. Refold and start making small slanted cuts that are very close together—about ½" from the fold.

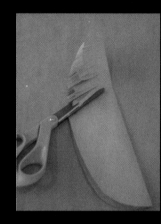

4. Continue making cuts all the way up the side of the folded paper and around the top of the feather.

> **SUGGESTION:** *The closer together your cuts are, the more featherlike your plumes will be.*

5. Unfold the paper and lay the feather flat, with the crease pointing downward.

6. To make the shaft of the feather, roll a piece of 2" × 5" craft paper into a long tube. Glue the edge of it to keep the tube tight.

7. Cut a piece of wire that is the length of the feather.

8. Starting from the end of the wire, glue about 1" of wire into the rolled-up tube.

9. Lay the wire onto the crease of the feather, and glue it down.

> **TIP:** *If the wire is hard to manage or difficult to attach, tape it into place with some very small pieces of tape until the glue dries.*

10. When the glue is dry, gently curve the wire.

11. About five of these will make a great arrangement. More will be even better!

SECRET–BOX BOOK

Everyone needs a place to hide some things. What better place than an old book? No one will ever discover your hidden items in this fantastic creation.

YOU'LL NEED:

- Old hardcover book, at least 2" thick
- Scrap of 8" × 12" × ½" plywood

> **SUGGESTION:** *If you don't want to use wood, very strong cardboard will work too.*

- Jigsaw, with a scroll blade
- Brush-on gold paint, any brand
- Craft knife
- Elmer's wood glue
- Craft paper

HERE'S HOW:

1. Cut out the pages by slicing through the front and back of the binding with your craft knife, being careful not to slice into the book cover. The meat of the book will come out easily.

2. Now you will need to make the walls of the box. (The front and back covers of the book are the lid and bottom of the box.) Carefully measure the width, height, and thickness of the book pages and use these measurements to make the pattern for the walls of the box on some craft paper.

3. When you measure your plywood for the walls of the box, make sure to account for the thickness of the wood. (The shorter pieces need to be shorter on each side by the thickness of the wood so that they fit together properly with the longer pieces.) So, subtract the thickness of the wood (½") from the measurement of the width of the pages. For example, if your pages are 5" × 8" × 2", then your measurements would be two pieces cut 4" × 2" and two pieces cut 8" × 2".

4. Use Elmer's wood glue to put your box together, making sure the walls fit inside of the book and create a box the exact size of the pages you just cut out.

5. When the glue is dry, attach one long side of the box to the book's binding and the bottom edges of the wood to the back cover. Make sure that the cover of the book can open easily.

6. Paint the walls of your box with gold paint, and let it dry.

7. Enjoy your new secret hiding place!

TIN-CANDLE ALLEY

At Christmastime, my family used to line our driveway with candles inside brown paper lunch bags. We filled the bottoms with sand to keep them in place, and, as simple as the decorations were, they looked absolutely beautiful. I always like the idea of candles lighting a path, and this is my more permanent alternative to paper bags.

YOU'LL NEED:

- Several aluminum cans (emptied and cleaned)
- Tin snips
- Sharpie marker, any color
- Spray paint, in silver metallic (or a color that matches your house)
- Work gloves (to protect yourself from sharp edges)
- Tea lights

HERE'S HOW:

1. Divide your can into four equal parts by drawing short vertical lines with your Sharpie around the lip of your can at quarter turns.

2. Draw four petals evenly around the can, inside the lines you've marked.

3. Cut off the rim of the can with the tin snips.

4. Cut out your petals.

5. Carefully bend the petals outward, so the can looks like an opening flower.

6. Cover the petals with silver metallic spray paint.

7. Make as many as you need to line your driveway or patio, and put a tea light in each one to light the way.

YOURS TRULY
(CREATIVE CORRESPONDENCE)

Every week I write a letter to my family. Either I handwrite a postcard, or I make a fun note card and a fantastic envelope to go with it. I like to keep in touch and let them know the details of my day-to-day life so that we don't feel so far away from one another. I also want them to know that I think of them more than just during the few minutes we are on the phone each week. When you read a card or letter from someone, it's a special moment; much more special than reading an e-mail. It shows that that person was thinking of you and spent some time honoring your relationship. On another note, I also happen to think my mail lady is really cool, and I want to do my part in making sure she has a job. Every day we chat for a minute and talk about her daughter and the weather.

I can't imagine getting only e-mail for the rest of my life. Getting a letter is like getting a little present, and I still get excited when the mail comes!

STITCHED CARDS AND ENVELOPES

I really like using discarded books for projects, and occasionally, while walking down the streets of Manhattan, I find piles of books waiting for me to give them another life. To the authors of these books, please understand. It was either make them into cards, or let them go to a landfill.

YOU'LL NEED:

- A children's book (or any book), with fun images

- Cardstock, in different colors (8½" × 11" sheets are perfect for making cards.)

- Pencil

- Sewing machine, with zigzag or straight stitch capability

- Thread, in a variety of bright colors

- Scissors

- Craft paper, any color

- Glue stick

FOR THE STITCHED CARD:

1. Cut your 8½" × 11" cardstock in half, either lengthwise or widthwise. Either way is fine, and will yield two folded cards measuring 5½" × 4¼".

2. Fold the pieces in half lengthwise, if you cut them widthwise, or vise versa.

3. Cut your book images to fit the fronts of the cards, making sure to leave enough of the cardstock showing to create a nice border.

4. Use a glue stick to attach the image to the card.

> **HINT:** *To keep your sewing machine needle free from glue, apply the glue only in the center of the image, to keep it in place.*

5. With your sewing machine set on straight or zigzag stitch, stitch around the edge of the image.

FOR THE STITCHED ENVELOPE:

1. Use the envelope pattern below to trace and cut out your envelope from craft paper.

2. Make the folds as if you are assembling the envelope, but don't glue the edges just yet.

3. Cut a small piece of cardstock (about 3" × 3"), to serve as your address label, and stitch it onto the front of the envelope using your sewing machine's straight or zigzag stitch.

4. Glue the edges of your envelope together.

5. Stitch all the way around the very edge of your envelope with the flap open so your flap will also have a decorative edge. By going around the very edge with your stitch, you will avoid the glued area of your envelope.

6. Now get in touch with someone!

¼" **Scale:** ¼" = 1"

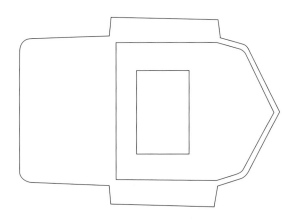

STITCHED-LOTERIA NOTE CARDS

Loteria is a Mexican card game that uses pictures. (Even young children can play.) It's thought that the game may date back as far as the time of the Aztecs. I have seen sets of loteria cards from as far back as one hundred years that are extremely beautiful. Look for loteria cards at a dollar store or at a Mexican supermarket, or order them online; they are pretty easy to find. Loteria cards are beautiful and perfect to work with for art projects and note cards, and you get a taste of another culture while you are creating.

YOU'LL NEED:

- Deck of Mexican loteria cards

- Sewing machine, with zigzag or straight stitch capability

- Thread, in a variety of bright colors

- Scissors

- Cardstock, different colors (8½" × 11" sheets are perfect for making cards.)

- Glue stick

HERE'S HOW:

1. Follow steps 1–2 for the stitched cards project on page 307.

2. With a glue stick, attach a loteria card to the cardstock.

> **HINT:** *To keep your sewing machine needle free from glue, apply the glue to the center of the loteria card, to keep it in place.*

3. With your sewing machine set on straight or zigzag stitch, stitch around the loteria card.

> **SUGGESTION:** *For some extra excitement, add sequins, or stitch all the way around the edge of the card-stock, too.*

SPRAY-PAINTED ENVELOPES

People will be so excited to receive mail from you if you start making your own envelopes. Do this project, and then prepare to become more popular!

YOU'LL NEED:

- Paper, white or light colored, to make your envelopes (or use already-made envelopes)

- Lace or athletic fabric (to use for your stencil)

- Spray paint, in two different colors

- Glue stick (if you are making your own envelopes from scratch)

- Scissors (if you are making your own envelopes from scratch)

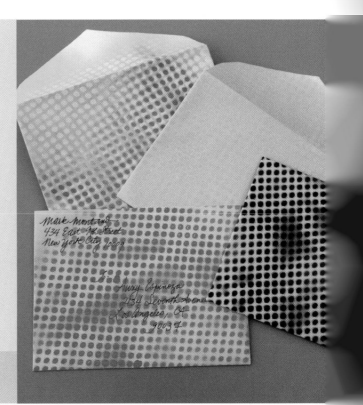

HERE'S HOW:

1. Working on one side of the envelope, lightly spray the lighter of the two colors of spray paint onto your envelope or your paper.

2. Wait a few minutes for the paint to dry.

3. Lay the lace or athletic fabric over the side you have just sprayed.

DON'T WORRY: *About securing the lace. I like the haphazard way this project looks.*

4. Lightly spray on the second color.

NOTE: *You don't have to use too much paint; a little will cover the paper nicely.*

5. Let the paint dry, and then write a nice letter to your mother!

GLAZED CARDS

These classy cards will inspire you to keep in touch with even your most distant relatives.

YOU'LL NEED:

- Images, any size, black-and-white or color
- Cardstock, any color
- Tempera paints, in different colors
- 1"-wide artist's brush
- Scissors
- Craft knife

- Glue stick
- Ruler
- Pencil
- Cup of water
- Access to a black-and-white copy machine

1. Reduce or enlarge your images on a copier, so that they fit into a 4¼" × 5½" space. (This is a quarter of your standard 8½" × 11" paper.)

2. Use your pencil and ruler to lightly draw two lines onto a piece of cardstock, so that your paper is intersected into four equal parts. This will be your master copy.

3. With the glue stick apply two images to the bottom of the page, one per quarter. They should be right side up, so if it's a picture of a person, the head would be near the center line and the neck at the bottom edge.

4. Run your master copy through your copy machine, using cardstock to print duplicates.

5. Cut out your cards along the center vertical line.

6. Lightly score along the fold lines of your cards with your craft knife.

7. Fold your cards in half.

8. Water down your tempera color so that it's translucent, making it more of a tempera wash or a stain.

9. With the card folded, brush the tempera wash over the image.

10. Let the wash dry for about half an hour.

DON'T WORRY: *If the cards curl. Just put them in between some books so they will flatten out.*

SUGGESTION: *Make your couture envelopes by following the instructions for the stitched envelopes on page 307.*

---

11. Let a friend know how special he or she is by picking up a pen and pouring your heart out.

STICKY BACK FOAM STAMPED NOTE CARDS

This is the perfect way to personalize a letter or stationery. Whether you make a stamp of your initial or of flowers, just go crazy and stamp away.

YOU'LL NEED:

- Sticky Back Foam Sheets, any color

- Small blocks of wood, at least 2"× 2"

- Large ink pads, any color

- Cardstock, any color (Lighter colors work well for this project.)

- Pencil

- Graphic design

SUGGESTION: *Try anything from simple flowers to sophisticated abstract images.*

- Scissors

1. Cut out a square of Sticky Back Foam to the size of the wood block, and adhere it to one end of the block. This additional layer of foam will give your stamp some extra cushion.

2. Trace your graphic design onto another square of Sticky Back Foam the size of your block, cut it out, then apply it to the foam on your block.

> **DON'T WORRY:** *If you don't like your design, just peel it off and try something else! You'll be surprised how terrific a few simple shapes will look once they are repeated on large sheets of paper.*

3. When you are happy with your design, press it onto the ink pad to see how your stamp comes out on a piece of scrap paper.

4. After you get the hang of it, try stamping your design onto a piece of cardstock. I promise, your notes will be even more special now that you've put your personal stamp on them.

COUTURE ENVELOPES

I love e-mail and how quickly you can get in touch with someone, but it will never replace the handwritten note and the excitement you get when you open the mailbox and see a beautiful envelope with your name written on it. As I've said, it's like a gift. Well, these couture envelopes are like the fancy wrapping paper for your letter. Make them for your own correspondence or make a set of ten to give to a friend as a gift.

YOU'LL NEED:

• Interesting sheets of 8½" × 11" or larger paper

SUGGESTION: *Use magazine pages, shopping bags from interesting boutiques, wrapping paper, enlarged book images, or printed papers from a craft store. Once you start, you'll find a million different papers out there to use!*

• Paper, in a color that complements your interesting paper

• Sticker labels (on which to write addresses)

• Pencil

• Scissors

• Glue stick

1. Use the envelope pattern on page 307 to trace and cut out your envelope from your interesting paper.

2. Cut out your envelope liner from your plain paper.

3. Glue the liner about ⅜" from the edge of the envelope's flap, avoiding where the glue would be to seal a regular envelope.

4. Fold the paper to form your envelope, starting at the bottom first, then the sides, and finally the flap.

5. Use your glue stick to adhere the side edges of your envelope.

6. Turn your envelope over and stick your label on the front.

7. Put a label on the back for your return address too.

8. Now reach out and let someone know you are thinking of him or her!

BUBBLE STATIONERY AND ENVELOPES

This is a terrific way to give plain white envelopes and lined paper an amazing look. And it's just plain fun to do. I love blowing bubbles, I love making a mess, and I love writing letters. This lets me do all three!

YOU'LL NEED:

- Food coloring, any colors
- Writing paper, lined or unlined
- Plain envelopes, any size
- Small bowls, to mix your colors
- Straw
- 1 teaspoon dishwashing soap, any brand
- 1 teaspoon sugar
- ½ cup water

HERE'S HOW:

1. Mix the water, soap, sugar, and about ten drops of food coloring, any color, into a small bowl.

2. Stir until the sugar is dissolved.

> **SUGGESTION:** *Food coloring comes in primary colors, so you can make any color you want by mixing them together. Experiment and have a blast!*

3. With one end of your straw at the bottom of the bowl, gently blow bubbles until they extend above the rim of the bowl.

4. Lightly place your paper/envelope on top of the bubbles so that the bubbles pop when they touch.

5. Repeat until the paper/envelope is covered with a bubble pattern.

6. Let the paper/envelope dry, then repeat steps 1–5, using another color.

7. After you've achieved the pattern you want, write a bubbly letter to a friend!

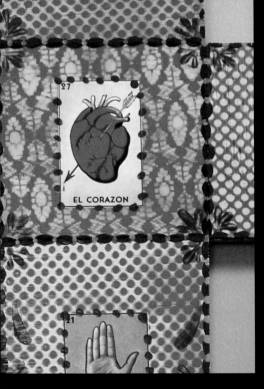

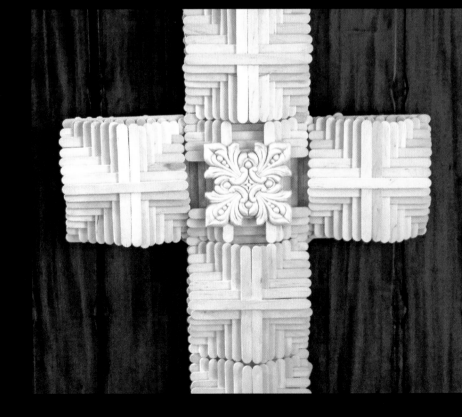

DON'T GET CROSS

have a religious family, and there were crosses everywhere in our house as I was growing up. But to me they were more than symbols, they were also beautiful objects in our home, and I fell in love with each one. I appreciated the meaning as well as the unique designs. Now, you may not be into crosses the way I am, but you can use the ideas in this chapter to make other beautiful, one-of-a kind pieces of art for your home.

POPSICLE-STICK CROSS

Who doesn't like a Popsicle-stick project? And how many people can say they have a cross made out of Popsicle-sticks in their home? You can be one of the few!

YOU'LL NEED:

- Elmer's glue
- Approximately 250 Popsicle sticks
- Pressed wooden medallion
- Newspaper
- Pencil

HERE'S HOW:

1. Lay down eleven Popsicle sticks lengthwise, side by side, to form a square.

2. Glue a stick down on the left and right sides of the square, across the ends of the first eleven sticks, to hold them in place.

3. Glue a stick lengthwise (in the same direction as the first eleven sticks) on top of the two sticks you just glued down, overlapping at the corners.

4. Continue gluing sticks in twos, switching directions and moving them closer and closer to the center of the square with each layer, until you have two sticks touching in the center and only room for one going across the top.

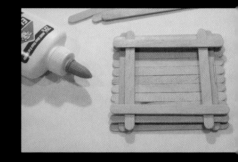

5. Repeat steps 1–4 so you have five of these structures.

6. Start a sixth structure, but stop when you have about four layers of sticks. This will be the center square, where the medallion will be placed.

7. After the glue is dry, it's time to join your pieces together. Place your six structures together on top of a piece of newspaper to form the cross, then trace around the cross with a pencil.

8. Remove the structures from the paper, then lay down Popsicle sticks inside the lines of the tracing. Cover that inside area with sticks. This will be the base onto which you adhere your square structures.

> NOTE: *When you are laying down the Popsicle sticks inside the lines of the cross, you need to make sure they are staggered, so that when you glue down your squares, a few of the Popsicle sticks will bridge the areas where the squares touch.*

9. Put glue on top of the sticks you placed on your tracing, and then put your structures on top. This will keep your structures together side by side in the shape of your cross.

10. Let the glue dry overnight.

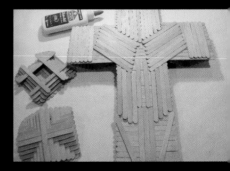

11. Glue the wooden medallion in the center, and you're done!

LOTERIA CROSS

You might be looking at this and wondering, What happened here? I enjoy mixing patterns and colors a lot. I like what happens when many different elements come together and start to make sense. I also really like crosses that have a Mexican flair!

YOU'LL NEED:

- ½"-thick plywood (I recommend a cross 24" from top to bottom and 18" across, with 5" wide beams, which will work for most standard and loteria cards.)

- 6" loteria cards, or other images (You might need to cut them to fit.)

- Spray paint, in five different colors (I used purple, yellow, pink, mint green, and light blue.)

- Liquitex Acrylics, in three different colors (I used dark blue, light blue, and forest green.)

- ½ yard of lace (to use as a stencil)

- ½ yard of nylon athletic fabric (to use as a stencil)

- Jigsaw, with a scroll blade

- Set of small artist's paintbrushes

- Elmer's glue

- Krylon Acrylic Crystal Clear

- Medium-grit sandpaper

- Blue painter's tape

- Newspaper

1. Use a jigsaw to cut out your cross from the plywood.

2. Sand the sides of your cross to make it smooth.

3. Divide your cross into sections. Each section will be painted differently and will feature a card in the middle.

4. Use blue painter's tape and some newspaper to cover up the sections of the cross that will not be painted.

5. Cover the exposed section with a color of spray paint, to make a solid background.

6. Wait a few minutes for the paint to dry, then repeat the process until all the sections are painted a different color.

7. With your tape and newspaper, section off one of your painted squares (but not the middle) and lay the nylon athletic fabric over it. Spray the section with a contrasting color.

> **SUGGESTION:** *You can secure the nylon fabric or lace by simply laying some rocks onto the edges while you spray.*

8. Wait one minute, then remove the fabric to reveal your pattern.

9. Repeat steps 6–7 for the rest of the cross, except the middle section. In the middle section, use lace instead of nylon fabric, to break up the pattern on the cross and add some interest.

> **DON'T WORRY:** *If you don't like your color combinations, you can always spray over the section you don't like with a different color.*

10. When the paint on your cross is dry, glue your loteria cards onto the center of each section.

11. With the darkest color of Liquitex and an artist's brush, make a decorative scallop pattern all the way around the cross and in between each of the sections that you've painted.

12. After the paint is dry, dot a lighter color of Liquitex in between the scallops.

13. After the second color is dry, take your third color of Liquitex and place dots around your loteria cards, and small leaves around the edges of the cross.

14. After the third color is dry, spray your cross with Krylon Acrylic Crystal Clear to give it a nice, protected finish.

WOOD BLOCK CROSS

This is such a gorgeous project. I love the simplicity of it!

YOU'LL NEED:

- ½"-thick plywood (My cross was 12" × 15" with 3" beams.)
- 100 small wood scrap blocks
- Jigsaw, with a scroll blade
- Medium-grit sandpaper
- Acrylic paint, any color
- 1"-wide paintbrush
- Elmer's wood glue
- Krylon Acrylic Crystal Clear
- Cup of water

HERE'S HOW:

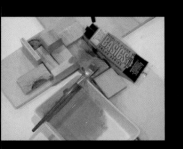

1. Use a jigsaw to cut out your cross from the plywood.

2. Sand the sides of your cross to make it smooth.

3. Start arranging your small wood scrap blocks onto the cross so you have an idea of how many of them you will need and where they will be placed. (Cut them if you need to.)

4. Sand the sides of the small wood blocks that will be facing outward.

5. Start gluing the blocks to the cross.

DON'T WORRY: *If you have gaps between blocks. You can fill them in later with smaller blocks.*

6. Once the plywood base of the cross is covered, let the glue dry.

7. Water down the paint to make a stain.

SUGGESTION: *Brush the stain on a piece of scrap wood you're not using, so you can see how it's going to look.*

8. Paint the cross, and let it dry.

9. Spray the cross with Krylon Acrylic Crystal Clear. Enjoy!

ALPHABET-BLOCK CROSS

This couldn't be easier, and it'll look great in a child's room. You can also use this process to make alphabet-block initials, if you don't feel like making a cross.

YOU'LL NEED:

- 26 wooden alphabet blocks
- Elmer's wood glue

HERE'S HOW:

1. Arrange your wooden blocks into the shape of a cross so you know how they will look when they are glued together.

2. Use Elmer's wood glue to glue your blocks together.

3. Let the glue dry overnight.

4. Display your creation with your collection of crosses.

IT'S IN THE TIN

While rummaging through the aisles at Home Depot and Lowe's a few years ago, I found something called "aluminum flashing." Aluminum flashing is thin sheets of aluminum, bought in squares and in rolls, that's easy to bend and work with. I bought some and went to town. I've manipulated this material into anything and everything: chandeliers, feathers, flowers, and frames are just a few of the project I've made using this material. My brother even made some items with it and torched them to make them look antique. A quick safety note before you get addicted to aluminum flashing too: Make sure you wear gloves when using tin and aluminum flashing, as it can be very sharp. Using tin snips will give it a serrated edge, so that it won't be as sharp. Now have fun!

TAPPED TIN FRAME

I love the way this frame looks when it catches the light. It makes the art really stand out, and it adds dimension to any room.

YOU'LL NEED:

- 14 inches of 10"-wide aluminum flashing

- Fitted canvas gloves

- 8" × 10" glass

- An image, to put behind glass (such as some art you made or a photo)

- Sharpie marker, fine point

- Pencil

- Tin snips

- Small hammer (a regular hammer will work too)

- 4 large 3"–4" heavy-duty nails

> **NOTE:** *Nails tend to dull, fall on the floor, or get lost or bent, so four nails will be enough to keep you tapping away.*

- Piece of flat scrap wood

1. Trace the pattern on page 330 onto your flashing with the marker.

2. Put on your canvas gloves and use the tin snips to cut out the pattern, making sure to be precise.

3. With a pencil, draw your decorative designs onto the tin. (Use swirls, zigzags, leaves, whatever—it will all look great. If you feel confident, make up your own. If not, just copy mine from the photo on the left.)

4. Put your flashing on top of your wood. Hold a nail over where you've drawn on the tin and tap it lightly with your hammer so you get an indentation in the flashing. Don't tap too hard, or it will make a hole.

5. Follow your lines, tapping every ⅛" or so, depending on how detailed you want your pattern to look.

6. When you're done tapping, center your glass on the tin, with the image behind it, and start folding the patterned edges around the glass, making sure to keep your glass in place.

> **NOTE:** *The tin is sturdy enough to hold the glass, so bending it over is fine.*

> **SUGGESTION:** *To hang this frame, you can take some ribbon or string, and thread a loop around the leaves in the front and hang it from a nail. It also looks terrific just leaning on a shelf. You might also try gluing a stand from another picture frame on to the back to prop it up.*

Tapped Tin Frame Pattern

½" Scale: ½" = 1"

Cut on solid lines

Fold on dotted lines

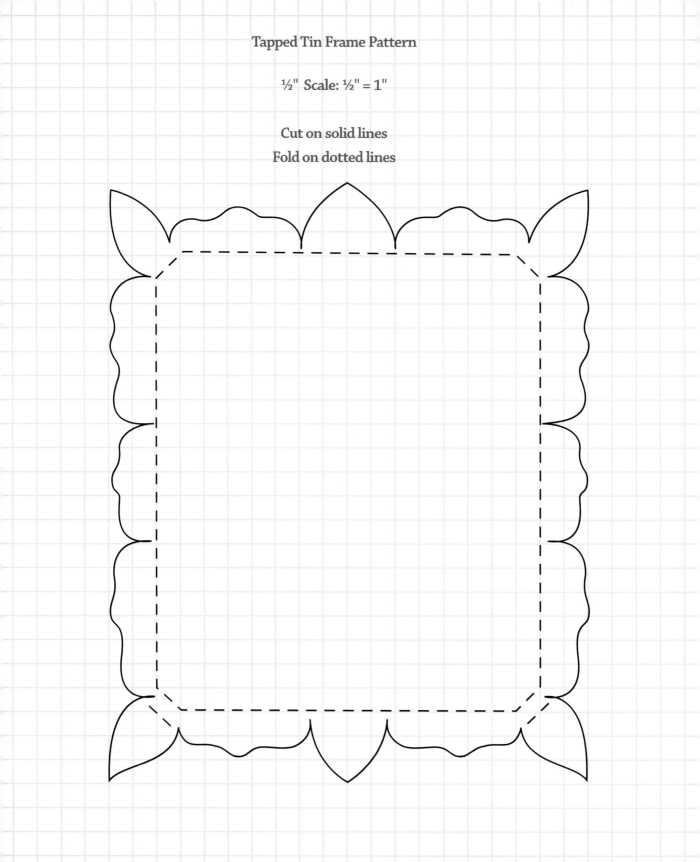

TIN FEATHER ARRANGEMENT

This is a great alternative to a flower arrangement, and it lasts forever. No water required (just a little dusting).

YOU'LL NEED:

- 4 feet of 8"-wide aluminum flashing
- Tin snips
- Sharpie marker, fine point
- Fitted canvas gloves
- Vase, with a thin neck

HERE'S HOW:

1. Draw about twelve feathers in different lengths and widths, with the Sharpie marker, onto your aluminum flashing.

SUGGESTION: *Make them 5"–15" long and 2"–3" wide.*

2. With your tin snips, carefully cut out the feathers.

3. Starting on one side, start making slits, about ⅛" apart, all along your feather's edges.

4. Repeat step 3 for all your feathers.

NOTE: *The feather will naturally curve while you are cutting, which gives it a great shape.*

5. Once you are done cutting, arrange them in a vase and admire your work.

TERRIFIC TIN TEA–LIGHT WALL SCONCE

I think sconces are an easy way to dress up any room. Lighting fixtures can really make a living space, and this one looks fantastic and is easier to make than it looks.

YOU'LL NEED:

- 3 feet of 10"-wide aluminum flashing
- Small hammer (a regular hammer will work too)
- 4 large 3"–4" heavy-duty nails
- 5" × 7" glass
- Image (to put behind your glass)
- Fitted canvas gloves
- Sharpie marker, fine point
- Pencil
- Tin snips
- Piece of flat scrap wood
- Tea light

1. Follow steps 1–5 for the tapped tin frame on page 329, except use the pattern below for this project.

2. When you're done tapping, place your glass onto the tin, with the image behind it, above the fold line marked A on your pattern.

3. Fold lines B and C over the glass to keep it in place.

4. Fold along the line marked A, so that it creates a shelf on which your tea light will rest.

5. Fold B, C, D, E, and F, in that order, as indicated on the pattern, to make the box in which your tea light is placed.

6. Tap a hole at the top of your sconce so you can hang it on the wall.

7. Put a tea light on the shelf, and you're done!

¼" **Scale: ¼" = 1"**

Cut on solid lines
Fold on dotted lines

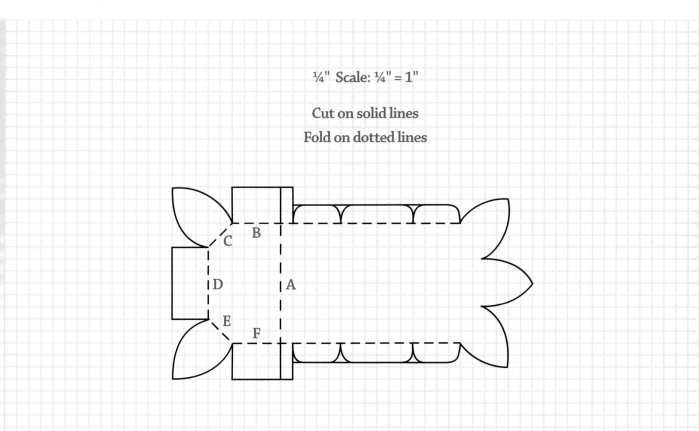

TIN-FLOWER TOMATO-CAGE CANDLE TOWER

I saw something similar to this in Mexico and couldn't wait to make my own. It's truly my favorite decorative piece to use for an evening meal outdoors.

YOU'LL NEED:

- 33"-high galvanized-wire tomato cage
- 5 feet of 12"-wide aluminum flashing
- Tin snips
- Small-gauge wire
- Household Goop glue
- Sharpie marker, fine point
- Needle-nose pliers
- 4 large 3"–4" heavy-duty nails
- Small hammer (a regular hammer will work too)
- Piece of flat scrap wood
- 14 tea lights

HERE'S HOW:

1. Use needle-nose pliers to break off the extra wires toward the top of the cage by bending them back and forth until they break off.

2. Use the pattern at the top of page 336 to trace out fourteen of the flowers and thirty stems with leaves on each end from the aluminum flashing. Cut them out with the tin snips.

3. Put your flashing on top of your wood. With the hammer and large nail, tap designs into the aluminum cutouts.

4. Pound two holes side by side into the center of each flower. These holes will allow you to thread a wire through the flowers so that you can attach them to the tomato cage.

5. Bend alternate petals of each flower upward until your flowers take shape.

6. Take a 3" piece of wire and thread the ends of the wire through the flower's holes (one end per hole), so they come out on the underside of the flower. Repeat for all your flowers.

7. Twist the two ends of each wire around the tomato cage wire until the flower is securely in place.

> **DON'T WORRY:** *If you don't like where you put your flowers. You can move them around until you're happy with the way they are positioned.*

8. After all your flowers are in place, turn the tower upside down and put a glob of glue under each flower to make them even more secure. Make sure the flowers are all straight and facing the right direction.

9. After the glue is dry, twist your leaves around the exposed wires.

10. Place a tea light in the center of each flower, and you're ready for an amazing dinner party.

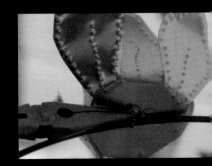

Tin Flower Tomato-Cage Candle Tower Pattern
½" Scale: ½" = 1

Tin Napkin Ring Pattern
½" Scale: ½" = 1

Napkin rings add class to any table, and these have a wonderful modern feel.

YOU'LL NEED:

- 2 feet of 10"-wide aluminum flashing (This will make four napkin rings.)
- Tin snips
- Fitted canvas gloves
- Sharpie marker, fine point
- 4 large 3"–4" heavy-duty nails
- Small hammer (a regular hammer will work too)
- Needle-nose pliers
- Household Goop glue
- Transparent tape or masking tape

HERE'S HOW:

1. Trace the pattern at the bottom of page 336 onto the aluminum flashing with your marker.

2. Cut out the shapes with your tin snips.

3. With your hammer and large nails, start to tap out any design you'd like around the shape, making sure not to puncture the tin. (The punctures will catch on the fabric of the napkin and snag it!)

4. Fold up the petals (except the two long leaves on the sides) so that they make a flower.

5. Use needle-nose pliers to curl the ends of each petal, to give them a more interesting shape.

6. Bend the leaves in the opposite direction of your petals so they overlap and form a ring.

7. Dot some Household Goop glue wherever the leaves meet, and tape them together until the glue dries.

8. Remove the tape after the glue has set, and serve up some dinner!

CHURCH CANDELABRA

In case you haven't figured it out, I believe that lighting is one of the most important elements in a home. Lighting fixtures can transform a room, and this candelabra is one of my favorites.

YOU'LL NEED:

- 2 16"-long metal plant brackets
- 4 8"-long metal plant brackets
- 3 feet of 12"-wide aluminum flashing
- Tin snips
- 5 feet of 1×1 wood (for the stand)
- Household Goop glue
- 4 large 3"–4" heavy-duty nails
- Small hammer (a regular hammer will work too)
- 12"–14½"-long wood screws
- Drill and screw bit
- Krylon Premium Metallic spray paint, in 18KT Gold
- Large needle-nose pliers

1. Use your screws, drill, and screw bit to attach your 16"-long plant brackets to opposite sides of the 1×1 wood, at the top end, making sure the brackets are flush with the top.

2. Drill in the 8"-long brackets onto the bottom end of the wood to create the base of your stand, making sure the brackets are all flush with the bottom.

3. Trace the flower pattern at the top of page 336, from the candle tower project, onto your aluminum flashing seven times, then cut out the shapes with the tin snips.

4. Trace the leaf pattern from the candle tower project, also at the top of page 336, onto your aluminum flashing two times, then cut out the shapes with the tin snips.

5. With your hammer and large nails, tap dots all the way around the edges and down the center of each leaf and petal.

6. Bend up every other petal on your flowers until they take on the shape of a flower.

7. Curl the ends of the petals with the needle-nose pliers to give them some more shape.

8. Use Household Goop glue to adhere the flowers evenly across the two 16"-long metal brackets.

9. Glue the leaves to the wooden post, right below the center flower.

10. Cover the entire candelabra with gold spray paint.

11. Fill each flower with a tea light, and you'll instantly have a romantic room.

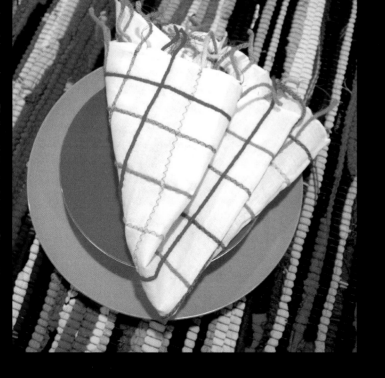

SEW DARN EASY

've tried to make these sewing projects as easy as possible, but you *will* have to make friends with your sewing machine before you get going. Don't worry, you'll find that if you practice your sewing just a little bit, you will quickly improve. And don't get frustrated. Relax and enjoy the process, and remember that you can always rip out the stitches and start over if you don't like what you've done.

As I was working on the following projects and attempting to simplify them, I fell in love all over again with the zigzag stitch. You can make anything with it, and the visual effect is a nice bonus. Run a zigzag stitch over some fabric, and you'll see how cool it looks. And just wait until you see it in action throughout this chapter!

OLIVE ULTRASUEDE PILLOW

Want to add a nice, rustic touch to any sofa or armchair? This pillow is just the thing.

YOU'LL NEED:

- 1 yard of Ultrasuede (for the base fabric), any color

- ¼ yard each of Ultrasuede (for the olives), in two different colors, with at least one color contrasting with your base color

- Sewing machine, with zigzag and straight stitch capabilities

- Thread, in a color that matches your Ultrasuede

- Sewing needle

- Craft paper, any color

- Box of straight pins

- Pillow stuffing (I buy inexpensive pillows, rip them open, and use the stuffing.)

- Pencil

- Scissors

OPTIONAL: *2½ yards of brown piping (for the edges)*

HERE'S HOW:

1. Cut two 18" × 18" squares of Ultrasuede from your base color.

2. Using the pattern on page 343, draw two ovals, one small and one large, onto craft paper. Put them against your squares to get the size and shape you like.

3. When you are happy with your patterns, trace two of each size onto two contrasting colors of Ultrasuede and cut them out. (The large ovals should be one color and the small ovals another color.)

4. Zigzag stitch the smaller ovals onto the larger ovals.

5. Zigzag stitch the olives you've created onto one of your squares, making sure they're at least 2" from the edges of the fabric.

NOTE: *If you want to add piping, match the flat edge of your piping onto one edge of your olive-covered pillow square, then sew all the way around the edges. (Remember, the tube part will be facing the olive and the flat part will be on the edge of the pillow.) When you get to where the ends of the piping touch, overlap them into the seam allowance.*

6. Pin the pillow squares together (with the olives facing inward) and sew around the edges of each side with a straight stitch. (If you added piping, try to get as close as you can get to the piping on the pillow edge.)

7. Leave a 6" hole on one side so that you can fill the pillow with stuffing.

8. Turn the pillow inside out, so your olives are now on the outside.

9. Fill the pillow with stuffing, then sew the hole closed, using a needle and thread.

10. Curl up on the couch with your new pillow, and eat some olives!

¼" **Scale:** ¼" = 1"

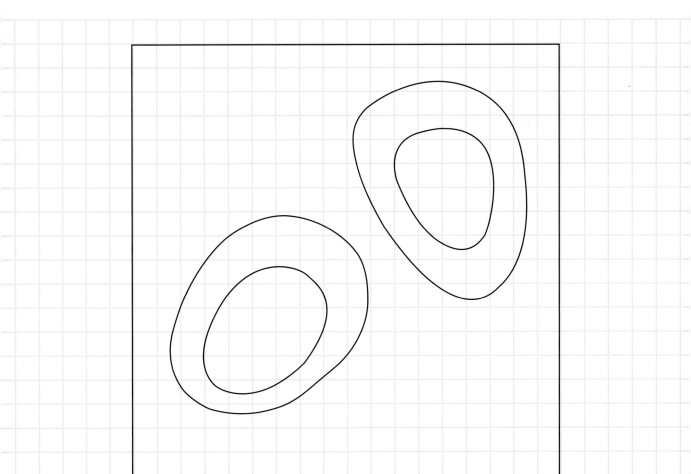

SCRAP-FABRIC LEAF RUG

I have tons of small scraps of fabric that I don't want to toss, so I decided to cut out leaves from the heavy-duty fabric and felt scraps to create a shaggy leaf rug. It was surprisingly easy, and I was able to accomplish it in about two hours. Take your time and don't feel like you need to cut out leaf shapes, like I did; cutting out circles and squares would also work. Experiment and have some fun.

YOU'LL NEED:

- 1 yard of heavy-duty fabric, such as denim, cotton twill, or Ultrasuede

- Sewing machine

- Thread, in a color that matches your fabric

- Tons of fabric scraps

- Pinking shears

- Sewing needle

HERE'S HOW:

1. Cut out as many 3"-long leaves from your scraps as you think you will need for your project. (The number of leaves you need depends on the size of the rug you are creating. You will need about three hundred leaves for a rug that is 18" × 24". It seems like a lot, but if you camp out in front of a good movie while you cut them, the time will fly by.)

2. Starting at one corner of your heavy-duty fabric, use the sewing machine to stitch leaves all along the edges.

3. Once you've covered the edges of the rug with leaves, work inward, overlapping each new row over the previous row, to cover the stitching. Keep going until you reach the center of the fabric.

4. After you have covered the center with leaves, hand sew several leaves, to hide the stitching of the last row.

SUGGESTION: *To keep the rug from slipping, add some strips of hot glue across the underside of the rug, then let it dry before flipping it over. This will create some traction.*

5. To clean your rug, hand wash it, then lay it flat to dry.

6. Now when fall leaves blow in your front door, you won't even notice!

SKULL PILLOW

How punk! This pillow will give any room a little edge.

YOU'LL NEED:

- 1 yard of canvas, in white

- 1 yard of canvas, satin, or Ultrasuede, in black

- Sewing machine, with zigzag and straight stitch capabilities

- Thread, in black and white

- Pillow stuffing (I buy inexpensive pillows, rip them open, and use the stuffing.)

- Scissors

- Box of straight pins

- Sewing needle

HERE'S HOW:

1. Using the outside edge of the skull pattern on page 347, draw the pillow shape on the white canvas twice, then cut them out.

2. Draw the skull onto the black fabric, then cut it out.

SUGGESTION: *If you are inclined, cut out two skulls, one for each side of the pillow.*

3. Carefully center the skull on the white canvas, then pin it on.

4. Zigzag stitch around the eyes, mouth, nose, and outside edge of the skull with black thread.

5. Pin the two sides of the pillow together, with right sides in (the skull(s) should be facing inward), and straight stitch around the edges of the skull with a ½" seam allowance.

6. Leave a 5" hole so you can stuff your pillow.

7. Turn the pillow inside out, then stuff your pillow with the stuffing.

8. With needle and white thread, stitch up the hole by hand.

9. Keep this on your bed and the bogeyman will think twice before trying to get you!

¼" Scale: ¼" = 1"

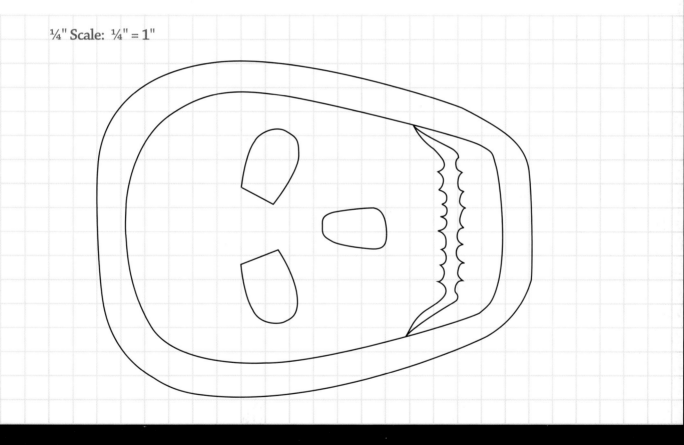

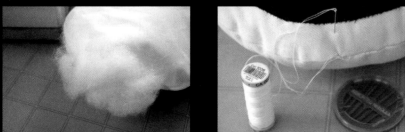

GRANNY-CHIC TOTE BAG

I know that knitting is relaxing, but for some reason I can't master the technique. I just don't have the patience for it! But I do have to say that I love the way it looks. And every time I'm at a thrift store and I see the beautiful knitted blankets made by all of the wonderful grannies out there, my heart breaks (so I buy them and give them a home). This tote bag is my homage to every granny out there who took the time to make us blankets when we were growing up. Thanks, Gram!

YOU'LL NEED:

- Medium-sized knitted blanket to cut up

- Sewing machine, with zigzag and straight stitch capabilities

- Yarn, in a color that matches the blanket

- Sewing needle

- 1½ yards of heavy cotton, in white (or another light color)

- Thread, in a color that matches your yarn, and in white or whatever color matches your cotton

- Box of long ball-point straight pins

1. Cut one 24" × 36" rectangle from the cotton, for the lining of the tote.

2. Cut two 4" × 24" rectangles from the cotton, for the facing at the tote's mouth.

3. Trim your granny blanket into a 24" × 36" rectangle.

4. Lay your granny-blanket rectangle over the cotton lining, and pin all the way around the edges.

5. Zigzag stitch all around the edges, to secure the blanket to the lining. This is the body of your tote bag.

6. Take your 4" × 24" cotton pieces and zigzag stitch along the edges of the long sides. This will keep the edges of the facing from fraying.

7. Now that you have your facing and tote-bag body ready, place a 4" × 24" piece along one of the 24" edges of the bag, sandwiching the granny fabric between the cotton lining and facing pieces. Use a straight stitch and ½" seam allowance to stitch across. Repeat for the other side of the tote.

8. Fold the bag in half widthwise, with the granny fabric on the inside and the facings on the outside, and stitch up the sides using a straight stitch and a ½" seam allowance.

9. Turn the bag right side out.

10. Fold the facing inward, then hand stitch down on the side seams and in the center of the bag, to keep the facing down.

> **SUGGESTION:** *You can iron down the facings, to help you out a bit, but use a low heat setting.*

11. Cut eighteen pieces of 36"-long strands of yarn to begin making your handles.

12. Bundle the strands together and tie a knot at the top. Separate the strands into three sections—with six strands per section—and braid the sections together. Tie a knot at the bottom of the braid.

13. Cut the braid in half and tie a knot at each loose end.

14. Hand stitch the knots of one braid to one of the top edges of the tote bag, about 7" apart, making sure to use plenty of thread and a lot of stitches (since you will be carrying things in this bag, and you want it to be sturdy).

15. Watch out! This tote bag will turn even the sweetest granny into a purse snatcher!

GRANNY-CHIC PILLOW

Okay, I spend my days making things and experimenting with crafts, but this project turned out even better than I thought it would. I love the colorful look of these pillows, and I think they will be a huge hit in any home.

YOU'LL NEED:

- 1 yard of medium-weight cotton, in white (or another light color)

- Sewing machine

- Scissors

- Knitted blanket to cut up

- Pillow stuffing (I buy inexpensive pillows, rip them open, and use the stuffing.)

- Box of ball-point straight pins

- Thread, in white

- Sewing needle

1. Cut two squares of white cotton to the same size. (Mine were 20" × 20".)

2. Cut a square of your blanket that's the same size as the cotton squares.

3. Use ball-point straight pins to secure the blanket square to one of the white cotton squares.

4. Zigzag stitch the blanket square to the cotton square.

5. Place the other white cotton square over the blanket square, so that you are sandwiching the blanket in between the cotton pieces.

6. Pin your squares together along the edges.

7. Use a ½" seam allowance and sew all the way around the pillow with a straight stitch, leaving a 6"-long hole on one side of the pillow.

8. Turn your pillow inside out, then fill it with pillow stuffing.

9. Use your sewing needle and thread to hand stitch the hole closed.

10. Dress up your couch or bed with your new creation!

GRANNY-CHIC SCARF

This scarf is yet another way to keep granny close, and look like you've mastered the art of knitting! It's also a great gift for your friends.

YOU'LL NEED:

- Knitted blanket to cut up

- 1 skein of yarn, in a color that matches the blanket

- Sewing machine, with zigzag stitch capability

- Thread, in at least one color that matches the blanket

- Scissors

HERE'S HOW:

1. Trim your blanket to the size that you want your scarf to be. (The blanket I used was 45" long, and I cut a 10"-wide strip from end to end.)

2. Zigzag stitch around the edges of the scarf so that it doesn't fray and come apart. Make sure to use the smallest zigzag stitch, which creates stitches that are close together.

3. For the fringe, cut 14"-long pieces of yarn, bundle them into groups of three, and knot them evenly onto the ends of the scarf by looping them through the knitting along the edges. (The knitting should be loose enough to squeeze your yarn through.)

4. Wrap yourself up, and go show off your granny chicness!

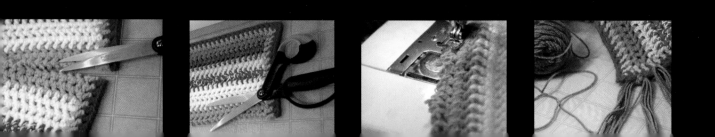

STITCHED-YARN NAPKIN

This technique is an excellent way to spruce up some very simple fabric and make your table unique. All it takes is some very basic sewing-machine skills and an imagination.

YOU'LL NEED:

- Napkin or men's handkerchief, in white
- Sewing machine, with zigzag stitch capability
- Thread, in bright colors
- Balls of yarn, in colors different from the thread

HERE'S HOW:

1. Cut your yarn into strands about 6" longer than your napkin or handkerchief.

2. Place the pieces of yarn over the handkerchief into any pattern you'd like, so that you get an idea of what your design will look like.

3. Set your sewing machine on the widest zigzag stitch it can make. (This means when you zigzag, the needle goes as far as it can from one side to the other.)

4. With a few inches hanging over the edges of the handkerchief (you will cut them down later), zigzag stitch the yarn to the fabric.

5. Continue sewing until you have your pattern stitched down.

6. Trim the edges of the yarn so that they are even all the way around.

> **DON'T WORRY:** *About the extra threads hanging off. I think it contributes to the handmade quality of the project.*

7. Now go crazy and zigzag stitch yarn on everything!

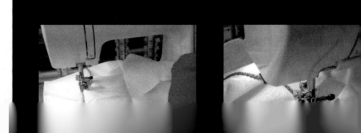

FANTASTIC AIRPLANE BLANKET

The motion sickness medicine I take when I fly makes me so drowsy that when I exit from the plane, I am so out of it I almost always don't notice that I still have an airplane blanket wrapped around my shoulders. I have quite a collection of airplane blankets now, and this zigzag yarn technique (see page 353) is how I kick them up a notch so I can use them around the house as throws, tablecloths, or picnic blankets.

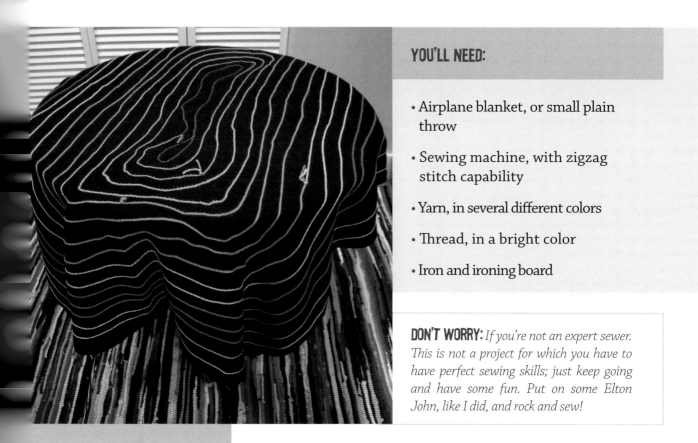

YOU'LL NEED:

- Airplane blanket, or small plain throw

- Sewing machine, with zigzag stitch capability

- Yarn, in several different colors

- Thread, in a bright color

- Iron and ironing board

DON'T WORRY: *If you're not an expert sewer. This is not a project for which you have to have perfect sewing skills; just keep going and have some fun. Put on some Elton John, like I did, and rock and sew!*

HERE'S HOW:

1. Starting with one color of yarn, zigzag stitch the yarn onto your blanket, around the edges. When you get to the end, don't cut your yarn, but continue working inward and sew another line around the blanket, inside your first.

2. Join your first yarn color to the next color with a knot, and keep zigzag stitching, spiraling inward until you have another two layers of your next color.

3. Repeat step 2 until you reach the center of the blanket.

4. Clip your threads when you're done, iron your blanket, and enjoy your new throw.

WARHOL-LITHO PILLOW

Maybe you think it's weird to sleep on a pillow with your own face on it, but I don't! (Perhaps if I had someone special, I could sleep on that person.) Till that special someone comes along, I'm content sleeping with myself.

YOU'LL NEED:

- 1 yard of 60"- or 45"-wide cotton, in a light color

- 2 Avery T-shirt Transfers

- Sewing machine

- 2 Warhol litho images (See pages 31-3.)

- Sewing needle

- Thread, in a color that matches your fabric

- Iron and ironing board

- Scissors

- Box of straight pins

- Pillow stuffing (I buy inexpensive pillows, rip them up, and use the stuffing.)

HERE'S HOW:

1. Cut two 18" × 18" squares from the cotton.

2. Iron your Warhol litho images onto each square, following the directions on the transfers package.

3. Place your fabric squares together, with the images facing inward, and pin them together every few inches along the edges.

4. Using a ½" seam allowance, sew around the pillow, leaving a 5" hole on one side.

5. Clip the corners of the pillow at a forty-five-degree angle, just outside the corner stitch.

> **TIP:** *Clipping the corners of your pillow, while inside out, will create less bulk in the corners when it's turned right side out.*

6. Turn the pillow right side out, and fill the pillow with stuffing.

7. Hand stitch the hole closed, and enjoy!

GIANT OCTOPUS

I had to make this. I have nieces and nephews galore, and when they sit down to read on this thing, they are incredibly happy. Also, they fall asleep on it right away, allowing me to get some much-needed peace and quiet during our visits. It's easier to put together than it looks, but it does take up a lot of room, so be prepared.

YOU'LL NEED:

- Large beanbag chair, any color

- Large trash bags

- 4½ yards of 60"-wide fabric, in a color that matches your beanbag

- ¼ yard of heavy cotton or felt, in black

- 8 bags of pillow stuffing

- Sewing machine, with zigzag and straight stitch capabilities

- Scissors

- Box of straight pins

- Seam ripper

- Sewing needle

- Heavy-duty thread, in a color that matches the fabric

1. Cut two large ovals from your black cotton/felt, for the eyes, and two smaller ovals from the 60"-wide fabric, for the inside of the eyes.

2. Zigzag stitch the smaller ovals onto the larger ovals.

3. Cut out a mouth from the black fabric.

4. Pin the eyes and mouth in place on the beanbag.

5. Unzip and empty the stuffing from your beanbag into the trash bags, and store them somewhere. (You won't need them until later.)

6. Zigzag stitch the eyes and mouth onto the beanbag.

7. Cut eight 6' × 15" strips of the 60"-wide fabric, for your legs.

8. Straight stitch each one of these strips to look like a long tube sock (you're folding the strips in half lengthwise), leaving one end open.

9. Turn them inside out, and fill them with pillow stuffing.

10. Figure out where the legs are going to be attached to your beanbag.

> **NOTE:** *Most beanbag chairs are sewn like a beach ball, with several seams joined all the way around to form the shape. You could use a seam ripper to make an 8" hole in each seam, to put in your octopus legs, and trap the ends of the legs in the seams as you sew up the holes. Or you could sew the legs around the outside without cutting the holes; it's up to you. If you have ripped slits in your beanbag, place the open ends of the legs inside the slits, then sew the legs to the bag from the inside. If you have not ripped slits in the beanbag, then fold the open end of each leg inside itself about 1" to cover the raw edges, so it looks neat, and top stitch each one onto the outside of the beanbag.*

11. Refill the beanbag with its stuffing.

12. Don't forget to zip the beanbag back up, or your stuffing will go everywhere, much to the kids' delight!

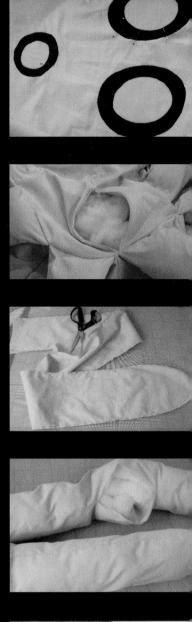

YOU'VE BEEN FRAMED

You might want to slap me for saying this, but there is nothing sadder than an ugly baby. No matter how much you want to say, "What a beautiful baby!" you just can't. Maybe it's the crossed eyes, or the misshapen head, or the similarity between the baby and a half-plucked Thanksgiving turkey, or the fact that there is a patch of Mohawk that protrudes from the kid's forehead. It's just sad, and hopefully time will be kind. It usually is. Remember the not-so-handsome guy in high school who is now posing for the covers of romance novels? The same thing will happen to that cross-eyed baby, so don't worry about it. Not that this has happened to me, but if you ever get a photo from a good friend or family member of an ugly baby, and you *have* to display the photo, the best thing to do to make the baby more attractive is put the photo in a fantastic frame. Then people can comment on the frame rather than the kid. Oh, and here's a tip: The next time you see an ugly baby, just lie or comment on how cute his or her outfit is. *Under no circumstance should you ask why the baby's eyebrows are so big.*

CHOP–CHOP–CHOPSTICK FRAME

I've used chopsticks for craft projects, but never in this way—not until I started working on the book! Pick them up in Asian grocery stores or order them through the Internet. Wherever you find them, just get a bunch and start having some fun. There is no right or wrong way to do this. You have to experiment! At the very least you can play pick-up sticks.

YOU'LL NEED:

- 150 wooden chopsticks
- Elmer's glue
- Transparent tape

OPTIONAL: *Glass from a cheap picture frame*

HERE'S HOW:

1. Lay down four chopsticks end to end, to make a square. (See the top layer in the photo on the left.)

2. Take four more chopsticks and glue them at diagonal angles on top of that square, forming a diamond. Let the glue dry. It will look like an eight-point star, with the top layer a diamond rather than a perfect square.

3. Glue down six chopsticks, one next to the other, onto each side of the diamond, making each side seven chopsticks wide. Let the glue dry.

4. Glue ten chopsticks next to one another across the top points of the diamond, and ten chopsticks next to one another across the bottom points of the diamond.

5. Glue ten more chopsticks next to one another, across the previous two sets of ten on each side of the diamond, creating an open square on the back.

6. Glue two more onto the top and bottom of the diamond, as in the photo on the left.

7. Keep crisscrossing chopsticks onto the back, across the top and across the sides of the frame, until you have created an area that fits your photo.

8. Tape a photo on the back.

TIP: *You can glue a piece of glass onto the back of your chopstick frame, then tape your photo to the face of the glass.*

361

ROLLED-MAGAZINE FRAME

Who doesn't have a million old magazines and shoeboxes lying around? I don't know why we feel the need to save them, except to make these fantastic frames.

YOU'LL NEED:

- Shoebox lid
- Craft knife
- Magazine
- Elmer's glue
- Clear packing tape
- Scissors
- Glass, from a small frame
- Krylon Color Creations Crystal Clear Top Coat

HERE'S HOW:

1. Follow steps 1–2 on page 280 for the rolled-magazine bowl project.

2. Use a craft knife to cut out a square in the middle of the shoebox that is ¼" smaller on all sides than the piece of glass you are using.

3. Chop off the ends of the sticks so that you have nice, even ends.

HINT: *Cut the straws to the sizes you need to make sure that the shoebox lid is covered with the straws.*

4. Glue the sticks down side by side onto the shoebox lid, one by one, until the whole box is covered.

5. Coat the straws with Krylon Color Creations Crystal Clear Top Coat, then let it dry.

6. Tape the glass onto the inside of the lid, then tape the photo behind the glass.

7. You're ready to hang your new frame!

BROOCH FRAME

Have you ever rummaged through your mom or grandma's old jewelry? Or found a box of costume jewelry at a yard sale? You want to take it because it sparkles and shines, but you just don't know what you'd do with it. Maybe you wouldn't actually wear any of it, but wow, it's fun to look at and play with. The next time you stumble across a box of old brooches and necklaces, grab them and glam up a picture frame. It's the best way to add some glitz to a deserving photo.

YOU'LL NEED:

- A selection of old jewelry
- E6000 glue
- Simple picture frame

HERE'S HOW:

1. Use the E6000 glue to glue jewels evenly all the way around your frame, or just add one big brooch to the top of the frame.

2. Fill the frame with the most glamorous photo you can find.

THINGS I USED FOR THE PROJECTS IN THIS BOOK

These are great things to have around the house for whenever you get inspired to make crafts.

ALUMINUM FLASHING: This comes in rolls of different widths. It's great for the tin projects because it's easy to cut and holds its shape when it's bent. Also, it doesn't rust!

BALL-POINT PINS: These will help you hold tiny things in place. The long ones come in especially handy.

BOOKS, OLD AND DISCARDED: You can use the paper for everything, from making leaves for your Poe-tree to a background for small art projects, and you can use the covers for boxes and art projects.

BUCKETS WITH LIDS: Hit the dollar store for big buckets. Great for storing large batches of papier-mâché and for keeping water and sponges nearby while you work.

BUTTONS: Beginning today, start collecting buttons. All kinds of buttons. Get them anywhere and glue them on anything. They are decorative, great for flower centers, and neat for mosaic projects. Just always have tons around. My favorite buttons are from the dollar store. They're tiny, flat, and come in many different colors.

CLAMPS: When you are gluing things together, these will help keep things in place while the glue dries.

CLOTHESPINS, WOOD AND PLASTIC: You can find these at the dollar store. The plastic ones are great little clamps for holding things together while they dry, and the wooden clothespins are perfect for gluing around and on projects, to give them a very handmade feel.

COFFEEMAKER: Okay, I threw this one in because let's face it: When you are having a good time making something, and you get tired, sometimes one good cup of coffee will keep you awake until you finish!

CRAFT KNIFE: You need tons of these around. They're perfect for making clean cuts. I use Olfa cutting knives, but you can also try X-Acto knives. They are both great. You can usually get a package of decent box cutters at the dollar store, so give that a try too. I use so many of them, I always have several around as backup.

CRAFT PAPER: You know, the brown stuff that looks like what they use to make paper bags out of. Perfect for patterns, wrapping paper—you name it.

CRAYOLA FINGER PAINTS: They come in great colors and are washable. Drip them on anything and have a blast!

DECORATIVE SCISSORS: You can get these in so many different shapes at Michaels arts and crafts stores, and you will want them all. It's a great way to give your paper projects beautiful borders—from antique photo edges to wild zigzag edges.

DRILL AND DRILL BITS: Get a nice drill. Mine is from Skil, and it's sturdy and strong. A nice selection of drill bits will last you forever, as long as you take care of them. Black & Decker makes a great set. Stay away from cheap tools; they just don't last!

ELMER'S GLUE: The basic white stuff is great for all craft projects. Especially decoupage.

ELMER'S WOOD GLUE: For small wood projects, where getting a tiny nail in place is almost impossible, this stuff will really keep your work together. It's also great for securing pieces of furniture that might be wobbly. Just fill in the cracks, and you'll see what a difference it makes! I use it all the time on old furniture.

EXTENSION CORDS: Let's just say that sometimes your glue gun does not quite reach your worktable.

FAUX FLOWERS AND LEAVES: Stick them in flower pots, use them for jewelry, spruce up a lampshade, but also have extras around for your projects, as they will always come in handy.

FELT: Just a great fabric that does not fray at the edges. Perfect for putting on the underside of your projects to protect your tabletops, and great for graphic fabric projects, such as pillows and tablecloths.

FLORAL TAPE: Floral tape is that green tape that doesn't really stick to anything but itself. In this book I've used it to wrap my faux flowers to a ballpoint pen, but it's also great for wrapping bunches of real or faux flowers together, so they arrange nicely.

GLITTER GLUE: Michaels arts and crafts store has a great selection of this stuff. Glitter glue is perfect for sprucing up any project. I love it, and never leave the house without some in my backpack!

GLUE STICKS: What would we do without them? They're perfect for greeting-card and envelope projects, and a nice, clean way to use glue.

GOOGLE.COM (IMAGE SEARCH FEATURE): If you want some ideas on how to paint your African masks or want to research what colors are usually found in a Mexican fabric, just get on your computer and do an image search. It's an easy way to find inspiration for your projects.

GOOP GLUE: Goop has a huge selection of different glues that bond everything. The E6000 is the best, and sticks just about anything to anything.

HAMMER: A must for every toolbox. Try a smaller craft hammer for tiny nails and projects.

HOT-GLUE GUN: You can get these anywhere. Although I am not a huge fan of the hot-glue gun, there are great things you can do with it, and as long as you use another adhesive along with it, it's perfect for keeping something in place.

JIGSAW WITH DIFFERENT SIZE BLADES: I use a Skil jigsaw with a scroll blade for many of my projects. It works like a charm.

LAMINATING MACHINE: If you can afford one, and like the projects you make with them, then get one. It's a blast to have in the house!

LEVEL: This is a must in any home and for any craft project—from making tables to hanging pictures. You can pick up a level anywhere these days. Get a small one that is no more than 1' long.

LIQUITEX ACRYLIC PAINTS: Great colors, perfect for any craft project. Nice quality, too.

MAGAZINES: Old magazines are full of inspiring pictures and great ideas for new projects.

METALLIC SPRAY PAINTS, GOLD AND SILVER: As any Southern girl will tell you, everything looks better sprayed silver or gold.

NEEDLE-NOSE PLIERS: Super for picking up tiny things and bending small wires.

NEWSPAPERS: You need these to keep your work area clean, and for papier-mâché.

NIGHT-LIGHTS, PLUG-IN: One of the easiest ways to light a project is to plug in a night-light to the end of an extension cord. It's safe and gives off a very nice low-wattage glow.

OLFA CUTTING MAT: This is a piece of plastic that you can use your craft knife on, over and over again, without harming it. It's perfect for all of the precise cutting you do. It also has a 1" square grid for easy measuring.

OOK: What is an OOK, you ask? It's a self-leveling saw-tooth hanger made by a company called OOK, and it's great for hanging your projects.

PAINTBRUSHES: Get them anywhere—from the dollar store to fine art stores—and make sure you take care of them.

PAINT CHIPS: It's always good to have color references around you, and paint chips allow you to see what colors work well together.

PAINT THINNER: This stuff is flammable, so be careful. It's great for getting rid of all kinds of messes, and can even remove some gooey glue. Just dab a bit onto a cotton swab, and you have a very useful item.

PAPER CLIPS: In case you need a wire hook, these are handy to have around. Just unbend them and twist them into shape.

PAPER CUTTER: Perfect for making straight edges and long cuts. It's also great for cutting several sheets at once. I used mine for my bookbinding and greeting-card projects. Get one at Staples for a good price.

PAPER SHREDDER: I got mine on sale at Staples for fifteen dollars. Great for making huge batches of paper strips for your papier-mâché projects.

PAPER TOWELS AND OLD RAGS: What can I say? The more messes I create, the more I'll need them! You need an arsenal of cleanup supplies at your disposal.

PENCILS: You can never have enough pencils. You'll use them for marking measurements, tracing, sketching, outlining . . . and they can be part of the actual projects, too!

PINKING SHEARS: Shears with notched blades; used to finish edges of cloth with a zigzag cut for decoration or to prevent unraveling or fraying. I love them! I have one pair for paper and one pair for fabric.

PLASTER OF PARIS: Experiment and have fun with this stuff. I like to fill old plastic dolls with it and make them into sculptures.

PLASTIC DRINKING STRAWS: You can pick these up anywhere. Go to town with them and use them for anything from lanterns to flower arrangements. Check out pages 68 and 82 for ideas.

PLYWOOD, BIRCH, $\frac{1}{2}$", $\frac{3}{4}$", AND 1" THICK: Great for all of your wood projects. Birch plywood has a nice finish and is a higher grade than other plywood.

POPSICLE STICKS, CHOPSTICKS, AND WOODEN COFFEE STIRRERS: Use these and lots of Elmer's wood glue to make sculptures, frames, trivets, what have you.

Q–TIPS: Perfect for dabbing on small bits of glue or taking off a little drip of paint while you work.

RECYCLED CONTAINERS: C'mon, how many times do you need somewhere to store your old brushes and pencils? Use what you have around the house.

RIBBONS IN FAILLE AND SATIN: Great for finishing edges on projects and for hanging picture frames the old-fashioned way. You can even hot-glue ribbon onto the edges of curtains or around the lids of boxes.

ROCKS TO USE AS PAPERWEIGHTS: It's always good to have some smooth rocks around to hold things down while you work. I work outside a lot, and I just gather some and keep them beautifully arranged in a corner somewhere. You will be surprised at how handy they are.

RULERS: Have a few of these on hand at all times. You will need them for everything. Be sure to get a metal ruler for making cuts with your craft knives.

SAFETY GOGGLES OR GLASSES: It doesn't matter if you are only drilling or sawing or hammering for one second. You need to protect your eyes!

SANDPAPER: I like to scrape smooth items before I add glue or paint to them. The rough surface it gives will give the glue something to stick to, and a little sandpaper is perfect for scoring.

SCISSORS FOR PAPER AND FABRIC: Invest in your fabric scissors. I like Fiskars, but there are other brands out there. For paper, it's good to have several pairs, so you don't have to waste your time sharpening. Try the dollar store for a decent pair. I use mine for everything.

SCRAPS OF WOOD: Check out the scrap pile of a local wood worker to see if you can get a bag of scrap wood for a good price. Check out the mirror on page 226. It's all made from wood scraps sanded and glued to a base!

SCREWDRIVER SET: No home should be without a set of screwdrivers. Paint the tops of the Phillips-head screwdrivers one color so that you know what you are picking up from the toolbox. I swear, whenever I want a Phillips I get a flat head, and vice versa!

SCREWS AND NAILS: Get them from the dollar store or anywhere you can pick them up. Small, long, fat, wood, metal—they will always be useful.

SCRUBBERS: You know how messy you can be. Always have some small ones on hand.

SEWING MACHINE: Need I say more?

SHADOW-BOX FRAMES IN DIFFERENT SIZES: I think these are a wonderful alternative to a regular frame. They give dimension even to flat items, and you can put anything in them. Even resting on a shelf, they are amazing to look at. Many of them come with Velcro and a fuzzy back, so that you can mount just about anything.

SHARPIE PERMANENT MARKERS: These will write on most any surface, so try to have them around. I like to use them on metal.

SMALL-GAUGE WIRE: I'm constantly wiring things together. Keep these around for everyday use.

SNAP-IN SOCKET-AND-CORD SET WITH SWITCH, 6": These are great for all of your lamp projects. They use a candelabra bulb (a smaller bulb), and they are safe to use and don't need wiring.

SPRAY ADHESIVE: 3M and Krylon make wonderful spray adhesives. It's a spray glue that leaves a nice, even coat of glue on your projects. There are strong- and light-tack ones, and depending on the tack, you can reposition your work until it dries, which is very helpful when you're decoupaging images.

SPRAY BOTTLE: Next time you empty out a spray bottle of glass cleaner, save it and fill it with water for your workroom. Spraying water on your projects that use paint can produce wonderful effects. It can cloud ink and make spray paint gather and dry into terrific patterns.

STAPLE GUN, HEAVY-DUTY: JT21 is great for small upholstery projects. And the staples are easy to pull out if you make a mistake.

STAPLER: You'd be surprised how you can use your stapler for projects in ways other than clipping a pile of papers together.

STICKY BACK FOAM: Kids have always known how fun Sticky Back Foam is. Now you get to use it too. My favorite use is for stamp making.

STICKY FELT: Great for adhering to the bottoms of your projects so that they don't scratch the surfaces of your tables. Also great for appliqués so you don't have to use pins while you are sewing.

TAPE: Painter's tape, masking tape, transparent tape. You need them all! Have plenty around for your projects.

TEMPERA PAINTS: My favorites are the metallic-sheen tempera paints made by Artworks. They give your greeting cards and art projects an amazing effect.

TIN SNIPS: Hand shears for cutting sheet metal. There are so many beautiful projects in this book using sheets of aluminum. You will want to have a nice pair of tin snips that make cuts with a serrated edge so the edges are not sharp.

TOMATO CAGES: Need a structure to make that fancy lamp? This is a great place to start. You can do so much with these, and they come in tons of sizes. Also, they are quite inexpensive!

TURPENTINE: Great for cleaning oil-based paint off brushes.

TWINE: From tying up your recycled newspapers into bundles to wrapping a lampshade, twine is your friend, and now it comes in fantastic colors. Stock up and use it!

WATER-BASED CLEAR LATEX (SUCH AS KRYLON OR MINWAX CLEAR COAT): I like to coat everything I make in latex for protection.

WIRE CUTTERS: Get a pair with spring action. They are much easier to work with. This way, you have more control when you are working on your projects.

WIRE PLANT BASKETS: What a discovery. Cover them with fabric, use them with papier-mâché—go nuts. They come in all sizes and are very sturdy. I like them for hanging-lantern projects.

WOOD FILL: Comes in a tube, great for cracks in your wood.

WORK GLOVES IN COTTON, CANVAS, AND LEATHER: Find a pair that fits, so that you can really use your fingers.

RESOURCE GUIDE

AMAZING GOOP CONTACT ADHESIVE AND SEALANT

www.amazinggoop.com

You cannot go wrong with these products. They work better than most glues out there, and they have a comprehensive line of adhesives for any project you might be tackling.

CALICO CORNERS

www.calicocorners.com

This is by far one of the best stores for fabric. They give you swatches and even mail them to your house when they don't have them in the store. The prices are great, and the fabrics are some of the best I've seen at any major chain.

THE CONTAINER STORE

www.containerstore.com

I rely on this place to keep myself organized and when I want to find containers for all of my creations.

DOLLAR STORE

What a great resource for just about anything you might need. Glass plates, candles, toothpicks, Popsicle sticks—you name it. You can't depend on the stock, but more often than not, you will find a piece of your crafting puzzle there for only a buck.

ELMER'S

www.elmers.com

You can find these glues most anywhere, but just in case you want to see what the company makes and sells in bulk, this is a good place to start. I like to buy the white glue by the gallon, since I use so much of it.

FANCIFULSINC.COM

www.fancifulsinc.com

The only resource for brass charms and rubber stamps. I used my charms for the Ultrasuede-covered containers on page 61. This is a mom and pop business that I fully support. The prices are great, the service is amazing, and once you start shopping here, you'll keep coming back for more.

FEDEX KINKO'S OFFICE AND PRINT CENTER

www.kinkos.com

If you don't have a Staples nearby, this is my second choice. It's still a great place to get things done, such as copying and enlarging.

FISKARS

www.fiskars.com

An amazing company that makes everything from wonderful sewing scissors and decorative hole punchers to paper cutters and pinking shears. Check out the website for all of their products and where to buy them. They are of great quality, and I use them for all of my craft projects!

GOODWILL STORES AND SALVATION ARMY STORES

www.goodwill.org

www.salvationarmyusa.org

If you need a table and you're prepared to add a little pizzazz to it, this is the place to look. Same goes for if you're looking for a chair to spruce up and paint. The money goes to a good cause, and it's fun to recycle something. Check out these places before you head off to a furniture store for something brand-new.

HOME DEPOT

www.homedepot.com
You can get anything here, from lamp-making parts to lumber. It's a great place to roam around and get inspired.

JOANN FABRICS

www.joann.com
Terrific national fabric chain with wonderful remnants at great prices. Pick up lace here for your spray-painting projects, felt for your felt creatures, Ultrasuede for your art cases, and every sewing supply you could ever need!

KRYLON

www.krylon.com
Krylon products are available everywhere. They truly are the best paint and spray paint around. The paints dry easily and make a great finish, and Krylon has everything you can imagine, from frosted-glass paint to reflective paint to make your own mirrors.

THE LAMP SHOP

www.lampshop.com
This is the best site I've found to get lamp parts, if you are making your own lampshades. You'll be inspired just by looking their website!

LOWE'S

www.lowes.com
It's a joy to shop at Lowe's. It's organized, the staff is knowledgeable, and you can find just about anything you need there for your projects.

MICHAELS

www.michaelscrafts.com
A nationwide craft supply store that has everything. I was there constantly while working on this book, and you will learn to love it too.

OLFA

www.olfa.com
A great manufacturer of cutting mats and blades. Check out their site for locations and new products.

ORIENTAL TRADING COMPANY, INC.

www.orientaltrading.com
More than twenty-five thousand fun products for every occasion! Great online resource for craft supplies. If you can't find a craft supply, it's on this site!

PEARL RIVER

www.pearlriver.com
The perfect place for all your Asian craft materials, from lanterns to fabrics. If you are going for an Asian theme, start by checking out this site. They ship to everywhere, and the prices are great!

ROSS

www.rossstores.com
Ross has an amazing home decor section. I like it because you can often find beautiful sheets that are easily turned into window treatments and tablecloths in a snap. It's also a great place to find a throw pillow or a vase at a very reasonable price. Frames are of good quality and inexpensive here too.

SKIL

www.skil.com
These are the only power tools I use for my projects. They are of a good quality, fairly priced, and powerful. The sanders are my favorite because you can handle them easily, and the drills are fantastic. I promise you will be happy with any Skil tool you purchase.

STAPLES

www.staples.com

Get your copying done here. Staples has the papers and other things you might need, so if you're trying to cross a lot of things off your list at once, Staples is the way to go. Look for sales on things like glue sticks and pencils when the school year starts.

STRATHMORE PAPERS

www.strathmoreartist.com

When you are creating something and you want it to last, use quality products. Papers especially, because in time they will change. Not Strathmore products, though. They are high-quality papers that will last a lifetime. I love the watercolor blocks, and I always have a Strathmore sketchbook with me. The paper is smooth, and you can erase and erase all you want and it won't tear.

USI, INC.

www.usi-laminate.com

I could not live without my laminating machine from USI. I use it for everything—from making place mats to photo books, or even lampshades. It's wonderful to have one around. Really, you can do a million projects with it.

YOUR GROCERY STORE

I know this is obvious, but I like to be thorough. When making your homemade cosmetics and body scrubs, this is the place to go for the sugar, Crisco, lemons, olive oil, and salt.

YOUR IMAGINATION

We all have one. I challenge you to use yours to take the projects in this book and make them your own. Give them your very special stamp and while you're embarking on your crafty journey, remember that there is not right or wrong way to be creative.

YOUR TRASH BIN!

I believe that we have to recycle as much as we can, so why not start by using what we discard to make our projects? Cans, yogurt cups, plastic soda bottles—you name it, they are all perfect starts to many projects.

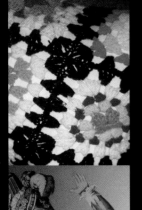

CRAFTYTOWN.COM